101 Questions & Answers Series

Constitutional Law

101
QUESTIONS & ANSWERS
SERIES

CONSTITUTIONAL LAW

CHARLES P REED
LLB, Barrister

OLD BAILEY PRESS

OLD BAILEY PRESS
200 Greyhound Road, London W14 9RY

ISBN 1 85836 091 9

British Library Cataloguing-in-Publication Data

A catalogue record for this book is available from the British Library.

5 4 3 2 1

Printed and bound in Great Britain

Contents

Foreword

This book is part of a series designed specifically for those students studying at undergraduate level. Coverage is not restricted to any one syllabus but embraces the main examination topics found in a typical examination paper.

This book is concerned with constitutional law in the context of examinations. Each chapter contains an Introduction setting out the scope of the topic, important recent cases and articles, and other helpful advice as to likely examination questions on that topic.

Additionally, in each chapter there are Interrograms and Examination Questions. The Interrograms are designed as short questions testing knowledge of the fundamentals of the topic being covered. The Examination Questions are a selection of actual questions taken from papers set by a university, and have been selected because they represent the most typical examples of how knowledge of the syllabus is tested. It is intended that students should work through the Interrograms and Examination Questions before checking their knowledge (and presentation style) against the suggested answers contained in each chapter (skeleton answers for Interrograms, full-length essay answers for the Examination Questions). The answers state the law as at 1 January 1998.

Acknowledgement

Examination questions are the copyright of the University of London.

The questions are taken or adapted from past University of London LLB Degree for external students examination papers. Our thanks are extended to the University of London for their kind permission to use and publish the questions.

Caveat

The answers given are not approved, sanctioned or endorsed by the University of London and are entirely the Publishers' responsibility.

Table of Cases

1

The Nature and Sources of Constitutional Law; the Separation of Powers and the Rule of Law

Introduction

This chapter is concerned with introductory concepts and certain constitutional fundamentals. Among the themes explored are the arguments for and against written constitutions; the distinction between rigid and flexible constitutions; the particular role of conventions in the British Constitution; and the continuing relevance of traditional doctrines such as the separation of powers and the rule of law to a modern democratic system of government.

It is necessary to be familiar with the basic characteristics of the British Constitution in order to compare and contrast them with other constitutions - the American Constitution provides a useful comparative model. There is much pressure for constitutional reform in the United Kingdom which may eventually lead to a new constitutional settlement. However, the traditional response to such pressure has been of a pragmatic, evolutionary kind, so that changes are likely to be in the form of a step-by-step process rather than a 'big bang' type. For a summary of the Labour Government's 1997 proposals for constitutional reform: see Hazell [1997] PL 424.

One feature of the British Constitution which has significantly distinguished it from other constitutions is the part played by conventions.

Any critical analysis of conventions will need to explore their purpose, scope adaptability, utility, and relationship with legally enforceable rules of the constitution. A knowledge of the political history of a constitution is important in order to illustrate this analysis, for example the suspension of the convention of collective ministerial responsibility in 1975 in order to permit some Cabinet ministers to campaign against continuing membership of the European Economic Community, even though such membership was recommended by official government policy. Did this episode involve a serious breach of constitutional practice or merely a sensible waiver of unwritten convention so as to avoid a political crisis and possible collapse of the governing party?

Constitutional theories such as the separation of powers and the rule of law also need to be subjected to particular critical scrutiny. Such scrutiny will need to examine the traditional definitions of these theories and how they have been adapted or modified to suit modern democratic principles. Has there been a danger of dilution for the sake of political expediency? The role of the judiciary is crucial to both doctrines, so it is important to examine the ways in which the independence and impartiality of the judiciary are maintained. The growth of judicial review of administrative action over the past 40 years may be described as a modern constitutional fundamental in upholding the rule of law against executive misuse of power, although at times such review has been criticised for involving judges in political inference, thereby undermining the separation that ought to exist between law and politics.

In a typical examination paper two questions can be anticipated on the main sources and theories of constitutional law. Such questions often take the form of quotations describing some aspect of these sources or theories, which then needs to be subjected to critical analysis.

Questions

INTERROGRAMS

1 Outline the main features of the British unwritten Constitution.
2 What is the purpose of conventions in the British Constitution?
3 Should conventions be codified as law?
4 Define Montesquieu's theory of the separation of powers.
5 Define Dicey's theory of the rule of law.

QUESTION ONE

Argue the case for and against codification, in a legal form, of the conventions of the British Constitution.

London University LLB Examination
(for external students) Constitutional Law June 1985 Q2

QUESTION TWO

Sir Ivor Jennings states that as between constitutional conventions and rules of law 'there is no distinction of substance or nature'. Do you agree?

London University LLB Examination
(for external students) Constitutional Law June 1995 Q2

QUESTION THREE

Discuss the nature and effect of the constitutional conventions which regulate the public conduct of the Sovereign as Head of State in the United Kingdom.

London University LLB Examination
(for external students) Constitutional Law June 1996 Q2

QUESTION FOUR

'Phrases like the "Separation of Powers" and the "Rule of Law" have no application to the British Constitution which rests solely on the principle of parliamentary sovereignty.'

Discuss.

London University LLB Examination
(for external students) Constitutional Law June 1988 Q4

QUESTION FIVE

'Our unwritten constitution rests upon a separation of powers. It also rests upon a mutual recognition of those powers. It is for Parliament to make new laws and to amend old laws, including the common law. It is for the courts to interpret and enforce the law. It is for the government to govern within the law. Each in its own sphere is supreme.' (Lord Donaldson of Lymington MR, *M* v *Home Office and Another* (1992)).

Discuss.

London University LLB Examination
(for external students) Constitutional Law June 1994 Q2

QUESTION SIX

In what respects does the British Constitution conform to, or contradict, the doctrine of the Separation of Powers?

London University LLB Examination
(for external students) Constitutional Law June 1996 Q1

QUESTION SEVEN

Does any aspect of Dicey's definition of the Rule of Law still have relevance today?

London University LLB Examination
(for external students) Constitutional Law June 1992 Q8

Answers

ANSWERS TO INTERROGRAMS

1 Traditionally the British Constitution has been described as an 'unwritten' one because it has lacked formal legal constraints on the exercise of governmental power. Unlike the American Constitution, there has been no devolution of power through a formal federal system, and no formal separation of powers or functions since the institution of Parliament combines membership of the legislature, the executive and the judiciary. The common law doctrine of parliamentary sovereignty has been a barrier to an entrenched Bill of Rights protecting civil liberties, so that British judges have been unable to act as 'guardians' of the constitution in the manner of their

American counterparts. Instead reliance has been placed on unwritten conventions to restrain excess or abuse of power.

However, the modernisation of the British Constitution is giving it features which strongly resemble a written constitution. Membership of the European Union involves consent to an external written constitution which is superior in the event of conflict with the British internal constitution. In 1999 considerable legislative powers will be devolved to a Scottish Parliament and deliberative powers to a Welsh Assembly. During 1998 the European Convention on Human Rights will be incorporated in a non-entrenched form into English law.

2 Generally all conventions share a common purpose, namely, filling the gaps within the legal structure of government in order to facilitate the exercise of public powers. Professor Dicey also suggested that conventions share a common moral basis, giving public officials a set of political ethics so that government can be operated in a fair and democratic manner. It is possible for the purpose of a particular convention to undergo change so as to reflect changes in public attitudes to such issues as standards in public life. For example, the convention of individual ministerial responsibility was traditionally concerned only with accountability for political decisions, but in recent years it has also become concerned with personal fitness for office (eg, ministers resigning because of scandalous behaviour in their private lives).

3 Codification of conventions as law would ensure certainty and enforceability, thereby preventing party political manipulation of conventions for short-term reasons of expediency. Critics of conventions argue that their lack of legal enforceability means that citizens have no guarantees against abuse of powers but are asked to trust the integrity of those in public office. Judicial review would provide a method of determining whether a suspension of a convention is a legitimate waiver or an unconstitutional breach.

However, it might be impossible to identify every convention for the purposes of a formal code of law, and even if it were achieved new conventions would probably develop to accommodate unforeseen political events. Enforcing conventions through the courts might damage the impartiality and independence of the judiciary by involving them in controversial political issues. It might, therefore, be preferable to clarify the contents of conventions through a non-enforceable charter or declaration, thereby obtaining greater certainty but without sacrificing flexibility or bringing judges into the political arena.

4 Montesquieu propounded his theory of separation of powers in an influential work called *L'Esprit des Lois* (*The Spirit of the Law*) in 1748. It provided the model on which the American Constitution was based in 1787. The theory contends that the three main powers of government, namely the legislative, the executive and the judicial, should be organically and functionally separated so as to avoid the risk of abuse of power. The theory requires that no member of one organ of government should at the same time be a member of another organ, and that no-one should exercise more than one of the three main functions of government, namely: (a) law-making; (b) policy-making and administration; and (c) interpretation and application of law.

5 Professor Dicey propounded his theory of the rule of law in *Introduction to the Study of the Law of the Constitution* (1885) and it has remained of considerable influence ever since. Dicey suggested three formal elements:

a no-one should be penalised except for a distinct breach of the law established in the ordinary legal manner before the ordinary courts;

b no-one should be above the law; every person, whatever his or her rank or condition, should be subject to the ordinary law and answerable to the ordinary courts;

c the general principles of the constitution, such as the right to personal liberty and the right of public meeting, are the result of judicial decisions.

Dicey summarised his theory as a device for ensuring the supremacy of regular law as distinct from the influence of arbitrary power. He included within his definition of artbitrary power wide discretionary authority enjoyed by public officials.

SUGGESTED ANSWER TO QUESTION ONE

General Comment

This is a very straightforward question involving discussion of conventions of the constitution, the differences between law and convention and the arguments for and against the codification of conventions in a legal form. Students should remember to stick to the specific points raised in the question. Don't write everything you know about conventions and don't simply produce a list of conventions.

Key Points

- Introduction - what are conventions; why are they obeyed?
- Distinction between law and convention - Dicey's views contrasted with those of Jennings
- Why maintain a distinction between law and convention?
- The advantages of codification of conventions in legal form (clarification of the present vague and undefined rules of conventions, the provision of a clear legal definition of unconstitutional behaviour and certainty)
- The advantages of retaining conventions (helps to bring about constitutional change without formal change in the law and flexibility helps to keep the judiciary out of political controversy)

Suggested Answer

A great many rules of the British Constitution, which are observed by the sovereign, the Prime Minister, ministers, Members of Parliament, the judiciary and civil servants, are not contained in Acts of Parliament or judicial decisions, but are to be found in those rules of conduct called constitutional conventions. These have been described as 'rules of constitutional behaviour which are considered to be binding by and upon those who operate the constitution but which are not enforced by the law courts ... nor by the presiding officers in the Houses of Parliament': Marshall and Moodie, *Some Problems of the Constitution* (1971, 5th ed), pp22-23. These conventions of the constitution are obeyed by those to whom they apply not because of the threat of any legal sanction in case of breach, but because of the political difficulties which may follow if they are not obeyed: Jennings, *The Law and the Constitution* (1959, 5th ed), p134.

Conventions therefore differ from laws in that unlike laws they are not enforced by the courts. According to Dicey (*The Law of the Constitution* (1959, 10th ed)), conventions are not 'laws in the true sense of the word, for if any or all of them were broken, no court would take notice of their violation'. Laws are rules enforced and recognised by the courts whereas conventions are 'a body not of laws but of constitutional or political ethics - the constitutional morality of the day, not enforced or recognised by the courts'. However, this approach is too simplistic. Conventions of the constitution are sometimes recognised by the courts. For example, in *Carltona Ltd* v *Commissioners of Works* (1943), the court recognised the convention of individual ministerial responsibility. Also some rules of strict law may be non-justicable. According to Jennings (above), the real distinction between law and convention lies in the fact that legal rules are either formally expressed, or illustrated by a decision of a court, whereas conventions arise out of practice. Law and convention are however closely interlocked. Conventions, he said, 'provide the flesh which clothes the dry bones of the law; they make the legal constitution work; they keep it in touch with the growth of ideas'.

The question therefore arises, why maintain the distinctions between strict law and convention? Why not codify conventions of the constitution in a legal form? In theory, all the conventional rules of the constitution could be enacted in legal form by one or more Acts of Parliament. Indeed, this has been achieved under several Commonwealth constitutions. Such a step would have distinct advantages. Codification would for example clarify certain constitutional rules which are at present vague and undefined. It is unsatisfactory that major rules of the constitution remain indeterminate. For instance, under what circumstances may the Queen dismiss her Prime Minister? If the Queen were to dismiss or to refuse to dismiss the Prime Minister under certain circumstances this would undoubtedly provoke controversy, because of the uncertainty surrounding the Queen's power of dismissal. This controversy would be avoided if the circumstances in which the Queen can and must dismiss her Prime Minister were set out in legal form. Also, where the rules of the constitution are in legal form, legislative or executive acts which conflict with the constitution may be held to be unconstitutional and therefore illegal. In the United Kingdom the absence of any fully legal constitutional code means that 'unconstitutional' has no definition. It is not always easy to determine whether the boundary between constitutional and unconstitutional behaviour has been crossed.

However, while codification may have the advantage of clarifying particular rules the disadvantages of such a step are considerable. Conventions cover such a diverse area and they differ so much in character that they cannot logically be included within a single code. Even if such an attempt were made it would be impossible to stop the process by which formal rules are gradually modified by non-legal rules from starting all over again.

Conventions also have several distinct advantages over legal rules in the context of constitutional law. Firstly they provide a means of bringing about constitutional change without the need for a formal change in the law. For example, many conventions concern the powers of the sovereign. They allow the legal powers of the Queen to remain intact, thus lending dignity to the affairs of state, while at the same time allowing the democratically elected government to actually exercise those powers. It may also be difficult or even harmful to define some important constitutional conventions. Codification may bring certainty, but only at the expense of flexibility. Law is rigid and may be difficult to change. Conventions on the other hand allow the constitution to evolve and keep up to date with changing circumstances without the need for formal enactment or repeal of law. Law must also be followed in every case. Conventions, being flexible and unenforceable by the courts, allow discretion to be exercised and can be waived if the particular circumstances make this desirable. Most conventions also concern matters of a political nature. Their non-legal nature thus helps keep the judiciary and the courts out of politics and political controversy. Experience in the Commonwealth has illustrated the difficulty that can arise when the courts become involved in politically sensitive situations.

Therefore, so long as conventions are obeyed there is no need for legal codification. Nevertheless, if a particular convention is disregarded then it can, if necessary, be formally enacted and given legal status. For example, in 1909 the House of Lords ignored the convention that they must defer to the will of the House of Commons. The result was the enactment of the Parliament Act 1911 defining the relationship between the two Houses on a statutory basis.

SUGGESTED ANSWER TO QUESTION TWO

General Comment

This is a question which requires students to write about the relationship between conventions and straightforward legal rules. Care must be taken to define the terms used in the question before launching into an answer, or the use of examples. The comparative importance of different types of conventions and legal rules should be explored. The temptation to be prolix in answering must be avoided. The structure of an answer to this type of brief question is all-important to the marks that will be ultimately awarded.

Key Points

- Take issue with the detail of Jennings' statement
- Explain the terms 'conventions' and 'rules of law'
- Discuss enforcement of each
- Conventions: Queen in Parliament and the ceremonial state opening of Parliament
- The rule of law
- Distinction between constitutional legal rules and ordinary legal rules
- Conclusion

Suggested Answer

Ivor Jennings is perhaps being disingenuous when he states that there is no distinction between constitutional conventions and rules of law in nature, but perceptive when he states that there is no distinction in substance. A rule of law is not a term of art necessarily. Legal rules, if they are to be taken as the same thing, can be said to be either statutory or common law. Where a rule is created by statute it has been approved by the Queen in Parliament or passed by a system of delegated legislation. Such a rule occupies a very particular place derived from the sovereignty of Parliament. Common-law rules are created by the courts and are similarly susceptible to definition in the decisions of the judiciary. The way in which legal rules are reformed is clearly understood: the decision of a superior court that the rule is to be changed settles the question.

However, conventions are considerably less certain than rules of law. Conventions are understood ways of behaviour rather than explicit rules. It is not possible to know from one day to the next whether or not a convention retains the same level of authority as it did the day before. It is only possible to understand the importance of conventions by their observance over time. The ceremonial state opening of Parliament, for example, is an event which is loaded with convention dating from the days of Henry VIII, but it is not so important that its abolition would cause a constitutional crisis. The convention that the Queen must assent to any Bill before it becomes law is a more significant legal rule because it controls the validity of legislation.

Another aspect of conventions is that they are not observable in the same way as legal rules, and they are not horizontally equal. Some conventions are more important than others, as indicated above. The delineations of legal rules is more certain. Statutes are given effect over common-law rules, but the two codes are able to interact in a way that is controlled by the practices of the courts and the legal profession.

The rule of law, in Dicey's sense, is a different perspective on the concept of 'rules of law'. This is in itself a convention which underpins the understanding of democratic political systems. Law in this sense is placed at the centre of the orientation of political arrangements. It is also a convention that the principle that no one is above the law will be respected. However, this is a convention which is typically honoured more in the breach than the observance. It is unclear when the rule of law is broken in most circumstances because it is such an elastic rule, which seeks to guide behaviour rather than impose punishment for its breach. The fact that a convention may be breached without certainty as to whether or not it has been breached creates a very large difference from legal rules where, usually, not only is breach clear but the means of redress or punishment are set out or ascertainable.

Therefore, the nature of the rules of law and the constitutional conventions are very different. However, there is some similarity in their significance. With reference to the convention that the Queen in Parliament passes bills into Acts of Parliament by signing the Royal Assent, it is possible to say that when this convention is altered it would constitute a very great alteration in British constitutional arrangements. Therefore, one might conclude that there had been a significant change in the constitutional arrangements of the United Kingdom as a result. Similarly, where it is clear that there has been an alteration in a piece of legislation or a change in the common law by a superior court, there would be a change in the framework of the legal system within the United Kingdom. Many such changes in legal rules would, of course, not be of similar importance to the constitutional alteration caused by the end of the convention surrounding the Queen in Parliament. However, the incorporation of the European Convention on Human Rights would be of such importance. Therefore, it is possible to say that there are occasions where the alteration of a legal rule or a constitutional convention would be of similar importance and that, in those circumstances, there is no distinction in substance between the two.

SUGGESTED ANSWER TO QUESTION THREE

General Comment

This is a rather narrow question. It involves the role of the sovereign and is not an opportunity to deal generally with the executive use of the prerogative.

An understanding of the term 'convention(s)' is required. The candidate should also be able to discuss such issues as the appointment and dismissal of the Prime Minister and the related issue of the dissolution of Parliament. Historical examples are necessary when dealing with the influence of conventions upon the role of the monarchy. Also some knowledge of the 1975 Australian constitutional crisis would be useful.

Key Points

- Definition of conventions
- Royal Assent to Bills
- Appointment of ministers and the Prime Minister
- Dissolution of Parliament
- Conclusion

Suggested Answer

Constitutional conventions have been described by Dicey *The Law of the Constitution* (1959, 10th ed) as:

> '... understandings, habits or practices ... which are not in reality laws at all since they are not enforced by the courts.'

They do, however, make sense of the constitution, and in the words of Sir Ivor Jennings (*The Law and the Constitution* (1959)):

> '... they provide the flesh which clothes the dry bones of the law; they make the legal constitution work ...'

This is particularly true of the role of the monarch. The powers of the Head of State are limited by convention, and in the majority of cases the functions of the monarch have passed into the hands of other actors of the constitution or else the monarch has no discretion on how to act. This is correct, for example, at the basic level of how statutes come into existence. When a Bill has passed both House of Parliament (the Parliament Acts notwithstanding) the monarch is obliged to give it Royal Assent, or so the convention would indicate. The position is, however, slightly clouded when one looks at past events in constitutional history. The classic textbook example is that of Queen Anne in 1708 refusing to give her assent to the Scottish Militia Bill, thus seeming to indicate that the monarch is not obliged by convention to assent to each and every Bill. The facts are, however, somewhat more opaque in that not only did her ministers not object but in fact they rather approved of this course of action. In more recent times the issue was resurrected over the question of Home Rule for Ireland in the period of 1912–14. In April 1912 the Liberal Government introduced a Home Rule Bill in the House of Commons, and to avoid the nineteenth-century precedent of the Bill being rejected by the House of Lords stated that they would, if necessary, utilise the Parliament Act 1911 to by-pass the House of Lords' veto. The proposed legislation aroused strong opposition amongst the Ulster Protestant community and their supporters, the Conservative Unionists. The King (George V) had the theoretical power to thwart the progress of the Bill by insisting that an election be held before the legislation was passed or by refusing to assent to the Bill. A memorandum was in fact prepared by the King to Prime Minister Asquith but it was never sent because the outbreak of the 1914–18 war. The memorandum indicated that there might be occasions on which the King would be justified in refusing to assent to legislation. When this would occur is not completely clear, but the memorandum indicated that the Crown would only adopt this course of action if it would have the effect of diffusing a crisis. It is doubtful whether in today's political climate the monarch would contemplate such an action, even if proposed legislation would have the effect of abolishing the UK's position as a sovereign state (for instance, proposed legislation to join a federal European Union).

The sovereign (Queen Elizabeth II) has the theoretical power to appoint whoever she wishes as a minister, and she could in theory appoint somebody outside Parliament. In fact her power is regulated by convention, and ministerial appointments are made on the advice of the Prime Minister in relation to individuals who either sit in Parliament (meaning both Houses) or whom it is proposed will sit in Parliament by means of either a successful by-election or an elevation to the peerage. Such a constitutional arrangement does not generate controversy; in greater dispute is the sovereign's power to appoint a Prime Minister.

The Prime Minister (PM) is appointed from the contestants who are able to command an overall majority in the House of Commons. This does not normally present a problem, since because of the workings of the British electoral system one party usually commands an overall majority in the House of Commons and it is usually the leader of that party who then becomes PM.

Problems may arise if, for instance, an incumbent PM resigns. In the two leading political parties, Conservative and Labour, a method of electing the next leader is provided for. This was not always the case, and up to 1965 the Conservative Party leader used to 'emerge', which could theoretically leave the monarch with an area of discretion. In 1923 when the Conservative PM Bonar Law resigned, the Conservative Lord Curzon was put forward as his successor, but George V thought it appropriate to appoint the Conservative commoner Baldwin as the Labour Party was unrepresented in the Lords and the King was of the opinion that it would be inappropriate to appoint a peer as PM.

Such an event in unlikely to occur again, but in more recent history the question as to who should be PM was raised again. In February 1974 the election result proved inconclusive as no one party had an overall majority. The incumbent PM, Edward Heath (as he then was), only resigned after spending three days trying to construct a coalition government. The Queen waited until the situation sorted itself out and then called for the main opposition leader, Harold Wilson, to form a government. The possibility of such events repeating themselves would, of course be more likely if electoral reform is introduced and overall majority governments cease to be the norm. The role of the monarch in this area would be highlighted and the Queen would be able to exercise a discretionary function.

Of more constitutional significance is the role of the monarch in the dissolution or non-dissolution of Parliament. Whether or not Parliament is dissolved is not in fact governed by convention (contrary to popular belief). The request as to the dissolution of Parliament is made, since November 1918, by the PM. The Queen could in theory refuse to grant a dissolution, although this is not likely, particularly as the PM would probably then resign. The converse is also true, and the monarch could insist upon a dissolution of Parliament if the government of the day was planning controversial and unprecedented legislation. The example of George V in the decade before the 1914–18 war is a precedent for such action. Before George V would create the required number of Liberal peers to effect the passage of the Parliament Act 1911 he insisted upon the dissolution of Parliament and an election. This power is still vested in the monarch and it is correct to describe it as a personal prerogative rather than a conventional practice.

A more recent instance of this power of the monarch, and also the role of the monarch in appointing a PM, arose in Australia in 1975. The Governor-General of Australia represents the Queen and enjoys the power and privileges of the Head of State. As a result of an impasse between the House of Representatives and the Senate, the government was denied its financial support. In order to break the deadlock the Governor-General, Sir John Kerr, dismissed PM Gough Whitlam and called in the opposition leader as PM upon condition that he then requested a dissolution of Parliament. There would appear, however, to be no reason to suppose that the Governor-General, exercising the royal prerogative, could not insist upon a dissolution of Parliament.

The public conduct of the sovereign is largely determined by the operation of conventions. Although they are not laws, conventions are regarded by the sovereign as obligatory. Many matters, particularly relating to foreign affairs, such as the signing of treaties, are done in the name of the sovereign; they are not, however, associated with the public conduct of the sovereign. Those that are, such as the appointment of the Prime Minister, leave the sovereign with little discretion as to how to act. If an unpopular, in the eyes of Parliament, individual were to be appointed PM he or she would be unable to obtain a vote of confidence. It is the application of conventions that prevents the sovereign from becoming embroiled in political controversy and preserves the institution in a symbolic role.

SUGGESTED ANSWER TO QUESTION FOUR

General Comment

Not a difficult question, but an explanation of the doctrine of the separation of powers, and of the rule of law is required. The statement assumes that the British Constitution is based upon the doctrine of parliamentary sovereignty, and whilst this may well be true it is an assumption that needs to be considered.

Key Points

- Explain doctrine of separation of powers
- Provide examples of breach and observance
- Comment on importance
- Analyse the rule of law
- Consider Dicey's three propositions
- Example of each
- Conclusions on importance
- Consider the theory of sovereignty and what it means in practical terms for the constitution
- Give examples
- Conclusion

Suggested Answer

Is the doctrine of the separation of powers irrelevant in the British Constitution? The doctrine is based on the principle that the powers of the legislature, judiciary, and executive should be in different hands, so as to provide for a system of checks and balances between each branch of government. Under the constitution of the United States for example, the legislature, in the form of Congress, can veto the President's nominations for Supreme Court appointments. Similarly, the Supreme Court can invalidate legislation enacted by Congress, on the ground that it is 'unconstitutional'.

If one examines the British Constitution it is undoubtedly the case that one will find many examples of the doctrine being violated. Ministers, members of the executive, are allowed to sit as members of the legislative body, the House of Commons. Judges have a role in creating law, by virtue of their powers to 'discover' or develop the common law, a clear example of which is provided by *Shaw* v *DPP* (1962) (where a common law offence of corrupting public morals was invented by the judges); arguably this involves the judiciary in usurping, or at least duplicating, the functions of the legislature. Further many executive bodies such as tribunals and commissioners exercise 'judicial' functions, by determining the rights of an applicant to some benefit or compensation.

To suggest, however, that the doctrine of the separation of powers is thus of 'no application' to the British Constitution is, it is submitted, to go too far. One of the main purposes of the House of Commons Disqualification Act 1975 was to simplify the law relating to the involvement of members of the executive in the legislature. As a result, the number of government ministers permitted to sit in the House of Commons is strictly limited at 95. Civil servants must resign their posts in order to stand for election to the House; police officers and members of the armed forces are also disqualified from membership of the House. The doctrine of the separation of powers is also reflected in the fact that a Member of Parliament, although unable to resign from office, can disqualify himself by taking an 'office of profit under the Crown', such as Stewardship of the Chiltern Hundreds.

If the doctrine is really of little significance to the British Constitution, it is difficult to explain the importance attached to judicial review. By means of an application for judicial review judges are able to call upon their common law jurisdiction to adjudicate upon the legality of action taken by administrative agencies, which includes members of the executive such as ministers; for a striking example of this see *Padfield* v *Minister of Agriculture* (1968).

It is not easy to determine the importance of the rule of law to the British Constitution until one has explained what is meant by the concept. If one adopts a Diceyan approach the rule of law encompasses three notions, firstly the absolute predominance of regular law as opposed to the influence of arbitrary power, secondly equality of all subjects before the law, and thirdly that so-called constitutional law is simply the law of the land applied to the constitution.

As to the first of these notions, Dicey rejected 'arbitrary' power as being contrary to the rule of law, but in the modern state legislation is frequently enacted granting to ministers powers to act as they think fit in a given situation. The existence of such subjectively worded powers does not mean, however, that ministers can become a law unto themselves. Again one comes back to the significant role played within the constitution by judicial review. In *Padfield* v *Minister of Agriculture* (above), the House of Lords confirmed that the courts would not be inhibited from invalidating a minister's action simply because he purported to act within a broadly drafted power.

Equality of subjects before the law is perhaps less easy to establish in English law, if for no other reason than one party to litigation may be able to afford a more competent legal advisor than the other. Even if one takes the proposition to mean that no one is above the law and that the law applies equally to all, difficulties will still arise by virtue of the number of exceptions that can be cited.

Parliamentary privilege prevents MPs from being sued in respect of statements made in proceedings in Parliament, the immunities of foreign diplomats are well known, and judges enjoy various legal privileges as an incident of their holding office. Further, children under the age of ten are not subject to the criminal law. It is submitted, however, that these examples do not actually undermine the argument supporting the existence of the rule of law in the British constitution, but in fact add strength to it, since they are all examples of exemptions granted and recognised by law. It is certain that they could all be abolished or amended by law.

The third aspect of Dicey's theory of the rule of law is the most controversial, though recently it was invoked by Lord Steyn as justification for the common law enforcing minimum standards of fairness of executive action affecting fundamental human rights: *Pierson* v *Secretary of State for the Home Department* (1997) (a case concerning the Home Secretary's power to increase the trial judge's recommended sentence of imprisonment for a serious offender). Dicey's view seems to reject the idea that there could be a body of law known as 'public law' as distinct from the private law governing individual rights and duties. That Dicey should reject such an idea is not surprising given his suspicion that it might involve public bodies being above the law, or at least enjoying legal privileges in comparison with the private individual. Today it has to be accepted that there is a branch of law, dealing with government and administration which lawyers for convenience term as 'public law' but it has not necessarily resulted in the type of abuse Dicey might have feared.

Turning to parliamentary sovereignty, it would be foolish indeed to underestimate the importance of this doctrine to the British Constitution, since it is in many ways what marks it out as being different from many other constitutions. It does mean that the judiciary will refuse to invalidate legislation which has been enacted by Parliament, see ***Pickin* v *British Railways Board*** (1974). It also means that Parliament can enact legislation effectively nullifying a decision by the highest court, see ***Burmah Oil Co* v *Lord Advocate*** (1965) as followed by the War Damage Act 1965. Whether it is still as strong a constitutional force as it once was is, however, questionable. The contention that parliamentary sovereignty meant that no parliament could bind its successors has always seemed dubious as regards legislation granting independence to former colonies and dominions. Parliament could vote to repeal the Canada Act 1982, but it is unlikely that the Canadians would give any effect to such a measure by recognising it. The debate over whether membership of the European Union has resulted in loss of sovereignty has been raging for 25 years, but it is submitted that regardless of legal theory, there may well come a time when the United Kingdom is so firmly enmeshed in Europe that withdrawal ceases to be a practical option. What price parliamentary sovereignty then?

In conclusion, it is submitted that if one had to cite the most significant aspect of the British Constitution it would be parliamentary sovereignty, but this would not be on the basis that concepts such as the rule of law and the doctrine of the separation of powers were either redundant or irrelevant.

SUGGESTED ANSWER TO QUESTION FIVE

General Comment

This is not simply a question requiring discussion of the doctrine of separation of powers; more is needed. It is essential to weave the basic discussion of separation of powers into an analysis of Lord Donaldson's quote. This involves application rather than mere repetition of knowledge.

Key Points

- Judicial and academic views: *Duport Steels* v *Sirs* and de Smith
- Montesquieu's conception of separation of powers
- British Constitution as 'mixed' or 'balanced' - the Crown
- Position of Cabinet and the Lord Chancellor
- Separation of powers in law - House of Commons Disqualification Act 1975 and Act of Settlement 1700

- The role of conventions
- Functional overlaps
- Conclusions

Suggested Answer

Lord Donaldson here repeats the familiar judicial learning on the doctrine of separation of powers; as Lord Diplock said in an earlier case, 'the British Constitution, though largely unwritten, is firmly based on the separation of powers': *Duport Steels* v *Sirs* (1980). But it is important to note that not all agree. The late Stanley de Smith wrote that 'No writer of repute would claim that [the doctrine] is a central feature of the modern British system of government': *Constitutional and Administrative Law* (1985, 5th ed), p31. It follows that Lord Donaldson's dictum is based on an assumption: that 'our unwritten constitution rests upon a separation of powers'. It is thus necessary in discussing the quote to question whether this is a valid assumption.

The quote also posits two further assumptions: that legislature, executive and judiciary recognise the separation of powers; and that each organ of government concedes supremacy to the other in its proper sphere of operation. Parliament legislates, the judges judge, and the executive governs. These assumptions, too, are susceptible to challenge. This answer will attempt to challenge them.

The doctrine of the separation of powers as explained by the French jurist Montesquieu has it that 'All would be lost if ... the same body ... exercised these three powers, that of making laws, that of executing public decisions, and that of judging the crimes or the disputes of private persons': *L'Esprit des Lois* (1748), Book XI, Chapter 6. But the doctrine has never formally found a place in the British Constitution, which is best described as a mixed or balanced constitution; ultimately, the Crown is present in all three organs of government - the Queen in Parliament, Her Majesty's ministers and Her Majesty's judges. Thus, for example, the Cabinet is chosen by and from the legislature; but the admixture is best exemplified by the Lord Chancellor who at one and the same time is head of the judiciary, member of the Cabinet and presides in the upper chamber of the legislature.

It is true that elements of a formal separation are to be found in legislation: the House of Commons Disqualification Act 1975 restricts the number of ministers who may sit in the Commons, and disqualifies from membership holders of judicial office, as well as a significant number of members of the executive, including the police, civil service and armed forces; the independence of the judiciary was confirmed in the Act of Settlement 1700. And true, too, that separation is effected informally through the operation of constitutional conventions. In the House of Lords, for example, lay peers do not participate in judicial business and the Law Lords do not participate generally in contentious legislative business. But it is clear, as will be seen below, that there remain significant overlaps in function; it is thus hard to accept Lord Donaldson's assertion that the constitution 'rests upon a separation of powers'.

It is in these functional overlaps that most difficulty arises in accepting Lord Donaldson's assumptions that each organ recognises and respects the exclusive competence, the 'supremacy' of 'each in its own sphere'. Thus, the executive enjoys significant legislative powers by way of delegated legislation; and, although formally Parliament retains control of powers delegated, the likelihood is that a government with a sufficient majority controls Parliament. Members of the executive are closely involved in the administration of justice: the Home Secretary in exercising the prerogative of mercy and the law officers of the Crown in civil and criminal proceedings.

The judges, in developing the common law, enjoy at least a quasi-legislative role (*Shaw* v *DPP* (1962)), and regularly perform 'executive-type' functions chairing commissions or inquiries (see, for example, the Scott Report on the Arms to Iraq Affair (1996)). The functional division between legislature and executive is compromised, at least to the extent that government ministers must be members of one or other House of Parliament; and, as the High Court of Parliament, the legislature retains a judicial role in enforcing parliamentary privilege.

In conclusion, it would seem that Lord Donaldson's dictum paints too simplistic a picture. It is clear from the above discussion that the idea of the separation of powers is of importance in the British constitution and, to that extent, de Smith's view is also suspect. But to claim that the constitution 'rests upon a separation of powers' surely goes too far. Similarly, while there is certainly a degree of 'mutual recognition of those powers', the overlap in functions between executive, legislature and judiciary suggests that although each organ functions primarily within its own sphere, none is supreme therein. It is hard, therefore, to dissent from the view of the Donoughmore Report on Ministers' Powers in 1932 that the doctrine of separation of powers is no more than 'a rule of political wisdom which must give way when sound reasons of public policy so require'. It cannot be elevated, as Lord Donaldson seeks to do, to a fundamental of the constitution.

SUGGESTED ANSWER TO QUESTION SIX

General Comment

The question involves an understanding of the basic structure and workings of the British Constitution.

The candidate should be familiar with what is meant by the doctrine of separation of powers and how this idea is put into practice in the context of the unwritten constitution of the United Kingdom. This will also involve an appreciation of the workings of conventions and the role of important 'actors' in the constitution.

Key Points

- Definition of the doctrine
- Its strict application in other constitutional jurisdictions, eg the United States of America
- Relevance to the UK - the Westminister model - the comments of Bagehot - the role and functions of the Attorney-General, Lord Chancellor, the Law Lords
- In contradistinction, the independence of the judiciary, Act of Settlement, House of Commons Disqualification Act 1975 and the judiciary
- The status of the Crown
- Conclusion

Suggested Answer

The doctrine of separation of powers divides the workings of a constitution into three distinct branches. These are the legislature, the executive and the judiciary. The legislature passes the laws, the executive puts them into practice and the judiciary interprets them. The 'highpoint' of this doctrine is to be found in the works of the eighteenth century philosopher Montesquieu. In this book *The Spirit of the Law*, published in 1748, the author advances the view that the best foundation for individual liberty and good governance is to separate the three branches of government. The three branches of government will have distinct functions and none will be powerful enough to dominate the others. Montesquieu wrongly believed that this formula applied to the England of his time, but the theory served to influence the founding fathers of the American constitution, which does apply the doctrine in practice. A member of the United States Congress is forbidden, for example, to be a member of the United States government: art 1, s6.

How, then, is this doctrine relevant to the United Kingdom? First, the UK constitution is characterised by the blending of the executive and the legislature. It is unusual, as a result of constitutional conventional practice, for a member of the executive not to be a member of the legislature. If the government of the day wishes to bring in an outsider - a non-professional politician - into government then that individual must be found a seat in the legislature, either in the House of Commons through election or in the House of Lords through ennoblement. Walter Bagehot in his classical work *The English Constitution* (1867) describes the constitution as displaying 'the close union, the nearly complete fusion of the executive and legislative powers'.

He then went on to argue that the fusion takes place in the Cabinet, a body which he graphically described as:

> '... a combining committee - a hyphen which joins, a buckle which fastens the legislative part of the state to the executive part of the state. In its origin it belongs to the one, in its functions it belongs to another.'

The Cabinet and government only come into existence because the majority of the legislature wish it so, but, as Bagehot points out, the Cabinet (and now the Prime Minister) may request a dissolution of Parliament and 'annihilate the legislature'. In contrast, the United States' President cannot dissolve the Congress, nor is his existence dependent upon a majority in the legislature. The amalgamation of the executive and the legislature and the answerability of the executive to the legislature, demonstrated in Question Time, is one of the fundamental characteristics of the Westminister model of government.

The role and functions of particular offices in government display this amalgamation of the branches of government. The Attorney-General has a function as a quasi-judicial officer of the Crown. In this role he decides in a limited number of offences and cases whether or not to initiate a prosecution. In this he is answerable to Parliament - usually the House of Commons - and may in theory be removed by them in a vote of no confidence. The Attorney-General is a member of the government, although not a member of the Cabinet, a convention which resulted from the alleged pressure which was placed upon the then Attorney-General, Sir Patrick Hastings, who withdrew a prosecution against J R Campbell, acting editor of a Communist paper, for 'incitement to mutiny'. The Attorney-General does take into account the views of the Cabinet when performing his functions, but he is not bound by the views of the Cabinet or Prime Minister. When Lord Denning, in an inventive phase, tried to make the Attorney-General answerable to the courts, this was firmly repudiated by the House of Lords in *Gouriet* v *Union of Post Office Workers* (1977). Similarly, the Divisional Court in *R* v *Solicitor-General, ex parte Taylor* (1995) reiterated that the Attorney-General, or the Solicitor-General acting on his behalf, is not amenable to judicial review of his official decisions.

It is with the officer of Lord Chancellor that the absence of separation of powers is most marked. The Lord Chancellor is a member not only of the government but also of the Cabinet. He is chosen by the Prime Minister, and previous Lord Chancellors, such as Lord Hailsham, have had an active political career before ascending to the office. Indeed, Lord Hailsham once ran for the leadership of the Conservative Party. The Lord Chancellor has important administrative functions to perform in connection with the judiciary and is responsible for law reform, some of which may be politically controversial. The Lord Chancellor is also a judge and may preside over the judicial committee of the House of Lords. This office also entitles the holder to sit in the legislature (in the House of Lords), and the Lord Chancellor acts as Speaker of the upper chamber, performing a Janus-type role of acting as an umpire - although less active than the House of Commons Speaker - and participant. The Lord Chancellor is also instrumental in the appointment of members of the judiciary in practice and theory. Justices of the Peace (JPs) are appointed by the Lord Chancellor on the advice of local advisory committees. Without the benefit of an advisory committee he appoints, for instance, High Court judges, Circuit Judges and Recorders. He also has the power to remove members of the judiciary below the status of superior court judges.

While an adherence to the doctrine of separation of powers would imply the disconnection of the judiciary and the legislature this is not found with regard to the role of the Lords of Appeal in Ordinary. The Law Lords can and do play a part in the proceedings of the upper chamber, and while it used to be correct to say that they avoided politically controversial issues, this is not now strictly the case. The response of Lord Taylor, the then Lord Chief Justice, in 1996 to the Home Secretary's proposed reform of sentencing casts doubt over the previously accepted view.

Considering the above discussion then how may Lord Diplock accurately state that 'the British Constitution is firmly based upon the separation of powers': *Duport Steels* v *Sirs* (1980) Presumably what is meant by this statement is the adherence to the concept of the independence of the judiciary. The Act of Settlement 1700 provided that the superior court judges should hold office upon 'good behaviour' rather than the 'King's pleasure' as had been the case. The independence of the judiciary and the inability of the executive to remove them is one of the hallmarks of the separation of powers. Since 1700 superior court judges can only be removed by the Crown on an address presented to it by both Houses of Parliament. It has to be said, however, that Circuit Judges and Recorders may be removed from office by the Lord Chancellor for 'inability or misbehaviour'.

Also, in accordance with the separation of the judiciary from the legislature and the executive is the statutory prohibition of full time members of the judiciary from the House of Commons: House of Commons Disqualification Act 1975.

All of the above, of course, is based upon the conventional (in the technical sense) role of the monarchy. While the Queen is forbidden to enter the House of Commons this is of little or no practical significance as her Ministers dominate the chamber. One may nevertheless conclude that although under the Westminister model the theory of separation of powers is more honoured in the breach than the observance; nevertheless the adherence to the practice of the independence of the judiciary has meant that the courts may maintain an independent and separate existence from the law-makers.

SUGGESTED ANSWER TO QUESTION SEVEN

General Comment

This is a fairly straightforward consideration of Dicey's formulation of the rule of law. One needs to be familiar with its three aspects and have examples to illustrate each in terms of the modern state. The consensus view is that it remains a useful theoretical yardstick with questionable modern application.

Key Points

- Define the rule of law
- Consider each of three aspects (predominance of regular law, equality before the law and the constitution as part of ordinary law)
- Provide examples for each
- Conclusion - recent use of rule of law during a judicial review (*Pierson* v *Secretary of State for the Home Department*)

Suggested Answer

When Professor Dicey formulated his concept of the rule of law in *The Law of the Constitution* (1885), he was not the first theorist to consider the phrase. However, his definition of the rule of law as one of the main features of the constitution of the United Kingdom has had such an influence on constitutional theory that the phrase has become firmly associated with Dicey. Whether the phrase is relevant to modern constitutional practice is less certain.

To Dicey, the rule of law had three separate aspects. Firstly, that 'regular law' was absolutely predominant over the influence of arbitrary or widely discretionary power. In other words, only by a breach of law established by an ordinary court could a person be made to suffer any penalties.

Secondly, the rule of law meant the equality of all before the law - and before the same law. For example, conflicts between the individual and the state were not dealt with in administrative courts. Thirdly, the constitution was the result of the ordinary law of the land which determined and protected the rights of the individual. There was no 'higher' constitutional law.

How relevant are these aspects of the rule of law today? Dealing with Dicey's first concept, the modern state is to a great extent run by discretionary powers. For example, Parliament delegates wide discretionary power to ministers. The use of this power, as, for instance, in the compulsory purchase of land, will often have far-reaching effect. That does not make the power 'arbitrary' but neither - in Dicey's terms - does this power emanate from the 'regular law'. The emphasis today is on the control of that power, such as by the courts through judicial review, as in *Padfield* v *Minister of Agriculture* (1968).

Personal freedom within the modern state can certainly be infringed without a breach of the law being established. Police powers of arrest where there are 'reasonable grounds of suspecting' (Police and Criminal Evidence Act 1984) are one example. The suspension of rights allowed by the Prevention of Terrorism (Temporary Provisions) Act 1989 is another. The detention of suspected terrorists in Northern Ireland under the powers of internment in the early 1970s would be a notable abuse of Dicey's concept. However, all of these are based upon powers granted by Parliament. It appears difficult, therefore, to reconcile the Rule of Law on the one hand with the power of Parliament to legislate on the other.

Dicey's second concept - equality before the law - was not in terms of discriminatory provisions. If it were, then anti-discriminatory legislation such as the Race Relations Act 1976 and the Sex Discrimination Act 1975 would no doubt have appealed to his theories. What Dicey had in mind more was the resolution of conflicts between individual and state. In France, the droit administratif (French public law) dealt with such matters separately and - in Dicey's view - with advantage to the state. This was not the case in the United Kingdom.

While it is true that administrative law does not form a separate code, it is a separate branch of the law and there are many tribunals - as opposed to the regular civil courts - which deal with such matters. Of course that does not mean they are partial and appeals from such bodies may take one into the regular structure. However, to some extent there is a parallel system with its own procedures and remedies.

Dicey was also referring to no person being above the law. One can easily list exceptions - the Monarch's immunity under the Crown Proceedings Act 1947, MPs' freedom from liability for anything said in Parliament, diplomatic immunity, judicial immunity in respect of the exercise of judicial functions (*Anderson* v *Gorrie* (1985)). However, these exceptions are granted and recognised by law and many existed in similar terms in Dicey's day. Their existence does not deny the rule of law, but certainly qualifies this second aspect.

With regard to the third aspect, it is true that there is still no superior constitutional law, though this may change after the incorporation of the European Convention on Human Rights (expected during 1998).

Dicey's formulation of the rule of law was set against the background of the nineteenth-century state. In that sense, much of it has become outmoded and cannot be said to describe the modern state. However, the relevance of a theory is not determined only by its practical application. It is submitted that Dicey's formulation of the rule of law remains a useful yardstick for measuring the position of the individual in relation to the state, and a good recent example can be found in Lord Steyn's use of the third aspect (above) to enforce minimum standards of fairness of executive action affecting fundamental human rights: see *Pierson* v *Secretary of State for the Home Department* (1997), where judicial review was granted so as to quash the Home Secretary's decision to increase arbitrarily the recommended sentence of imprisonment passed by the trial judge on a serious offender. Lord Steyn's judgment shows that Dicey's rule of law is very much alive in the modern British Constitution.

2

The Sovereignty of Parliament and Membership of the European Union

Introduction

This chapter is concerned with the most fundamental rule of the British Constitution, namely the doctrine of parliamentary sovereignty. The concept of legislative supremacy has been the subject of much critical analysis. Particular themes to consider are its relationship to other constitutional tenets, such as the separation of powers and the rule of law; possible limits to legislative sovereignty, whether in the form of practical, political or legal limits; and the effect on parliamentary sovereignty of membership of the European Union. For this purpose a background knowledge of the institutions and sources of Community law is essential, and it is also necessary to understand the implications for national sovereignty of leading cases in Community law such as *Van Gend en Loos* [1963] ECR 1, *Costa* v *ENEL* [1964] ECR 585, *Marleasing SA* v *La Comercial Internacionale de Alimentacion SA* [1990] ECR I-4135, *Francovich* v *Italian Republic* [1993] 2 CMLR 66, and the *Factortame* cases, particularly *Factortame (No 2)* [1991] 1 AC 603 and *Factortame (No 4)* [1996] 2 WLR 506.

Much of the reasoning in these cases is complex and controversial. It has been argued that the European Court of Justice, the main judicial organ of the European Union, has adopted a political interpretation of Treaty obligations so as to facilitate the movement to a federal system of government. There is no room for concepts such as parliamentary sovereignty so far as such a doctrine of national law may impede political union of the 15 Member States.

It follows that any analysis of sovereignty needs to distinguish clearly between the European dimension and purely national or domestic issues. For example, the moves towards legislating for a Bill of Rights (expected to be completed during 1998) revive the old arguments over whether it is possible to 'entrench' such legislation. Competing theories as to the nature of sovereignty need to be examined: the 'continuing concept', the 'self-embracing' concept and the 'redefinition theory' need to be analysed with reference to possible precedents on changes in sovereignty such as the Parliament Acts 1911 and 1949 and the European Communities Act 1972.

If, however, an issue arises involving a conflict between UK and Community law, traditional concepts of sovereignty need to be analysed in the context of the 'new legal order' created originally by the Treaty of Rome 1957 and developed by later inter-governmental agreements such as the Treaty on European Union (Maastricht). New concepts such as 'subsidiarity' may have come to replace traditional notions of national sovereignty; art 3b of the Treaty on European Union provides that, in areas which do *not* fall within the exclusive competence of Community institutions (known as the 'occupied field'), the Community shall take action only if and so far as the objectives of proposed action cannot be sufficiently achieved by Member States and can be better achieved by Community institutions.

In a typical examination paper at least one question can be anticipated on the doctrine of parliamentary sovereignty, and in recent years the emphasis has been on the impact on sovereignty of membership of the European Union, either in a problem-type question involving a conflict of laws or an essay-type question requiring critical analysis of such impact. It is useful when answering such questions to make use of academic contributions in the leading law journals. Recent examples include: Wade (1996) 112 LQR 568, Craig (1997) 113 LQR 67, Eekelaar (1997) 113 LQR 185, Allan (1997) 113 LQR 443, Spink (1997) 113 LQR 524 and Marshall [1997] PL 1.

Questions

INTERROGRAMS

1 What is meant by the 'sovereignty of Parliament'?
2 Is it possible to reconcile sovereignty with the rule of law?
3 Is it possible to entrench legislation?
4 Outline the constitutional implications of ss2 and 3 of the European Communities Act 1972.

QUESTION ONE

'It is often said that it would be unconstitutional for the United Kingdom Parliament to do certain things, meaning that the moral, political and other reasons against doing them are so strong that most people would regard it as highly improper if Parliament did these things. But this does not mean that it is beyond the power of Parliament to do such things. If Parliament chose to do any of them the courts could not hold the Act of Parliament invalid.' (*Madzimbamuto* v *Lardner-Burke* (1969), *per* Lord Reid).

Discuss.

London University LLB Examination
(for external students) Constitutional Law June 1995 Q1

QUESTION TWO

'Attempts to entrench legislation by legal means will inevitably be futile unless the basic rule of the United Kingdom's Constitution is abandoned.'

Discuss.

London University LLB Examination
(for external students) Constitutional Law June 1991 Q1

QUESTION THREE

It is now over 25 years since the United Kingdom entered the European Economic

Community (now known as the European Union). To what extent have British courts taken account of this constitutional change?

Adapted from London University LLB Examination
(for external students) Constitutional Law June 1992 Q1

QUESTION FOUR

'The *Factortame (No 2)* [1991] 1 All ER 70 decision marks a significant departure from the traditionally accepted view of parliamentary sovereignty.'

Critically assess this statement.

Adapted from London University LLB Examination
(for external students) Constitutional Law June 1994 Q1

QUESTION FIVE

Discuss, by reference to decided cases, the legal status of European Community law within the United Kingdom and its priority in relation to provisions in domestic Acts of Parliament.

London University LLB Examination
(for external students) Constitutional Law June 1996 Q4

Answers

ANSWERS TO INTERROGAMS

1 Parliamentary sovereignty, as defined by Professor Dicey, means that the legislature can make or unmake any law whatever; and that the legality or validity of an authentic Act of Parliament cannot be challenged in any court or place outside of Parliament. It follows from this definition that a judge must give effect not only to an express repeal of legislation but also to any statutory provision which is inconsistent with any earlier statutory provision by treating the earlier provision as being impliedly repealed by the later statute: *Vauxhall Estates Ltd* v *Liverpool Corporation* [1932] 1 KB 733.

2 Although the theoretical supremacy of Parliament cannot be legally constrained by measures designed to uphold the rule of law, Professor Dicey suggested that practical and political realities would prevent the legislature from using its sovereign powers to undermine the rule of law. No Parliament, said Dicey, would pass a law to authorise the killing of all blue-eyed babies: *Introduction to the Study of the Law of the Constitution* (1959, 10th ed), p81. Apart from this extreme example, Dicey suggested that the 'internal' limit of MPs' consciences and the 'external' limit of political unrest would ensure that Parliament did not exercise its powers so as to infringe fundamental principles, such as the need to uphold equality under the law.

However, Dicey's analysis has been criticised for failing to take account of potentially oppressive uses of legislative power, what Lord Hailsham described in 1974 as the threat of an 'elective dictatorship'. The demand for a Bill of Rights as a device for checking such abuses of power grew so strong that it is expected that such a Bill will be enacted during 1998.

3 The traditional Diceyan definition of parliamentary sovereignty is based on the concept that sovereignty is 'continuing', ie that Parliament is a perpetual institution whose unconfined legislative power is created afresh every time it meets regardless of what previous Parliaments have enacted. If this is correct it would follow that one Parliament cannot legally limit in manner or form the legislative competence of a future Parliament. This view has received judicial support: see *Ellen Street Estates Ltd* v *Minister for Health* [1934] 1 KB 590.

However, critics of Dicey, notably Professor Jennings in *The Law and the Constitution* (1959, 5th ed), argue that whilst authority is a continuing concept the exercise of power by that authority is not so that it is possible for the sovereign authority to alter the manner by which it exercises its power for certain purposes. This is known as either the 'self-embracing' theory or the the 'redefinition' theory, and support for it is found in decisions of Commonwealth courts in countries which followed the Westminster system of parliamentary government. If British judges followed that approach, rather than the Diceyan approach, it would be legally possible to entrench legislation, eg by providing that a Bill of Rights could be amended or repealed only with the consent of the people in a referendum *in addition to* the ordinary parliamentary process.

4 Section 2 European Communities Act 1972 provides, in effect, that any existing or future Acts of Parliament must be interpreted and applied subject to directly effective Community law. This gives a special constitutional status to Community law. Judges are directed as to the order of priorities in the event of conflicts between Community law and United Kingdom law: Community law must prevail. It is not open to judges to treat such a conflict as an implied repeal of s2 of the 1972 Act because Parliament provided a new solution to replace the common law doctrine of implied repeal in this special situation. This solution (to give priority to Community law) operates on the assumption that any conflict is accidental, and that Parliament would wish the judges to deal with the matter by giving effect to the international obligations assumed by the United Kingdom under the Community treaties: see *McCarthys Ltd* v *Smith* [1979] 3 All ER 325. In this case, Lord Denning MR suggested, obiter, that in the event of a deliberate and intentional breach of Community law s2 could not be applied because ultimate parliamentary sovereignty remains intact.

Section 3 of the European Communities Act 1972 provides, in effect, that decisions of the European Court of Justice as to the meaning or effect of any Community treaty or instrument is binding on national courts, ie the European Court became the supreme court for the United Kingdom on matters of Community law. In a series of decisions starting with *Van Gend en loos* [1963] ECR 1, the European Court developed a line of reasoning to the effect that the Treaty of Rome 1957 had created 'a new legal order' for the benefit of which Member States have limited their sovereign rights. Any rule of national law, even a fundamental constitutional doctrine such as parliamentary sovereignty, became 'irrelevant' in this new legal order. This view was accepted by the House of Lords in *R* v *Secretary of State for Transport, ex parte Factortame (No 2)* [1991] 1 AC 603 as justification for disapplying the Merchant Shipping Act 1988 so far as it was found to breach art 52 of the Treaty of Rome 1957.

SUGGESTED ANSWER TO QUESTION ONE

General Comment

This question is a general theoretical problem which requires some discussion of basic constitutional theory. The candidate must take care with this problem and not merely launch into it because it appears to be straightforward. Obtaining a strong mark in very generally based questions can be difficult unless the candidate is scrupulous to ensure that the answer is well structured. Beyond that, it is a question asking for a discussion of the interaction between Parliament and the courts, and an explanation of the possible limitations that exist to the theoretical absolute sovereignty of Parliament.

Key Points

- Comparison with the USA
- Discussion of the scope of judicial review in English law to review executive action
- Discussion of the Criminal Justice and Public Order Act 1994 as an example of courts' ability to control Parliament
- Use of statutory interpretation to control legislation partially
- Overall sovereignty of Parliament explained

Suggested Answer

There is a tension between the theoretical constitutional powers of Parliament and those acts which Parliament can perform without attracting political censure. The basic rule of constitutional law is that Parliament is the sovereign body and that any Act of Parliament passed by the Queen in Parliament supersedes any other rule or decree. Therefore, at least in theory, there is a possibility that Parliament can act in any way that it sees fit.

In the United States of America, the Supreme Court has the power to review any legislative act of the executive or the legislature. Therefore, the principle of sovereignty under United States constitutional arrangements is that the Supreme Court has a residuary power to find that any particular act is unconstitutional.

There is no such power in the United Kingdom legal jurisdiction. The English law doctrine of judicial review has led to a power in the High Court to review certain acts of public bodies or the acts of ministers in the exercise of the prerogative powers of the Crown. There is, therefore, a development of the ability of the courts to look at the powers of the executive and their exercise. However, these powers derive directly from the Supreme Court Act 1981 and therefore can be said to be constitutional 'long-stop' functions created by the powers of Parliament itself, rather than judicial powers to curtail the exercise of those of Parliament. Judicial powers are restricted to the categories of unreasonableness or breaches of natural justice: *Associated Provincial Picture Houses Ltd* v *Wednesbury Corporation* (1948).

It is important to note that judicial review cannot curtail the power of the legislature or executive by retaining a power to overturn legislation, nor can it affect the power of the legislature, Parliament, to pass legislation by exercising judicial review principles. There is no ability to say that an Act of Parliament offends some principle of natural justice or that it is *Wednesbury* unreasonable in some way. Therefore, there is no judicial control over Parliament.

As a result of a lack of judicial competence, and in the absence of a written constitution making plain any other control over the powers of Parliament, judicial review principles have grown to fill the gap. Indeed, it would be undesirable if it were possible for some agency other than Parliament itself to overturn its powers. That would lead to a political conflict outside the scope of the British constitutional arrangement of parliamentary elections and the sovereignty of the Queen in Parliament.

The question arises: to what extent does Parliament act against the interests of the constitutional order by doing things which are, per se, unconstitutional? The answer to that question is that Parliament does not tend to do things that are unconstitutional on such a regular basis that the constitutional order would be threatened. The system of democratic elections ensures that the House of Commons has a vested interest in not exercising powers which it would be unable to justify to the British electorate.

Therefore, legislation like the Criminal Justice and Public Order Act 1994 can be passed by Parliament, despite the fact that it seems to interfere with the rights of citizens to freedom of movement and action in prescribed circumstances. On the United States model, it would be possible for the Supreme Court to consider whether or not this exercise of power was unconstitutional. If it were found to be unconstitutional, then it would be possible to refer the legislation back to Parliament as constitutionally invalid.

The Westminster model, however, invests no such power in the courts. The Criminal Justice and Public Order Act 1994 cannot be declared invalid. The courts, however, are able to interpret it in such a way that the sense it appeared to have when passed through Parliament is tempered somewhat to ensure that it complies with a level of fairness on the facts of any case. In September 1995 (in an unreported decision), s70 of the 1994 Act was invoked against an individual claiming to be King Arthur. He sought to gain access to Stonehenge at the time of the Solstice. However, the police arrested him for criminal trespass on the basis that there were more than 20 people gathered together seeking to trespass on land. The court held that of the 20 or more people in attendance, most were not known to the defendant, being either television crews or simply bystanders. Therefore, s70 was held not to apply on these facts. This is an example of the way in which a court can interpret the wording of an Act to suit the court's view of what is appropriate in the circumstances. Contrast *DPP* v *Jones* (1997), where it was held that any assembly of 20 or more persons, even if peaceful and static and non-obstructive of the highway, would be a trespassory assembly and unlawful if there was an order in force under the Act prohibiting trespassory assemblies in the vicinity in question.

The fact that this legislation can be passed without any power to prevent it is perhaps more a testament to shortcomings in the democratic system than to the constitutional rules per se. It might be possible to vote for a different government which was committed to the repeal of this legislation; however, there is no political party currently committed in this way. Therefore, there is a gap between constitutional theory, which might hold that there has been a technical breach of some standard of natural justice, and the political realities of democratic power.

SUGGESTED ANSWER TO QUESTON TWO

General Comment

A question requiring an explanation of the terms used, particularly 'entrenchment', and 'the basic rule of the constitution'. It is important to explain how parliamentary sovereignty manifests itself thus indicating the difficulties with entrenchment. Obviously the impact of membership of the European Union (EU) upon parliamentary sovereignty also needs to be considered.

Key Points

- Explain nature of sovereignty
- Express and implied repeal - examples
- Nature of European Communities Act
- Decisions thereunder
- Implications of the *Factortame* litigation
- Conclusion

Suggested Answer

Entrenchment of legislation involves the enactment of clauses that prevent the Act concerned from being repealed by simple majority vote by the legislative body. A typical example is provided by art V of the United States' constitution under which two thirds of the members of Congress have to approve an amendment to the constitution, which in turn has to receive the support of three quarters of the state legislatures. The purpose of entrenchment is clearly to protect those constitutional measures which are seen as being particularly fundamental. A constitution that could not be altered at all would soon become obsolete and disregarded in practice. One that could be changed by a simple majority vote would be at the mercy of passing political trends, especially where a small party held the balance of power because an election had produced a 'hung' parliament.

The question under consideration refers to attempts at entrenchment within the British constitution being futile because of the constitution's basic rule. By this it is assumed that the question is referring to the doctrine of parliamentary sovereignty, under which Parliament has the ultimate power to pass or repeal any legislation it sees fit. In short it is being suggested that it will not avail Parliament to include entrenchment provisions in a piece of legislation in an effort to protect it, as a natural consequence of parliamentary sovereignty is that no parliament can bind its successor parliaments. To what extent does the operation of the British constitution support this view?

Traditionally, constitutional lawyers have pointed to the operation of two doctrines as evidence of the inability of any parliament to bind its successors; express repeal and implied repeal. Under the former, any Parliament could enact legislation expressly repealing existing legislation. Where two pieces of legislation appeared irreconcilable, but the later Act did not expressly state that its effect was to repeal the terms of the earlier Act, the doctrine of implied repeal would be brought into play by means of which the courts would assume that it was implicit in the passage of the later legislation that Parliament had intended to repeal the earlier legislation since they could not stand together. Attempts by Parliament to circumvent the doctrine of implied repeal in the earlier part of the 20th century met with little success.

This is illustrated by the cases of *Vauxhall Estates Ltd* v *Liverpool Corporation* (1932), and *Ellen Street Estates Ltd* v *Minister of Health* (1934).

In the first of these cases, the Corporation of Liverpool proposed a scheme for the improvement of a certain area of the city. The Minister of Health confirmed the scheme in an order which incorporated the provisions of the Acquisition of Land (Assessment of Compensation) Act 1919 and the Housing Act 1925. These two Acts each provided a different scheme of compensation for compulsorily acquired land. The 1919 Act provided in s7(1):

> 'The provisions of the ... order by which the land is authorised to be acquired, or of any Act incorporated therewith, shall in relation to the matters dealt with in this Act, have effect subject to this Act, and so far as inconsistent with this Act those provisions shall ... not have effect.'

The question arose as to whether the compensation due to the appellants should be calculated in accordance with the 1919 Act or in accordance with the 1925 Act. The appellants argued that, because of s7(1) of the 1919 Act, it must be calculated in accordance with that Act.

It was held that the compensation should be assessed in accordance with the later Act. Parliament had exercised its power of overriding the provisions of s7(1) of the 1919 Act by enacting in the later Act of 1925 a set of provisions totally inconsistent with those of the 1919 Act. Similarly, in the *Ellen Street* case it was held that the provisions of an earlier Act could always be repealed, by implication, by provisions in a later Act which were inconsistent with those in the earlier Act. Maugham LJ stated the effect of the doctrine as follows:

> '... the Legislature cannot, according to our constitution, bind itself as to the form of subsequent legislation, and it is impossible for Parliament to enact that in a subsequent statute dealing with the same subject-matter there can be no implied repeal.'

It should be clear from the above that the doctrine of parliamentary sovereignty depends in large measure on the adherence by the judiciary to the practice of applying the later Act in preference to an earlier one.

Membership of the European Union may require the assumptions implicit in the question to be re-assessed, however. Section 2(1) European Communities Act 1972 provides that all EC law became part of United Kingdom law with effect from 1 January 1973. Section 2(4) further provides that:

> '... any such provision (of any such extent) as might be made by Act of Parliament, and any enactment passed or to be passed, other than one contained in this Part of this Act, shall be construed and have effect subject to the foregoing provisions of this section ...'

In other words, any subsequent Act passed by the United Kingdom Parliament was to take effect only to the extent that it did not conflict with the provisions of EC law. This was clearly another attempt to bypass the doctrine of implied repeal, but it was one that was necessary if the United Kingdom was going to be able to abide by its obligations under the terms of the Treaty of Rome, which requires each Member State to give primacy to EC law: see *Costa* v *ENEL* (1964). The result has been that the domestic courts have modified the doctrine of implied repeal as regards domestic law and EC legislation, by holding that domestic law should always be interpreted in a manner that produces a result consistent with the United Kingdom's obligations under the Treaty: see *Macarthys Ltd* v *Smith* (1981) and *Garland* v *British Rail Engineering Ltd* (1983), wherein Lord Diplock stated that, in a case of clear conflict, domestic courts would still have to produce an interpretation of domestic law that ensured conformity with EC law, '... no matter how wide a departure from the prima facie meaning may be needed to achieve consistency'.

Following *R* v *Secretary of State for Transport, ex parte Factortame (No 2)* (1991), it is now clear that the domestic courts have to be prepared to go as far as suspending the operation of an Act of Parliament if it is impugned on the ground that it conflicts with EU law whilst that issue is being considered by the European Court of Justice. It is submitted that short of the United Kingdom expressly repealing the European Communities Act 1972, the Act effectively entrenches EU law, by making it impossible for any later Act to be applied in preference to EU law by means of implied repeal.

Note that this result is achieved because of the existence of bodies outside the United Kingdom (such as the European Commission and Court of Justice) given jurisdiction by the United Kingdom Parliament over matters formerly within its control, and further given power to invoke sanctions against the United Kingdom if it attempts to re-assert that sovereignty by indirect means.

SUGGESTED ANSWER TO QUESTION THREE

General Comment

This question requires a good knowledge of case law but is otherwise a straightforward discussion of the effects of European Union membership on the constitution.

Key Points

- Hoffmann J in *Stoke-on-Trent* v *B & Q plc*
- Effect of membership
- ECJ's view
- Doctrine of implied repeal
- *Macarthys Ltd* v *Smith* and the rule of construction
- The *Factortame* litigation
- Conclusion

Suggested Answer

In the case of *Stoke-on-Trent City Council* v *B & Q plc* (1991) Hoffmann J stated that the Treaty of Rome is the supreme law of this country and went on to say that Britain's entry into the European Communities:

> '... meant that (subject to our undoubted but probably theoretical right to withdraw from the Community altogether) Parliament surrendered its sovereign right to legislate contrary to the provisions of the Treaty.'

If this clear and unequivocal statement is an accurate reflection of judicial thinking then it suggests that over the last 25 years, the courts have recognised and embraced the constitutional changes created by our entry into the European Communities (now the European Union).

The different interpretations of s2 European Communities Act 1972 - the Act whereby the Treaty of Accession was incorporated - allowed initial confusion over the courts' role. While s2 gave direct legal effect to Community law, the issue of parliamentary sovereignty was unresolved. The view of the European Court of Justice was always clear: Community law should prevail over national law in all circumstances (*Costa* v *ENEL* (1964)).

However, English courts were faced with a potential conflict. By the doctrine of implied repeal, a later and conflicting Act impliedly repeals earlier legislation with which it is inconsistent: *Vauxhall Estates Ltd* v *Liverpool Corporation* (1932). Therefore, were Parliament to pass an Act which conflicted with Community law - either an article of the Treaty of Rome or Community legislation given legal effect by the European Communities Act 1972 - then in theory the later Act should prevail.

This problem faced the Court of Appeal in *Macarthys Ltd* v *Smith* (1979) where there was a potential conflict between domestic employment statutes and the equal pay provisions of art 119. Lord Denning MR recognised the constitutional change and presumed that Parliament, in passing legislation, intended to legislate consistently with Community law. This allowed the court to interpret domestic law in a way that was consistent with Community law, although recognising that Community law has priority. However, while implied repeal was effectively abandoned, Parliament's ability expressly to repeal remained.

The House of Lords in *Garland* v *British Rail Engineering Ltd* (1983) also adopted this approach, which might be termed a 'rule of construction'. However, both cases involved directly enforceable legislation. This compromise view, which recognised constitutional change but did not necessarily embrace it, would most likely have been sufficient, since a situation where Parliament passed an Act which openly opposed Community law was unlikely since it would amount to repudiation of membership.

However, the important *Factortame* litigation revealed the potential conflicts: *R* v *Secretary of State for Transport, ex parte Factortame (No 1)* (1989) and *(No 2)* (1991). The Merchant Shipping Act 1988 was arguably inconsistent with the anti-discriminatory provisions of art 52. An interim injunction pending resolution of the issue would effectively suspend an Act of Parliament. The House of Lords - and inferior courts - were doubly concerned with this suspension of sovereignty, as injunctive relief is not available against the Crown under s21 Crown Proceedings Act 1947.

While the outcome of the case determined that the Act was discriminatory and that injunctive relief was available, its constitutional significance was greater. Not only did it confirm the supremacy of EC law but it showed that the constitutional function of the courts is to enforce rights created by Community law.

Hoffmann J's dicta in *Stoke-on-Trent City Council* v *B and Q plc* therefore reflect political reality and it is submitted that they show judicial reality. However, there is a need for further discussion of the role of the courts if the effect of the constitutional changes brought about by membership of the European Union has also altered the balance between Parliament and the judiciary.

SUGGESTED ANSWER TO QUESTION FOUR

General Comment

A fairly straightforward question on the effect of membership of the European Union on the doctrine of parliamentary sovereignty. It is important to answer the question: that is, critically assess the statement. While it is possible to argue that *Factortame (No 2)* either is or is not a significant departure, the approach taken here will be that it is not.

Key Points

- Dicey on sovereignty
- Express repeal: *Macarthys Ltd* v *Smith*
- Supremacy in EU law
- European Communities Act 1972
- Implied repeal
- The *Factortame* litigation
- Conclusion

Suggested Answer

There is no doubt that the United Kingdom's membership of the European Union has had some effect on the traditionally accepted view of parliamentary sovereignty: in particular, the doctrine of implied repeal has been modified. To this extent the statement in the question is correct, although one might argue about the word 'significant'. In *R* v *Secretary of State for Transport, ex parte Factortame (No 2)* (1991) the House of Lords clearly accepted the doctrine of the supremacy of European Community law. But it is arguable that their Lordships did so by reference to the traditionally accepted view of parliamentary sovereignty; European Community law is supreme because Parliament has said so in the European Communities Act 1972.

Thus, the *Factortame (No 2)* decision, far from departing in any significant way from the doctrine of parliamentary sovereignty, is in fact in accordance therewith. To explain this argument it is necessary to consider: first, Dicey's traditional view of parliamentary sovereignty; second, the doctrine of supremacy in European Community law; third, the European Communities Act 1972 and its effect on the doctrines of implied repeal and express repeal; and, fourth, the *Factortame (No 2)* case itself. Finally, in conclusion, it will be suggested that that decision does not mark 'a significant constitutional departure from the traditionally accepted view of parliamentary sovereignty'.

Dicey explained parliamentary sovereignty in terms of two propositions: in its positive sense, it meant that 'Parliament ... has ... the right to make or unmake any law whatever'; in the negative, that 'no person or body is recognised by the law of England as having a right to override or set aside the legislation of Parliament'. It is hard to see how European Union membership affects the former proposition; as Lawton LJ said in *Macarthys Ltd* v *Smith* (1979), 'Parliament's recognition of European Community law and of the jurisdiction of the European Court of Justice by one enactment can be withdrawn by another'. And, while the European Court of Justice can require that a national court set aside domestic legislation, the source of the power of an English court to do so lies in the European Communities Act 1972 - an Act of Parliament.

As a matter of European Community law, there can be few propositions clearer than the doctrine of supremacy as developed by the European Court of Justice; in the event of conflict between European Community law and domestic law, the former must prevail: *Costa* v *ENEL* (1964); *Amministrazione delle Finanze dello Stato* v *Simmenthal SpA* (1978). The supremacy of European Community law was accepted doctrine at the time the United Kingdom joined the European Community in 1972.

Apart from the incorporation of both past and future European Community law via s2(1), s3 European Communities Act 1972 requires English courts to decide questions of European Community law in accordance with the principles laid down by the European Court of Justice - which include its jurisprudence on supremacy. Section 2(4) provides that the European Communities Act 1972 will have precedence over both pre-accession legislation and that, for Acts passed after 1973, these 'shall be construed and have effect' subject to European Community law; it is this latter which gives rise to arguments that membership has affected the Diceyan view of parliamentary sovereignty.

It seems clear that the courts have treated s2(4) as empowering them to depart from the doctrine of implied repeal (as laid down in *Vauxhall Estates Ltd* v *Liverpool Corporation* (1932) and *Ellen Street Estates Ltd* v *Minister of Health* (1934)), whereunder a later and conflicting Act impliedly repeals earlier legislation with which it is inconsistent: see, eg, *Garland* v *British Rail Engineering* (1983); *Litster* v *Forth Dry Dock and Engineering Co* (1990). But it is hard to find any statement in the dicta that express repeal has been abandoned; European Community law is supreme because English law says so, in the European Communities Act. This approach is exemplified in *Factortame* itself.

In *R* v *Secretary of State for Transport, ex parte Factortame (No 1)* (1989), the applicants argued that the Merchant Shipping Act 1988 was in conflict with European Community law; the Divisional Court sought a ruling on the question of compatibility from the European Court of Justice and, pending its reply, ordered that parts of the 1988 Act should be suspended in their application. Its decision was reversed by both the Court of Appeal and the House of Lords on the grounds that English law did not permit the award of interim relief against the Crown. Their Lordships referred a second question to the European Court of Justice: whether European Community law required that the Act be disapplied on an interim basis pending a final determination of the case on its merits. The European Court of Justice replied in the affirmative and the House of Lords complied: *Factortame (No 2)*, above.

But it is the reasoning of their Lordships that is most significant: as in the Divisional Court, where reliance was placed squarely on s2(4) European Communities Act 1972, Lord Bridge explained that such limitations as Parliament accepted on its sovereignty in 1972 were 'entirely voluntary'; the 1972 Act made it quite clear that United Kingdom courts were obliged to override any rule of national law found to be in conflict with European Community law; and there was 'nothing in any way novel in according supremacy' to European Community law.

In conclusion, there is little support for the view that *Factortame (No 2)* marks a significant constitutional departure from the traditionally accepted view of parliamentary sovereignty; it accepts the supremacy of European Community law, but it does so because to do so is in conformity with the will of Parliament. There is nothing in *Factortame (No 2)* to suggest that an English court would refuse to comply with an express repeal of the European Communities Act. Until such time, if ever, as that happens, the traditional Diceyan view of parliamentary sovereignty remains, modified no doubt, but largely intact.

SUGGESTED ANSWER TO QUESTION FIVE

General Comment

This is a relatively straightforward question involving the case law relating to the UK's membership of the European Union. The candidate should highlight the leading cases in this area and avoid getting enmeshed in a descriptive analysis of the plethora of cases in this area.

A detailed knowledge, inter alia, of the course and implications of the *Factortame* litigation is required.

Key Points

- UK's membership of the EU and the method by which treaties are signed
- Implications for domestic law of the signing of treaties
- Sections 2(1), 2(4) and 3 European Communities Act 1972
- Question of express and implied repeal
- *McCarthys Ltd* v *Smith*
- *Factortame* cases - art 177
- How the EU sees itself and conclusion

Suggested Answer

The United Kingdom as an international legal personality joined the European Economic Community (as it then was) by the act of signing and ratifying the Treaty of Rome under the power vested in the royal prerogative. This was not as such a departure from previous practice dealing with treaties. The power so to do cannot be impugned or questioned in the courts (*Blackburn* v *Attorney-General* (1971)). The royal prerogative is not, however, capable of enacting new laws and, as the *Case of Proclamations* (1611) established, the Crown is unable to make new prerogative powers or laws imposing rights or obligations upon the Crown's subjects. Therefore, in order to give domestic effect to the Treaty of Rome it was necessary to incorporate the Treaty into United Kingdom municipal law. This was done by the enactment of the European Communities Act 1972.

The terms of the statute are far-reaching. By s2(1) both primary - the Treaty - and secondary Community law is to be given legal effect in the UK. This applies to Community law past, present and future. Moreover, under s3 of the statute the interpretation of Community treaties and legislation is regarded as a question of law to be interpreted either by the European Court of Justice at Luxembourg (ECJ) or, if it is decided by the courts of the UK, the matter is to be decided in accordance with ECJ decisions. The wording of s2(4) presents the UK courts with the dilemma of how to interpret Community law and subsequent Acts of Parliament, stating that: 'any existing or future enactments are to be construed and have effect subject to the foregoing provisions of this section'.

This would appear to be constitutional nonsense. According to the traditional doctrine of parliamentary sovereignty one Parliament cannot bind future Parliaments. Sovereignty is continuing and one Parliament cannot set itself up as being superior to any future Parliament or Parliaments. A subsequent Act of Parliament may expressly or impliedly repeal any previous legislation. English case law contains a plethora of decisions substantiating the above proposition. In the case of *Ellen Street Estates Ltd* v *Minister of Health* (1934) Maugham LJ held, inter alia:

> 'If in a subsequent Act, Parliament chooses to make it plain that the earlier statute is being to some extent repealed, effect must be given to that intention just because it is the will of the legislature.'

Such is, or was, the theory. In the case of *Blackburn* v *Attorney-General* (above) Lord Denning chose to cast doubt on the orthodox theory and its relation to reality. Speaking obiter he said:

> 'We have all been brought up to believe that in legal theory one Parliament cannot bind another and that no Act is irreversible. But legal theory does not always march alongside political reality.'

He then went on to discuss the unlikely instance of Parliament reversing an Act of independence to a former colony, arguing 'Freedom once given cannot be taken away. Legal theory must give way to practical politics.'

What then is the position with relation to European Union law and any conflicting Acts of Parliament? In the case of *Macarthys Ltd* v *Smith* (1979) Lord Denning again turned his attention to this problem. Speaking obiter he hypothesised:

> 'Thus far I have assumed that our Parliament whenever it passes legislation intends to fulfil its obligations under the Treaty. If the time should come when our Parliament *deliberately passes an Act* - with the intention of repudiating the Treaty or any provision in it - or intentionally acting inconsistently with it - and says so in express terms - then I should

> have thought that it would be the duty of our courts to follow the statute of our Parliament. I do not, however, envisage any such situation.' (emphasis added)

Thus, Lord Denning is acknowledging that if Parliament intends to repudiate Community law, then the UK courts will give effect to it. In his judgment Lord Denning also provides for an escape clause from any possible conflict by talking about 'some oversight of our draftsmen' when a conflict with Community law is apparent. So what is 'the intention of Parliament' or what is 'an oversight of our draftsmen' is conveniently left to the UK courts to interpret.

Another aspect of the potential conflict between the two jurisdictions which the courts have had to tackle arises when there is a *perceived* conflict between the UK law and EU law. This is discussed in the series of *Factortame* cases.

The Common Market Fishing Policy devised a system to conserve fish by fixing quotas for national fishing fleets. The British government established a licensing system in 1985, which was expanded upon in the Merchant Shipping Act 1988 and which empowered the Secretary for Transport to make regulations and introduce a new register of British fishing vessels designed to prevent so-called 'quota hopping', whereby non-British Community nationals, Spanish fishermen, established companies in the UK in order to avail themselves of the British fishing quota. The question which arose before the UK courts was if a UK Act of Parliament supposedly infringed a party's Community rights - in this case as a result of discrimination based on the grounds of nationality - could that Act could be disapplied pending a final outcome? The House of Lords initially answered 'no' but referred the case to the ECJ, under art 177, for a preliminary ruling: *R* v *Secretary of State for Transport, ex parte Factortame (No 1)* (1989)

The ECJ in its preliminary ruling decided that the full effectiveness of Community law would be impaired if the UK argument that they could not disapply an Act of Parliament in such circumstances were to prevail. The ECJ in *R* v *Secretary of State for Transport, ex parte Factortame (No 2)* (1991) decided that, pending a final outcome, interim relief should be granted and the House of Lords granted the said relief. A temporary injunction was issued against the Secretary of State preventing him from enforcing the offending provisions of the statute. Injunctive relief was therefore granted against the Crown and an Act of Parliament was disapplied.

The legal revolution as a result of joining the European Community has also been commented upon in other areas of litigation. Hoffmann J (as he then was) put it succinctly:

> 'The EC Treaty is the supreme law of this country, taking precedence over Acts of Parliament. Our entry into the EC meant that Parliament surrendered its sovereign right to legislate contrary to the provisions of the Treaty on matters of social and economic policy which it regulated': *Stoke-on-Trent City Council* v *B & Q plc* (1991).

Whether or not the courts of the UK would disapply an Act of Parliament if it were to say 'notwithstanding EU law to the contrary' such and such is to apply is an open question. As it is the UK courts have clearly absorbed the philosophy of the ECJ in *Costa* v *ENEL* (1964), when it decided in effect that a new legal order had been created. The UK courts will now not only disapply the workings of a statute but will also entertain an application for judicial review from, for example, the Equal Opportunities Commission, for a declaration that UK law is incompatible with Community law: *R* v *Secretary of State for Employment, ex parte Equal Opportunities Commission* (1994). It is indeed true to say, as Lord Denning stated in *Bulmer* v *Bollinger* (1974), that 'the Treaty [ie the Treaty of Rome] is like an incoming tide. It flows into the estuaries and up the rivers. It cannot be held back'.

3

The Electoral System: Membership of the House of Commons

Introduction

This chapter is concerned with the operation of the British electoral system and proposals for its reform. Particular areas of study include the system of constituency boundaries, the conduct of election campaigns and the counting system for citizens' votes. Examination emphasis is usually on the method of counting votes (in the UK the 'first past the post' system) and alternative methods used in other democracies, either in the form of proportional representation or preferential voting. At present there is an independent Commission on Electoral Reform (chaired by Lord Jenkins of Hillhead) examining submissions on issues of electoral law reform. It is expected to report during 1998.

It is important to study the composition and functions of the four Boundary Commissions set up by the Parliamentary Constituencies Act 1986. Note that their recommendations are advisory only, and it is possible for a government to delay implementation of an unfavourable report until after it has held a General Election based on the existing boundaries (this happened in 1969, prior to the 1970 General Election).

In regard to the conduct of election campaigns, note the powers of the 'Election Court' (two judges of the Queen's Bench Division of the High Court). This Court enforces electoral law, most of which is contained in the Representation of the People Act 1983. Examples include rules relating to eligibility to vote and to stand for Parliament; and those for the spending of campaign money in constituencies. Note that there is no limit on *national* campaign spending by political parties. Consider critically whether reforms are needed to any of these rules.

The basic complaint against the 'first past the post' method of counting votes is that it produces only a very limited correlation between the votes that a party receives and the number of seats it wins in the House of Commons: see Loveland, *A Critical Introduction to Constitutional Law* (1996), p277 for a useful table of statistics illustrating this correlation for General Elections from 1945 to 1992. The statistics show that no party elected to office since 1945 has secured over 50 per cent of the vote, yet has always obtained a governing majority (sometimes a large one) in the House of Commons. The results of the General Election held on 1 May 1997 were as follows:

Labour	418 seats on 44.4 per cent share of vote
Conservative	165 seats on 31.4 per cent share of vote
Liberal Democrats	46 seats on 17.2 per cent share of vote
Others	29 seats on 7 per cent share of vote
Speaker	1 seat

(Total number of seats in the House of Commons is 659.)

The main alternatives are: proportional representation systems (such as the party list system and the single transferable vote system), designed to produce a closer relationship between the votes cast for seats won by parties; and preferential voting systems (such as the alternative vote system), designed to reflect the voter preferences between candidates and to produce candidates who can win majority electoral support in their constituencies. It is a common failing in examinations to give inadequate explanations of the workings of such systems. Hence it is important to undertake comparative research so as to give illustrations of the operation and effects of particular systems in other democratic states - Germany, the Republic of Ireland, Australia, France and Israel all provide useful examples, eg see Loveland's research, above, at pp280-284.

Questions on the electoral system are not regular annual features of a typical examination paper. They tend to come up when the subject becomes topical, eg close to a General Election or when a particular set of reform proposals have been announced. The most common form of question is an essay-type question requiring critical analysis of the method of counting votes and allotting seats in the legislature, although problem-type questions on other aspects of electoral law are occasionally set. Only one question on the electoral system will be set if the issue comes up for examination.

Questions

INTERROGRAMS

1 Outline the work of the Boundary Commissions.
2 What are the main rules regulating the right to vote and to stand for Parliament?
3 Summarise the advantages and disadvantages of the British 'first past the post' electoral system and the party list system of proportional representation.
4 Explain the operation of the single transferable vote and alternative vote systems.

QUESTION ONE

a During the course of a General Election Mr Smith, a political activist with no fixed party allegiance, published (at his own cost) and distributed 50,000 leaflets exhorting voters to express their dissatisfaction with the Conservative government's tax policies by abstaining from voting. On polling day the Conservative candidate lost the election, his previous majority of 30,000 votes being wiped out. The final result was Labour 15,000, Liberal Democratic Party 10,000, Conservative 5,000. 20,000 voters failed to vote.

The Conservative Party candidate wishes to challenge the legality of the result of the election.

Advise him.

b 'The detailed rules regulating constituency election campaigns are of little value given the absence of controls on national party campaigns.'

Discuss.

London University LLB Examination
(for external students) Constitutional Law June 1994 Q3

QUESTION TWO

What difference, if any, would reforming the electoral system make to the British Constitution?

London University LLB Examination
(for external students) Constitutional Law June 1987 Q2

QUESTION THREE

'In a really equal democracy, every or any section would be represented, not disproportionately, but proportionately.' (JS Mill).

Discuss this statement with respect to the British system of general elections.

London University LLB Examination
(for external students) Constitutional Law June 1995 Q3

QUESTION FOUR

Consider the view that 'our method of election to the House of Commons is in the highest degree unjust, unsatisfactory and dangerous'.

London University LLB Examination
(for external students) Constitutional Law June 1996 Q3

Answers

ANSWERS TO INTERROGRAMS

1 There are four Boundary Commissions - one each for England, Scotland, Wales and Northern Ireland. Each Commission is nominally chaired by the Speaker in order to symbolise its political impartiality, though in practice it is headed by a High Court judge, who is assisted by two other persons appointed by the government with the approval of opposition parties. Each Commission holds local inquiries every 15 years concerning the redrawing of boundaries to take account of population movements. Each Commission may, at its discretion, take account of: the need to ensure that constituencies do not cross county or London borough boundaries; the need to ensure that all constituencies are as near to a set electoral quota as possible (the quota is arrived at by dividing the total number of registered voters by the number of constituencies); and the need to depart from these two objectives if special considerations, such as the maintenance of local communities, make such departure desirable. The exercise of this discretion is a controversial one since it has produced substantial discrepancies in constituency size, thereby undermining the principle of 'one vote, one value'.

Each Commission must present a report containing its recommendations (which are advisory only) to the Home Secretary.

2 The main rules may be summarised as follows:

a Eligibility to vote: the right to vote is given to all citizens (other than the Monarch and members of the House of Lords) who are over 18 years of age and whose names are entered on the electoral register of the constituency where they reside. A citizen may only be 'resident' for voting purposes in one constituency; for example, a citizen who lives six months of the year in one constituency and six months in another constituency must choose in which constituency he or she wishes to cast his or her vote. Individual citizens lose the right to vote if serving a prison sentence, or suffering from serious mental incapacity, or have recently been convicted of electoral malpractice.

b Eligibility to stand for Parliament: a candidate needs to be nominated by ten registered voters. Citizens who are disqualified from standing are persons under 21 years of age, non-British citizens (other than Irish nationals), peers, Church of England and Roman Catholic clergymen, bankrupt debtors, and some categories of criminals and the mentally ill. Each candidate must produce a deposit of £500, which is forfeit if he or she fails to gain 5 per cent of the vote in his or her constituency.

3 a 'First past the post' (or 'plurality majority system'): used in the United Kingdom for parliamentary elections, it is non-proportional and non-preferential, usually producing a government elected on a minority of the popular vote and usually disproportionately penalising smaller parties who may attract a reasonable number of votes nationwide but not enough in concentrated areas so as to win many constituencies. However, the system is easy to understand, usually produces a quick and decisive outcome on election night, and usually produces stable, decisive administrations. It also ensures a close relationship between MPs and their constituents.

b Party list system: advantages are proportionality and fairness in matching seats to votes won. Stable governments can emerge if parties are willing to co-operate in long-term coalitions. However there is no constituency link between representatives and voters, raising risks of remoteness and alienation. The system also places complete control of candidate selection in the hands of party officials, raising risks of political nepotism. The emphasis on strict proportionality between votes cast and seats won can, unless there is a minimum threshold, allow very small, perhaps extremist, parties into the legislature which then may have opportunities to exercise disproportional influence.

4 Under the single transferable vote system there are multi-member constituencies in which voters mark candidates in order of preference. Parties may field more than one candidate so that preferences can be expressed between candidates representing different wings of the same party. A candidate is successful if satisfying the quota of votes for his or her constituency. The quota is obtained by the following formula:

$$\frac{\text{number of first preference votes} + 1}{\text{number of candidates} + 1}$$

The winning candidate's second preference votes are then allocated as new first preference votes to the remaining candidates. Any of these candidates who reach the quota are also elected, with their second preferences being redistributed in the same manner. The process continues until all the seats for that constituency are filled.

Under the alternative vote system voters list candidates in order of preference in single member constituencies. If a candidate secures at least 50 per cent first preference votes he or she is elected. If no candidate achieves this the least popular candidate is eliminated and his or her second preference votes are reallocated according to the marked preferences among the remaining candidates. The process continues until one candidate passes the 50 per cent threshold.

SUGGESTED ANSWER TO QUESTION ONE

General Comment

Although both parts to this question are straightforward, part (a) does require fairly detailed knowledge of a narrow area. One must always think carefully before attempting a two-part question; usually, single questions are easier. Be careful always to ensure that you answer both parts! Ensure, too, that the answer to (a) does constitute advice to the Conservative Party candidate and is not just a general essay; and that that to (b) comprises a discussion of the quote.

Key Points

a
- Who may challenge? - s121 Representation of the People Act 1983 and Conservative Party candidate
- Grounds of challenge (corrupt and illegal practices (Representation of the People Act Part II), *R* v *Tronoh Mines Ltd* and *DPP* v *Luft*)
- Effect of challenge: void?

b
- Comparison between local and national controls
- Historical explanation: bribery and corruption
- Modern law (expenditure (Representation of the People Act Part II), advertising (*R* v *Tronoh Mines Ltd*), broadcasting (*Grieve* v *Douglas-Home*; Broadcasting Act 1990) and party funding)
- Conclusions

Suggested Answer

a Advice to the Conservative Party candidate falls conveniently into two parts: first, whether he can challenge the result; and, second, if so, the grounds of challenge. The conclusion will address the Conservative Party candidate's likely prospects of success.

Once an election has been held and the result declared, the only way to challenge that result is by way of a petition to the Election Court, comprising two judges of the Queen's Bench Division of the High Court: s120 Representation of the People Act 1983. Under s121 of the 1983 Act, petitions may be brought by voters, those claiming a 'right to be elected or returned at the election', or a candidate. Clearly, the Conservative Party candidate here falls within s121, probably under all or any of these headings. The petition itself is to be brought against the successful candidate, here the Labour Party candidate, as respondent or, if appropriate, the Returning Officers. The Election Court has power to determine that the respondent candidate was duly elected or that the election is void; it can order a recount or declare the runner-up elected.

The main grounds of challenge under the Representation of the People Act are that the successful candidate is disqualified, that the election has been conducted improperly by officials or that offences, such as corrupt or illegal practices, have been committed during the campaign. There is no indication on the facts either that the Labour Party candidate is disqualified from membership or that there have been any administrative irregularities in the conduct of the election. It follows that the Conservative Party candidate must rely in his petition on the commission of electoral offences.

The Representation of the People Act 1983 imposes strict controls on expenditure in the conduct of an election campaign. Under s75:

> 'No expenses shall, with a view to promoting or procuring the election of a candidate ... be incurred by any person other than the candidate, his election agent and persons authorised ... by the ... agent on account ... (b) of issuing advertisements, circulars or publications.'

Since the commission of corrupt or illegal election practices during the campaign may render an election void, the Conservative Party candidate will have to establish that Smith is in breach of this section.

While Smith's expenses fall within s75(1)(b), it is not clear whether Smith, a 'political activist', is himself a candidate, agent or authorised person. If he is not, there may be a breach of s75. (If he is, a further question will arise in respect of the limits imposed in s76.) However, s75 applies at the local constituency and not the national level. In *R* v *Tronoh Mines Ltd* (1952) it was held that the prohibition applied to local constituencies, not national expenditure, and thus the defendant company's advertisment in *The Times* warning against the 'perils of socialism' was not in breach of the Representation of the People legislation. Although not clear from the facts, it appears as if Smith's leaflet campaign is conducted in the local constituency and could therefore be in breach of s75.

Smith may argue that his expenses are not incurred 'with a view to promoting or procuring the election of a candidate' but were rather intended to prevent the election of the Conservative Party candidate. In *DPP* v *Luft* (1977) it was held that the offence was made out where, as on the facts here, unauthorised expenditure was incurred through a leaflet campaign designed to prevent the election of a candidate; the House of Lords accepted that expenditure designed to prevent the election of one candidate could indirectly promote the election of others.

In conclusion, the Conservative Party candidate may be able to challenge the result of the election on the grounds of the commission by Smith of electoral offences, although we are not given sufficient information to conclude definitively. If Smith has acted in breach of s75, the Election Court may declare the election void and a new election could be held. In the absence of any apparent link between Smith and the successful candidate, it might be doubted whether the Court would do so.

b It is undeniably true that there is something of a contradiction between the rules regulating the conduct of elections at constituency as opposed to national level. The former are indeed quite detailed, particularly in the limits put on expenditure on the election. It is therefore somewhat anomalous that, despite these strict controls, there are few equivalent controls on national expenditure, for example on broadcasting or advertising in newspapers and billboards. However, to claim a total absence of controls goes too far: some control exists, both at national level and, more especially, when 'national' expenditure 'spills over' and directly affects the local campaign. Second, it does not follow that, even if there is a disparity between national and local control, local rules 'are of little value'.

The reason for this disparity is found, as so often in constitutional law, in history. Up until the beginning of the present century, bribery and corruption were rife during election campaigns; not until the Parliamentary and Municipal Elections Act 1872, introducing a secret ballot, and the Parliamentary Elections (Corrupt and Illegal Practices) Act 1883, imposing strict controls on expenditure, was it possible to establish an effective framework to stamp out such practices. This framework has remained largely in place in the Representation of the People Act 1983 Part II. In its inception, therefore, the system of local control was both necessary and justified.

Since then, however, the development of the party system and the growth in national campaigning has not been met with attempts to impose equivalent controls at a national level. It is true that the legislation makes 'no attempt to control the purchasing of victory on a national scale': Rawlings *Law and the Electoral Process* (1988), p137. However, it is important to appreciate that the paucity of national control does not, in itself, deny the validity of the local controls; these still perform an essential function in ensuring aspects of the fairness of elections by preventing (or limiting) corrupt and illegal practices.

Moreover, the detailed rules regulating local elections may impinge on national situations. In *R* v *Tronoh Mines Ltd*, although it was held that expenditure on national advertising was not caught by the prohibition on local expenditure, this was because the campaign was not intended to support a particular candidate in a particular constituency but rather a particular party generally. Clearly, where a national advertising campaign did have such an effect, it could fall within the detailed local rules.

It is, however, clear from *Grieve* v *Douglas-Home* (1965) that national expenditure on party political broadcasts is not caught by the provisions of the Representation of the People Act and, to this extent, there is no real control on the levels of expenditure at the national level. The Election Court justified its decision on the grounds that broadcasts transmitted information of general public importance, and were not designed to procure the election of individual candidates. Again, a broadcast designed to procure an individual's election might yet be caught.

The absence of specific controls on the national campaign in the Representation of the People Act 1983 does not mean that the application of the general law is excluded. Thus, for example, controls on broadcasting exist under the Broadcasting Act 1990, imposing a statutory duty of impartiality in broadcasting news and political programmes and, therefore, challenge may be brought for breach of this duty. Limited controls over advertising also exist in general law, for example under planning law regulating billboard advertising. It is true, though, that the effect of *Tronoh Mines* (above) is largely to exclude national advertising from effective control. The most glaring area of disparity lies in the general absence of rules regulating the financing of political parties at national levels; although the greater spending power of the Conservative Party did not prevent its devasting defeat at the 1997 General Election, so perhaps the influence of national spending on the minds of the electorate has been exaggerated.

In conclusion, although there is a significant lack of control over national election campaigns, legal controls are not wholly absent. Nor does absence necessarily cast doubt on the validity of local controls. That the detailed local rules do nothing to control national campaigns suggests not so much that these are of little value - they continue to play an important role - but rather that their value would be enhanced were a more comprehensive system of national control to be instituted.

SUGGESTED ANSWER TO QUESTION TWO

General Comment

This is a straightforward question involving discussion of the present electoral system and the effect reform would have on the British Constitution. The election of the Labour Government on 1 May 1997 is a significant event as the new government is committed to electoral reform.

Key Points

- Introduction - the operation of the relative majority system
- The problems with the present system (parliamentary seats not allocated on a proportional basis, discrimination against small parties, wastage of votes and problems with constituency size)
- The advantages of the present system (simplicity, results in strong government and constituency link with MP)
- Effect of reform (loss of the advantages of the present system and election of a Parliament but not a government)
- Proposals of Labour Government, elected on 1 May 1997

Suggested Answer

Under the present parliamentary electoral system the United Kingdom is divided into 659 parliamentary constituencies, each of which returns a single member to the House of Commons. Each elector may vote for one candidate only and the successful candidate is the one who receives the highest number of valid votes in the constituency. This system of 'first past the post' is known as the simple (or relative) majority system as wherever there are more than two candidates in a constituency, the successful candidate need not have received an absolute majority of votes, but simply a majority over the runner-up. This system has the advantage of being very simple, but as a means of providing representation of the electorate in Parliament it is very crude. It is a system which, according to its critics, is not truly democratic and one which has several inherent disadvantages, which, it is argued, can only be overcome by reform.

Certainly any reform of the present electoral system will seek to remedy the major problem that at present the system does not ensure that the distribution of seats in the House of Commons is in any way proportionate to the national distribution of votes. There is no consistent relationship between the number of votes cast nationally for a political party and the seats which they obtain. This is well illustrated by the June 1983 election results. The Conservative Party polled 42.4 per cent of the votes cast and won 397 seats. The Labour Party polled 27.6 per cent of the votes cast and won 209 seats. But the Liberal/SDP Alliance polled 25.4 per cent of the votes cast and won only 23 seats. The Alliance therefore was under-represented in relation to their national vote, while the Conservative Government achieved the largest parliamentary majority since the war, but received one of the smallest percentages of votes cast. Under this system a Conservative vote thus carried more weight than an Alliance vote.

This tendency of the system to exaggerate the representation of the large parties and reduce that of the smaller parties leads to the allegation that the present electoral system makes no provision for the representation of minority interests. It discriminates against the smaller parties whose support is evenly spread throughout the country rather than being concentrated in particular constituencies. Votes for the smaller parties are, in effect, wasted votes. It doesn't matter whether the person elected has one more or twenty thousand more votes than his nearest rival. So where there are more than two candidates a person may be elected by less than 50 per cent of the total votes cast in that constituency. The votes for the losing candidate have no parliamentary importance, they are in a sense wasted. This system, it is argued, perpetuates the two party system and helps destroy any possibility of consensus politics in the United Kingdom.

A further problem arises from the constituency basis of the present system. If votes are to carry equal weight throughout the country each constituency must be of equal size. The size of each constituency is determined by the Boundary Commissioners who keep the situation under constant review and try to ensure that each constituency has the same number of voters in it. However disparity does exist between constituency populations and as a result the weight of your vote may vary according to where you live.

Reforming the electoral system would therefore help remove these problems and help achieve fairer representation for all political parties in the House of Commons. But it must always be remembered that the present electoral system has considerable advantages and that these advantages may be lost as a result of any reform. For example the voting procedure itself is very simple and easy to understand, ensuring quick results. The outcome of the election is known within a matter of hours of the close of poll. The system also ensures a close link between the Member of Parliament and his constituency. The constituents know who their parliamentary representative is and can approach him with their problems. He in turn will serve their interests, in the knowledge that their continued support is necessary if he is to be re-elected.

But the major advantage claimed for the present system is its tendency to produce an absolute majority of seats in the House of Commons for one party. The function of a general election is to elect a government as well as a Parliament and the present system does precisely that, producing strong government. The United Kingdom system avoids the problems, often found in European countries, which use various kinds of proportional representation, of coalition or minority governments which can find it difficult to govern effectively because of their unstable electoral position.

Despite these advantages there is a case for reforming the electoral system so as to secure better representation of minority parties and a distribution of seats which bears some relation to the votes cast, the most favoured alternative systems being the alternative vote system, the party list system and the single transferable vote system. The adoption of any one of these systems would bring about changes to the British constitution which, while welcomed by some, would be abhorrent to others.

The major result of adopting these systems is that they will help achieve legislative representation which accords with the relative electoral strengths of the political parties. Minority parties and independent candidates will therefore stand a better chance of election and the number of wasted votes will be reduced. But while these systems may to an extent maintain a local basis for representation, they may weaken the link between members of Parliament and constituents. These systems of election are also complex. Most important, however, is the likely result that the traditional two party system may be destroyed. To some of course this may be no bad thing but, if the European experience is repeated and one party is less likely to secure an absolute majority of seats in the House of Commons, this will lead to minority or coalition governments giving smaller parties political importance out of all proportion to their popular support. Such a system of government is totally alien to the British tradition.

The Labour Government, which was elected at the General Election on 1 May 1997, is committed to carrying out a review of electoral law which may result in a referendum being held on any proposed change to the method of counting votes. Other changes may include moving the traditional voting day of Thursday to Saturday, and the introduction of better facilities for postal and electronic voting. Such changes may help to increase voter turn-out, which has declined in recent years.

SUGGESTED ANSWER TO QUESTION THREE

General Comment

This is a beguilingly straightforward question about differing forms of electoral systems. The statement is brief and therefore gives a lot of scope to the candidate to use all the knowledge that can be amassed. The statement itself focuses on 'sections' of society rather than the individual voter. This aspect should be discussed to focus on the right aim for an electoral system, before considering the variety of possible electoral systems.

Key Points

- Discuss the detail of the statement in the question
- Discuss the pros and cons of the 'first past the post' system

- Discuss the pros and cons of the party list system
- Discuss the pros and cons of the single transferable vote
- Discuss the pros and cons of the alternative member system
- Conclusion

Suggested Answer

The question of the desirability of equality in systems of democracy is one that is easy to answer in rhetorical terms, but difficult to deal with in systemic terms. In general, it is possible to say that an ideal system of elections would aim to provide each citizen of majority age with one vote which would be of equal value to the vote of every other citizen. However, Mill's formulation of this proposition looks at society not in terms of individual citizens but rather in terms of 'sections'.

The difficulty with this formulation is that it requires it to be possible for every section to be identified in a two-dimensional format. To identify the opinions of the electorate as sectional interests casting their votes in the same manner is to ignore the broad range of issues which are active in the minds of the voters, and which may cause people of ostensibly similar backgrounds and with seemingly similar views to vote or act in very different ways. One may choose not to vote, whereas the other might decide that one should vote for the least worst option. Both are valid choices, but it is difficult to identify exactly which 'section' best represents each voter. Therefore, the individual citizen model, it is suggested, offers the better model for assessing whether or not a given democratic system is 'equal' or not.

Mill's conception of the issue is more useful when looking at the issue of proportional representation. While it is still focused on the notion of 'sections', it does identify the need to create a Parliament which does, to some extent, reflect the political composition and views of society. The result of an election is the creation of a Parliament which enacts the political programme of the majority party or a coalition of parties.

The 'first past the post' system fails to admit the views of the minority interests in society. Where there is insufficient support for a particular interest or shade of opinion in a given geographic region, there will not be enough support to elect a Member of Parliament in any constituency. Therefore, special interest groups are unrepresented. The growing cynicism of the population with the political system can potentially be traced to the failure of the current electoral system to reflect adequately the opinions of the population in more than a two-party, two-dimensional format. The weight of a vote for Party A will be weaker in a constituency where Party A either stands no prospect of victory or where Party A is sure to win. A vote for Party A will be more important in a constituency where Party A might win or lose by a very few votes.

The advantages of this system appear in ways other than straightforward 'equality' or parity of votes. The constituency system does provide representation for a particular region through a given individual politician. Therefore, there is a mechanism for ensuring responsiveness from the political system to the local needs of a particular constituency. The conduct of representational and democratic politics can therefore be made more accountable to specific units of the population. Voting patterns mirror more closely the views of general geographic areas measured in trends large enough to affect those overall local majorities. The simple majority system also aids ease of comprehension, which makes it easier for politicians to analyse the views of the population and also, more importantly, for the population to understand the outcomes of elections.

The proportional representation models are many and varied. The simplest system is that used in Israel where people vote on a party list, non-constituency basis. The proportion of the total national vote obtained by each party is then attributed to that party. The percentage of the total that represents is then allotted to each party as a corresponding percentage of seats in the parliamentary assembly. The advantage of this system is that every vote has exactly the same weight. Similarly, each section in society is represented precisely.

The disadvantages with this system are, firstly, that there is no link between local people and any individual politician: therefore local democratic ties are very weak. Secondly, the system places enormous powers in the hands of the parties when selecting political candidates.

The single transferable vote method is a more complicated system of proportional representation. This system retains the use of large constituencies from which a number of candidates are elected at the same time. Voters mark their ballot papers with their candidates placed in order of preference. A threshold level of votes is calculated above which a candidate is elected. This threshold is itself calculated by reference to the mean number of votes required for the prescribed number of candidates to be selected out of the votes cast. This enables a broader range of preferences to be tested because, once a candidate crosses the threshold, the remaining votes for that candidate as first choice are reallocated to the second choice on the ballot paper. The drawbacks are the complication of the system and the loose ties which are established on a local democratic basis. There is also an element of mathematical chance involved with the reallocation of votes.

The alternative member system is practised in a variety of countries, and it enables the voter to vote for a constituency MP and then to have that vote counted a second time as a vote for a party-list candidate selected by the party. Therefore, there are two cadres of MP, one who represents the constituency and another who is selected by the political party. There is a drawback to having two streams of politicians in that it raises questions as to which of the two has a better mandate from the electorate. The electoral process is also slightly complicated by the use of this system.

It is clear that there are a number of means of carrying out elections. However, it is difficult to measure which is the best electoral system to use. Mill's conception points towards a simple party list system which may, in fact, diminish the service and representation which many constituents are able to obtain from the 'first past the post' system.

SUGGESTED ANSWER TO QUESTION FOUR

General Comment

This question invites a discussion of the workings of the present electoral system. Candidates should discuss not only the present electoral system but also its consequences in the representation of the parties in Parliament. The advantages and disadvantages of the system should be set out and the student must be willing to agree or disagree with the polemical statement. A brief summary of some of the alternative electoral systems needs to be included to complete the essay.

Key Points

- Introduction - the franchise in the UK
- Constituency basis of the MP
- 'First past the post'
- The reflection of 'first past the post' in the Commons
- Advantages of the present system
- Disadvantages of the present system
- Alternative electoral systems
- Conclusion - proposals of Labout Government, elected on 1 May 1997

Suggested Answer

The membership of the House of Commons is elected on the basis of universal adult suffrage. In order to vote in a parliamentary election the individual must be listed in the electoral register for a parliamentary constituency. To be placed on the register the individual must be a British subject, a Commonwealth citizen or a citizen of the Irish Republic (such citizens are not classified as aliens for electoral purposes), be eighteen years of age or be due to attain his/her eighteenth birthday within twelve months of the publication of the register, not suffer any legal incapacity and be resident in the constituency on the qualifying date for compiling the register.

The above is without controversy and has raised little or no political discussion. It is the electoral system rather than those eligible to vote which is the cause of political disquiet.

How then is the electoral system to the House of Commons based? The United Kingdom is divided into 659 parliamentary constituencies, each of which is represented by one member in the House of Commons. The constituency boundaries are determined by the Boundary Commission which works on the theory that each constituency should have the same number of votes within it to ensure that all votes in the country are of equal value. This is summed up by the maxim: 'one person, one vote, one value'. The Boundary Commission reviews the electoral population of the parliamentary constituencies and may recommend that extra constituencies be formed in an area under-represented owing to an increase in population, or an abolition of constituencies owing to a decrease in population. These changes largely reflect the change in the balance of the population away from urban areas and into the shires. The Boundary

Commission is not, however, obliged to reflect the voting population exclusively (Parliamentary Constituencies Act 1986).

This division of the UK by the Boundary Commission is normally accepted by the political parties but its findings are still capable of judicial review, as the Court of Appeal accepted in their judgment in *R* v *Boundary Commission for England, ex parte Foot* (1983).

Of much more controversy though is the electoral system. The UK system is categorised as 'first past the post'. Each elector is eligible to vote for one candidate only and the candidate who obtains the most votes within a constituency wins. It is possible, therefore, for a candidate to win even though the majority of the electorate in a constituency vote against him. If, for instance, J Bloggs obtains 10,000 votes, J Smith obtains 7,000 votes and J Jones obtains 6,000 votes, J Bloggs wins despite the fact the majority of the electorate voted against him. All the votes given to J Bloggs over 7,001 are 'wasted'. The number of wasted votes may be huge in a safe Labour seat, for example in South Wales, or in a safe Conservative seat, for instance in Surrey. There is no way in the existing system that the votes, or more accurately the surplus votes, may be distributed elsewhere in the country.

This system is reflected in the final outcome of the votes as there is litte relationship between the number of votes cast nationally for a party and the number of seats that party may obtain in the House of Commons. Thus, in the 1992 General Election the Conservatives obtained 41.9 per cent of the votes but achieved 51.6 per cent of the seats. Minority parties do particularly badly in this system, as illustrated by the Liberal Democrats who obtained 17.8 per cent of the votes in 1992 but only 3.1 per cent of the seats. As with racing, or even more so, there is little merit in coming second or third. Parties which come second in a significant number of constituencies, as with the Social Democratic Party in 1983, may as well have come third or fourth. The only minority parties likely to survive in such a system are those with a strong regional base, such as the Scottish Nationalists, or to some extent the Liberals in the 'celtic fringe'. They are able to target particular constituencies rather than have their votes spread out throughout the country.

It should be pointed out, however, that the 'first past the post' system has a number of advantages. It is simple and the electorate has a clear understanding of how it works. The results are easily arrived at and it avoids delays in establishing the winner on both a national and local level. It also establishes a link between the MP and his/her constituency; the other systems (see below) often fail to achieve this. The link between an MP and his/her constituency enables other institutions such as the Parliamentary Commissioner for Administration (PCA) to function effectively as the MP puts forward the complaints and grieviances of the constituent. An MP may also pursue a particular matter which is of concern to his or her constituents. For example, Members of Parliament who have a large proportion of immigrants amongst their constituents are more likely to be involved in immigration issues. In taking up an issue raised by a constituent the MP is obliged to help the constituent to his or her best ability no matter whether the constituent is likely to vote for the MP or not.

A further advantage of the present system is that it usually creates an absolute (overall) majority of seats in the House of Commons. At the end of the day the electorate can understand the result of the election, while in other electoral systems (see below) this is not necessarily the case. The majority of British elections do not result in inter- and intra-party manoeuvres as a government is trying to be formed. A proportional representation system, with its possible result of a 'hung' Parliament, would also have the effect of politicising the role of the monarch as she would have to exercise her discretion as to which candidate would be the most suitable Prime Minister.

While it may be seen as unjust in the manner in which it penalises minority parties, the present electoral system does have the beneficial effect of preventing extremist minority parties obtaining a presence in the House of Commons. In the 1930s the British Fascist Party led by Oswald Mosley failed to obtain a seat in the House of Commons because its followers were spread throughout the country and the party failed to gain enough following to achieve a majority in a single constituency. Indeed, some countries with a system of proportional representation have a threshold requirement of about 5 per cent before a party can enter Parliament, the purpose being to prevent extremist minority parties gaining a platform.

What then are the alternatives to the British electoral system? The main options are these systems:

a alternative vote;

b party list; and

c single transferable vote.

The alternative vote system operates by the voter listing the candidates in their constituency in order of preference. If no candidate gains an absolute majority of the first preference then the lowest candidate is eliminated and his/her second preference votes are distributed amongst the other candidates. This process can be repeated until one candidate emerges with an absolute majority. The principal inadequacy of the system is that the overall result does not reflect the actual proportions of the votes. The voter has the potential to be confused with the procedure and the winner might not have a clear mandate from the voters.

The party list system is perhaps the method which best reflects the real proportion of the votes. The country is classified as one constituency and the parties present lists of candidates and the electors vote for the whole party list. Seats in Parliament are allocated to the parties in proportion to the votes received by each party list. Such a system strengthens the party bureaucracy as potential candidates compete to be placed as near the top of the list as possible. The link between the MP and the constituency is destroyed and minority parties will be given greater potential power as they offer their conditional support to any putative government. This effect is increased as an outright winner in such a system is unusual (a classic example being Israel).

The single transferable vote (STV) is the system which is looked upon with most approval by the advocates of electoral reform. This system would see a diminution in the number of constituencies in Parliament, as it requires multi-member constituencies with between five and seven members. Voters list the candidates in order of preference. The candidate needs a quota of votes to be elected. The 'surplus' votes of the winning candidate are then redistributed among the other candidates in accordance with the voter's second preference. While this system would weaken the link between the MP and his constituents it is not unknown in the UK. In the nineteenth century multi-member constituencies (usually two MPs) were present in the UK Parliament.

The call for reform of the electoral system in the UK is heard especially from those parties such as the Liberal Democrats who are penalised by being minority parties. There is no manner in which their votes may be distributed. The Labour Party, or sections of it, frustrated after 17 years in opposition, also considered the idea of electoral reform, though its enthusiasm for electoral reform may be dimmed following the Labour Party's landslide victory under the 'first past the post' system at the 1997 General Election! Nevertheless the Labour Government is conducting a review of electoral law and there may be a referendum on any proposed change to the method of counting votes.

Unfortunately, the debate is often centred on the economic and social success of a particular country. The advocates of electoral reform point to the German voting system while the detractors point to Israel or Ireland. The message elsewhere is unclear; while New Zealand has introduced a system of proportional representation, Italy has moved away from it. One might conclude that our method of election is unjust and unsatisfactory, but so are all the others.

4

The Functions of the House of Commons and Parliamentary Privilege

Introduction

This chapter is concerned with several aspects of the parliamentary system of government. These include parliamentary scrutiny of legislation and of the executive generally. It is necessary to analyse critically the operation of such parliamentary devices as Question Time, debates and the committee system, and the extent to which the role of the backbencher in this system may be undermined by the pressures of party politics, notably through the use of the whip system.

A separate, albeit related, topic dealt with in this chapter is parliamentary privilege. It is a topic that deserves detailed critical scrutiny because it offends the rule of law by exempting Members of Parliament from ordinary civil liability for things said or done during the course of parliamentary proceedings. Members also enjoy extraordinary powers of self-regulation, including exclusive powers to punish for breaches of privilege and contempt of Parliament. There is considerable case law on the scope of parliamentary privilege and on the role of the courts in this area. In recent years attempts have been made to modernise the parliamentary system in order to make it more open and accountable. Scandals such as the 'cash for questions' affair (money paid to MPs in return for raising questions in the House) have led to the establishment of a Parliamentary Commissioner for Standards and a reformed Select Committee on Standards and Privileges. The election of the Labour Government at the General Election in May 1997 led swiftly to a reform of Question Time and to the setting up of a committee to examine ways of reforming parliamentary procedures, particularly on such matters as hours of work, since the length and timing of debates in the House has long been a source of dissatisfaction to Members of Parliament who wish to maintain normal family lifestyles.

A typical examination paper would usually include at least one question on parliamentary proceedings, either on the role of the backbencher in scrutinising laws and the administration, or on the scope and utility of parliamentary privilege. (It is unusual, though not unknown, for both subjects to come up in the form of two separate questions in the same paper.) Usually the questions require a critical analysis, though occasionally problem-style questions are set on the scope of parliamentary privilege.

Useful recent articles on reforms to the law of parliamentary privilege (s13 Defamation Act 1996) are as follows: Williams (1997) 60 MLR 388 and Sharland and Loveland [1997] PL 113.

Questions

INTERROGRAMS

1 Explain the operation and purpose of Question Time.
2 What is the value of the departmental select committee system?
3 Explain the contents of art 9 Bill of Rights 1688.
4 What is the effect of s13 Defamation Act 1996?

QUESTION ONE

'Parliamentary experience ... has demonstrated that collectively Members (of the House of Commons) can exercise the political will necessary to provide the parameters within which the Government can govern, albeit of necessity in a limited and generally negative way.' (Norton)

Discuss.

Adapted from London University LLB Examination
(for external students) Constitutional Law June 1990 Q1

QUESTION TWO

'The adequacy of parliamentary scrutiny of primary and secondary legislation is defective. Procedural reform is urgently needed.'

Discuss.

London University LLB Examination
(for external students) Constitutional Law June 1993 Q5

QUESTION THREE

'The two Houses justify the special rights, powers and immunities conferred by parliamentary privilege as being necessary for the welfare of the nation. Citizens denied legal redress against MPs or judged by the House of Commons to have committed a high contempt and a breach of its privileges, tend to be less impressed by these claims.' (de Smith)

Discuss.

London University LLB Examination
(for external students) Constitutional Law June 1985 Q4

QUESTION FOUR

Critically assess the respective roles of the House of Commons and the courts in regulating parliamentary privilege.

London University LLB Examination
(for external students) Constitutional Law June 1993 Q8b

Answers

ANSWERS TO INTERROGRAMS

1 In the chamber of the House of Commons MPs may orally question ministers at regular intervals on a rota basis concerning their departmental responsibilities. Two days' notice of such questions must be given to the department concerned since the primary purpose is to elicit factually accurate information. However, supplementary oral questions can be put for the purpose of ensuring that the minister knows his or her brief, or perhaps for the purpose of scoring party political points. Written questions and written answers can also be given. Traditionally the Prime Minister answered questions each Tuesday and Thursday from 3.15 pm to 3.30 pm during parliamentary sessions, but following the election of the Labour Government on 1 May 1997 Tony Blair, as the new Prime Minister, instituted a new session which takes place every Wednesday from 3 pm to 3.30 pm to replace the Tuesday and Thursday slots. The reform was designed to ease the burden on a Prime Minister (who prepares only once a week instead of twice a week under the old system) and to increase opportunities for more sustained questioning by Opposition party leaders and backbenchers (who found the old 15-minute sessions undermined by long-winded answers, heckling, interruptions, etc). Prime Minister's Questions are designed to produce statements of general government policies and to highlight the main differences between the Government and Opposition.

2 The value of the departmental select committee system is that it gives small groups of MPs the opportunity to carry out detailed investigations into the operation of government departments. A committee can choose an area of inquiry and then summon persons, including ministers and civil servants, to answer questions before it. Often these sessions are televised. Committees can also conduct inquiries by travelling on fact-finding missions outside Parliament, and by appointing specialist advisers to help them. Committees tend to maintain a non-partisan approach so as to secure unanimity when reporting to the whole House, thereby obtaining greater impact for their recommendations. Nevertheless, the operation of these committees tends to be undermined by lack of resources and lack-lustre publicity.

3 Article 9 Bill of Rights 1688 provides that 'the freedom of speech, and debates or proceedings in Parliament ought not to be impeached or questioned in any court or place out of Parliament'.

This provision gives absolute privilege to Members of Parliament during 'parliamentary proceedings', a concept which covers not only the transaction of official business within the physical precincts of Parliament but also the conduct of parliamentary business outside Parliament, though the exact scope of this privilege has never been satisfactorily settled: see the *Strauss Affair* (1957–58) HC 227 and view of Judicial Committee of the Privy Council in *Re Parliamentary Privilege Act* [1958] AC 331. The absolute privilege from the civil law of defamation has been criticised as a licence to defame capable of misuse by unscrupulous MPs, but the traditional justification for it has been the need to preserve for MPs the uninhibited discussion of matters of public interest.

4 Article 9 Bill of Rights 1688 has been amended by s13 Defamation Act 1996 so as to allow an MP to waive, for the purpose of defamation proceedings in which his or her conduct in relation to parliamentary proceedings is in issue, the protection of the art 9 privilege. This allows an MP to call evidence in a defamation action which he or she is bringing and which would otherwise be excluded by the art 9 privilege. At common law the privilege cannot be waived by an individual MP even though it is expedient to do so: see *Prebble* v *Television New Zealand Ltd* [1994] 3 WLR 970. MPs will continue to enjoy the art 9 privilege when *defending* defamation actions as s13 of the 1996 Act permits a waiver only for the purpose of an MP suing to maintain his or her reputation.

SUGGESTED ANSWER TO QUESTION ONE

General Comment

A question calling for a critical analysis of the parliamentary mechanisms available for scrutinising and controlling the activities of government

Key Points

- Definition of accountability
- Influence of conventions
- Parliamentary controls over public finance
- The select committee system
- Question Time
- Parliamentary Commissioner for Standards
- Conclusions

Suggested Answer

The starting point of the constitution is the representation of the electorate in Parliament, which is the supreme and sovereign law maker. Developed from this is the notion that the electorate thereby makes its preferred choice of government. However, for obvious practical reasons, elections cannot be held every year, nor can referendums be held on all points of importance that arise during a government's term of office. Thus, the accountability of government directly to the electorate is only periodic and it is this situation that gives rise to the fear of the possibility of an 'elective dictatorship', with a carte blanche to govern in whichever way it pleases for the term of its office.

To a certain extent this is an ill founded fear since the final reckoning will ultimately come with the dissolution of Parliament. Of more concern, however, is the situation that arises where, for the most part, a government's policies and style of government finds general approval, but where particular measures are potentially constitutionally threatening.

In such circumstances, government becomes directly accountable to the representatives of the electorate in Parliament and as such Parliament is termed the 'watchdog' of executive action. Since the Commons is the elected chamber and the focus of most political activity, without dismissing the important work of the Lords, it must clearly be the area where the ground rules of governmental activity are laid down.

Thus in purist theory, the political arm of the executive are collectively responsible to Parliament in general and to the House of Commons in particular. The idiomatic traditions of Parliament provide the forum for the supervision of government. The experience of recent years has brought much attention to bear on how effective these complex constraints and restrictions are when the Commons is effectively dominated by the party that holds office.

Before considering in detail the general parliamentary restrictions on government activity, it must be made clear that the mere fact that a party commands a majority in the House does not guarantee a majority of votes. Even where the whip system that urges members to comply is in strict operation, a member cannot be forcibly compelled to vote with the government. Although the price of such rebellion might be suspension from the parliamentary party, such defiance often has a profound political consequence and may be the prompt for revision of legislation when the action is taken in concert.

As well as such purely political considerations, the application of conventions relating to the accountability individually and collectively of ministers establishes a further set of checks which are enforced through Parliament. The intense political embarrassment caused by ministerial or departmental misfeasance usually finds its focus in parliamentary questions or debates, where, on serious issues, the choice of either a convincing explanation or resignation is expected to be forthcoming.

Similarly, where decisions are made at Cabinet level, ministers are held collectively to account to Parliament. As de Smith observed, if a minister dissents he should resign first, and then publicly distance himself from the subject in contention. However, the purist theory lacks a little in substance, since a suspension of the convention is possible and the government attitude seems to be enshrined not a little in Mr Callaghan's remark that '... I certainly think the doctrine should apply, except in cases where I announce that it does not.' This indeed indicates the extent of the 'flexibility' of our unwritten constitution. (Mr Callaghan was Labour Prime Minister 1976–1979.)

Parliament, if it feels so inclined, may censure the government with a motion of no confidence where the government is held to be collectively responsible. Of convention, such a motion, if it were successful, would prompt the resignation of the government. However, the significance of such a motion is to be viewed more in terms of a political tactic and a method of attracting media attention.

A more direct and effective control of government is the need for parliamentary approval for the financing of government initiatives. Since Parliament holds the country's purse strings, the government must inspire enough confidence in the Commons, at least to provide funding for new policies. The structure of government finance is necessarily complex, but the parliamentary system is structured so as to cope with these rigours. Central to this system is the Public Accounts Committee, which, although reflecting the parliamentary representation of the parties, has such a non-partisan reputation that it is, by convention, chaired by a member of the opposition. Although it primarily seeks out financial irregularities, it also monitors extravagant spending and imprudent contractual transactions.

Extensive powers of discovery and enquiry were conferred on the Treasury and Civil Service Committee, which was set up in 1979, to the extent that scrutinising Treasury policy is within the Committee's brief. In such ways Parliament tacitly defines the parameters within which the Executive can finance its policies.

Aside from these financial controls, the standing orders and procedures of the Commons provide adequate opportunities for confrontation of the government by the opposition and their own backbenchers on contentious issues. Debating opportunities on the Queen's Speech, budget and on Opposition Days, motions of censure and others and emergency debates take on more significance with the eye of the country fixed on television.

The committee system now mirrors the departmental organisation of central government with departmental select committees examining the expenditure, administration and policy of various designated government departments. Their powers are the same as those of the Treasury and Civil Service Committee and are brought together under the auspices of the Liaison Committee. The force of the House's authority and powers to punish for contempt are behind these committees.

The teeth of the Defence Select Committee were tested during the 'Westland Affair' (1986) when it sought to discover the names of civil servants who were responsible for the leaking of a letter from the Solicitor General. Although the government achieved a compromise, the Committee never conceded that in law there were any governmental restraints on the exercise of its functions.

The departmental select committee system is generally regarded as a forum for more in-depth and informed discussion than is available elsewhere in Parliament. Furthermore, their unanimous, but often powerfully critical reports, have certainly had effects on executive policy. However, the paucity of free debating time means that only a handful of the reports have had full discussion on the floor of the House of Commons.

Parliament's role as the arena for airing criticism of the government has been significantly augmented by the advent of television cameras, as we have observed before. Certainly the parliamentary proceeding that most captivates the imagination of the electorate is Question Time, when the government at least appears to be under the most stringent attack. Since taking office on 2 May 1997 the Labour Prime Minister, Tony Blair, has reformed Prime Minister's Question Time by scrapping the Tuesday and Thursday 15-minute sessions and replacing them with a 30-minute session every Wednesday. This was done to reflect his desire that more time should be spent for detailed questioning of the 'chief executive' of government, rather than for quick party political point-scoring which had seemed to dominate the shorter Tuesday and Thursday sessions. It is generally acknowledged that the change has been popular and successful with MPs and the viewing public.

The extent to which the request for oral or written answers to questions to any minister is actually laying down the parameters of government, rather than political point scoring, is somewhat questionable. However, it is clear that the electoral fortunes of a party or MP may be decided in the cut and thrust of these sessions, something of which the government is clearly aware. However, de Smith's view that 'a question to a minister is rather a method of ventilating a grievance than of securing a remedy' is perhaps the most realistic approach.

In addition to the practical limitations of parliamentary questions as a method of scrutinising the government, certain questions may be refused if they lie outside the sphere of competence of a minister. Answers may not be forthcoming if the matter is sub judice, or simply because an answer would cost more than the prescribed ceiling for expenditure on parliamentary answers.

A final method available to members to ensure the maintenance of the standards of government is by working with the Parliamentary Commissioner for Standards, a post set up after the Nolan Report (1993) on the 'cash for questions' scandal. A committee of MPs supervises the Commissioner's work and reports to the whole House.

Thus, having explored the way in which members might scrutinise the Executive, we must assess the truth of Norton's assertions. In our parliamentary system, strong reliance is placed upon adherence to conventions. The effect of disapproving motions relating to conventions of responsibility cannot be denied; however, the change in attitude towards, for example, the motion of censure, demonstrates that reliance on convention as a method of executive control is unsatisfactory, particularly when a government commands a sizeable majority in the Commons.

Equally, there are limits on the extent to which control of the government can be exercised by intermittent rebellions of back bench members, who stand to lose their status within the parliamentary party and with the electorate.

Financial control holds out the most practical promise as delineating the parameters of government, but once again is subject to the control of the majority party in the House, which is almost always subject to strict party discipline.

It is therefore in the arena of the debating floor and during Question Time, which, due to its high media profile, is of great significance in terms of public opinion, that the democratic check on the executive finds its strongest weapon. Where MPs collectively know that public opinion supports them against government policy, even back benchers of the party in power may find a reserves of courage to criticise and rebel.

Conversely, the committee system is increasingly being regarded as the part of the Commons where much of the serious work goes on. With its smaller and more informed membership, and its greater opportunities for detailed and lengthy scrutiny, as well as the tendency of committees to be less partisan or concerned with political point scoring, this forum has become in many ways a powerhouse of the democratic process. Opportunities exist not only to criticise, but to make searching enquiries of the way in which the process of government is carried on.

It is difficult to envisage, however, what Norton's conception of a positive way of providing the parameters within which government can govern would amount to. Obviously, the doctrine of the separation of powers prevents excessive interference by the legislature in executive functions. Thus, the positive function of members must be to maintain and enforce the constitutional safeguards against abuse of executive power. Since these safeguards are largely in the nature of conventions, then following the general view that they are adhered to since their breach would result in political embarrassment, Parliament's only significant function is to heighten the electorate's awareness of government threats to the constitution. It is arguable that this role is better performed by the media, although it cannot compel ministers to account. More importantly parliamentary committees can extract information in a way that need not be as self-consciously populist as the methods employed on the floor of the House of Commons.

In the final analysis, any weaknesses or limitations in the methods available to members who wish to lay down the parameters for good government have to be put down to the inherent weaknesses of our constitution. Additionally, it must be remembered that excessive interference in Executive functions by the legislature is constitutionally undesirable.

SUGGESTED ANSWER TO QUESTION TWO

General Comment

A straightforward question but one involving a considerable amount of material, so selectivity of issues for discussion is important. Equal emphasis should be given to primary and delegated legislation; it is tempting for students to revise only one of these areas and hence produce a one-sided approach. Such a question should be attempted only if the student is confident of having enough material to produce a balanced and critical analysis.

Key Points

- Control of primary legislation by the executive
- Effect of whips and patronage
- Uses of the guillotine
- Weaknesses of parliamentary control
- Proposals of the Hansard Society
- Critical evaluation
- Types of delegated legislation and weaknesses of parliamentary control
- Special problem of European Union legislation
- Threats to the rule of law
- Conclusions

Suggested Answer

In regard to primary legislation the executive controls business not only by setting a general timetable for discussing Bills but also the length of debates on individual issues through the use of its (in normal times) party majority to ensure the closure, guillotining or adjournment of debates. The control extends beyond the debating chamber to the standing committees in which Bills are scrutinised line by line. The effect of the whip and patronage systems to ensure party loyalty enables the efficient passage of legislation but at the price of reducing the independence of action of MPs, who may be unable to object to hasty or ill-conceived measures, or even simply poorly drafted ones, because of the priority given to complying with the government's timetable. An article by Ganz ([1990] PL 496) contains a devastating analysis of the frequency of the use of the guillotine during the 'Thatcher Years': more use was made of it than in the entire period of 1945-1979 (the Thatcher Years were May 1979 to November 1990).

In 1993 the Hansard Society, a non-party group, published proposals for reform of parliamentary procedures to ensure better examination of legislation. The price would be an agreed timetable with Opposition parties in which the latter would have to surrender their most valuable weapon, delay (filibuster) of government proposals. It may be that the price is one an Opposition will not be prepared to pay.

Among the Hansard Commission proposals (published 3 February 1993) are pre-legislative enquiries by MPs into the preparation of Bills and evidence-taking sessions after their publication. In this way more open consultation of interested parties could take place, which should be continued at later stages with more open meetings of standing committees. For this purpose the current minimum intervals between stages of Bills should be increased and more information should be made publicly available. A two-year legislative programme should be designed to replace the current one-year programmes to allow greater time for drafting Bills.

Such proposals are unlikely to go down well with the government civil service, which tends to view the passage of primary legislation like a military operation. The reforms might also be unpopular with MPs, who would be faced with more work on standing committees, stretching into mornings, evenings and weekends if all interested groups are to be heard fairly. As Peter Riddell commented:

> 'The trouble with proposals like those from the Hansard Society ... is that they take too idealistic a view of what MPs can, and want, to do. Most see themselves primarily as party politicians and ministerial aspirants. Only a minority regard themselves as legislators and champions of Parliament': (1993) The Times 3 February.

The scrutiny process is probably just as unsatisfactory when it comes to review of delegated legislation. The sheer quantity of such legislation makes it impossible for an amateurish group of 658 individuals (Speaker omitted) with other diverse responsibilities to exercise anything like detailed scrutiny of the content and effect of statutory instruments, orders in council, ministerial regulations, etc. Indeed, the flood of European Union delegated laws in the form of directives from the Council of Ministers and European Commission is so great that not even the specialist Select Committee of the House of Lords on the European Union can cope with it and the Hansard Report gives warning of this. Probably a Joint Committee of both Houses with co-opted experts is needed. The parliamentary Joint Committee on domestic delegated legislation in the form of statutory instruments seems to work reasonably well, but its reports are rarely read in the whole House and MPs simply do not seem to have the time to devote to such issues. A Select Committee on the Scrutiny of Delegated Powers was established by the House of Lords in 1992 to report whether the provisions of any Bill inappropriately delegate legislative power, or whether they subject the exercise of legislative power to an inappropriate degree of parliamentary scrutiny. Experiments with morning sittings devoted entirely to scrutiny of delegated legislation have proved failures, probably because, as Riddell said in his article above, many MPs are 'too old, too idle, too maverick or too preoccupied with their constituencies or outside business interests to play an active part'.

Yet the problem of inadequate scrutiny of delegated legislation has always been a considerable one, one not to shy away from, if one follows the Diceyan attitudes on the rule of law and accepts the need for curtailment of wide executive discretion:

> 'There is a clear threat to parliamentary government if power is delegated to legislate on matters of general policy or if so wide a discretion is conferred that it is impossible to be sure of what limit the legislature intended to impose': Wade and Bradley *Constitutional and Administrative Law* (1985, 10th ed), p612.

Consequently reformers should go on trying to persuade MPs of the need to devote more time and energy to this subject and to stop providing blank cheques for the Government of the day. If MPs need more resources to do this, by way of expert researchers and other assistants, so be it. Most modern legislatures, from the American Congress to the Australian and New Zealand Parliaments, spend enormous sums on ensuring proper scrutiny of subordinate legislation: finding, Hansard Report, above. Greater use of the second chamber (the House of Lords) as a means of scrutinising delegated legislation may also be a partial solution to an intractable problem.

SUGGESTED ANSWER TO QUESTION THREE

General Comment

A relatively simple question on parliamentary privilege dealing with two main criticisms of the doctrine from the point of view of the aggrieved individual. There are two issues to be considered: (i) the case of citizens denied legal redress where the MP hides behind his privileges; and (ii) the case of those adjudged to have committed a breach of privilege who are usually found 'guilty' following a procedure which breaches the rules of natural justice. Remember that the question is fairly specific. There is no need to go into detail regarding the various privileges. Freedom of speech in debate is the most relevant.

Key Points

- Introduction: definition of parliamentary privilege; the justification for the privilege; examples of privileges.
- Cases of abuse where the Member of Parliament hides behind privilege; example of freedom of speech in debate and the law of defamation. Effect of s13 Defamation Act 1996.
- Procedure for determining breaches of privilege: punishments available to those found guilty of contempt or breach of privilege; procedure for dealing with complaints - breaches of the rules of natural justice; recommendations of the 1967 Select Committee on Parliamentary Privilege.
- General conclusion: breach of the rule of law; breach of natural justice.

Suggested Answer

Parliamentary privilege forms part of the law and custom of Parliament evolved by the two Houses in order to protect their freedom to conduct their proceedings without improper interference by the sovereign, the courts, or other bodies or persons outside Parliament. It is defined by Erskine May as 'the sum of the peculiar rights enjoyed by each House collectively as a constitutional part of the High Court of Parliament and by members of each House individually, without which they could not discharge their functions, and which exceed those possessed by other bodies or individuals'.

The privileges enjoyed by the House of Commons include those 'ancient and undoubted privileges' claimed by the Speaker at the beginning of each new Parliament such as freedom of speech in debate, freedom from civil arrest, freedom of access via the Speaker to the sovereign and that the most favourable construction should be placed upon all their proceedings. There are also more privileges enjoyed by the House in its corporate capacity such as the right to regulate its own composition, the right to take exclusive cognisance of matters arising within the precincts of the House and the right to punish both members and non-members for breach of privilege and contempt. Similar provisions apply in respect of the House of Lords. These special rights, powers and immunities conferred by parliamentary privilege are said to be essential for the conduct of the business and the maintenance of the authority of the House.

There is no doubt, however, that while parliamentary privilege may be considered necessary for the welfare of the nation, there is wide scope for abuse by MPs especially as regards freedom of speech. Article 9 Bill of Rights 1688 provides that the freedom of speech, and debates or proceedings in Parliament ought not to be imposed or questioned in any court or place out of Parliament. Therefore no action or prosecution can be brought against an MP for any words used in the course of parliamentary proceedings. If an MP were to be sued for libel or slander in respect of words used in Parliament in the course of 'proceedings in Parliament', the writ should be struck out as disclosing no cause of action. If the case were to come to trial the court would hold that the MP was protected by absolute privilege in the law of defamation. Thus, an MP may make defamatory statements regarding an individual, in the course of proceedings in Parliament, knowing that even if there is no basis to his allegations he is protected from a civil action for damages in tort. No action would be against him even if his remarks were shown to be defamatory, untrue, malicious and unfair, no matter how much damage is caused to the individual as a result.

The privileged position of an MP has become even more controversial with the passage of s13 Defamation Act 1996 which permits an MP to waive privilege if he wishes to make use of parliamentary material during the course of a defamation action which that MP is bringing against an outsider or outside organisation. It is not possible for the MP, even if he/she wanted to do so, to waive privilege when *defending* a defamation action: *Prebble* v *Television New Zealand Ltd* (1994).

Further, the House still reserves to itself the right to treat the institution of legal proceedings against an MP in respect of a matter covered, in its opinion, by parliamentary privilege, as a breach of its own privilege and may punish the individual concerned for breach of privilege or contempt: the *Strauss Affair* (1957–58). Of course, an MP who abuses his privilege of freedom of speech may be subject to disciplinary sanctions by the House, but this is no great deterrent. The fact remains that every year innocent individuals are defamed by ill-informed, careless or even malicious MPs and suffer considerable damage to their reputation as a result, but are nevertheless denied any legal redress because the MP concerned hides behind his or her parliamentary privilege.

Those individuals adjudged by the House to have committed a high contempt and a breach of its privileges are also treated in a manner which is open to considerable criticism. Parliamentary privileges are part of the common law in so far as their existence and validity are recognised by the courts. But they are enforced not by the courts but exclusively by Parliament.

By virtue of its inherent right to control its own proceedings and maintain its dignity, the House of Commons in protecting its privileges may punish those who violate them or commit contempt of the House. Breach of privilege consists of either an abuse of a particular privilege by an MP, or any conduct which interferes with one of the privileges of Parliament. Contempt is a much wider concept and consists of any conduct which tends to bring the House into disrepute or detract from its dignity. No matter whether the offence is styled a breach of privilege or a contempt, or both, the penal powers of the House are the same. Offenders may be reprimanded or admonished by the Speaker. Members of Parliament may be suspended or expelled. Officials of the House may be dismissed and any MP or stranger may be committed to prison for the duration of the parliamentary session. However, it is the procedure by which complaints of breach of privilege are dealt with which is open to most criticism.

Complaints of breach of privilege may be raised by an MP or in the House by the Speaker. If the Speaker rules that a prima facie case has been made out a motion is proposed that the matter be referred to the Committee on Standards and Privileges. The motion may then be debated and voted upon. The Committee, comprising the most senior members of the parties in the House is the master of its own proceedings. It can compel the attendance of witnesses and the production of documents, failure to comply being a contempt. There is no requirement of legal representation, indeed the 'defendant' may not be given any hearing at all. At the conclusion of its investigation the Committee reports its findings to the House and may recommend the action that the House should take. The House need not accept the Committee's findings nor recommendations, but it almost always does. This procedure has been criticised. The Committee in 1967 recommended that persons directly concerned in the Committee's investigations should have the right to attend its hearings, make submissions, call, examine and cross-examine witnesses and, with leave of the Committee, be legally represented and apply for legal aid. These recommendations have however never been adopted.

It can be seen therefore that whatever the justification for parliamentary privilege may be, it is open to abuse by the less responsible members of the House, it is a breach of the rule of law, and the procedures for dealing with allegations of breach of privilege and contempt invariably breach the rules of natural justice. It is therefore an area ripe for reform.

SUGGESTED ANSWER TO QUESTION FOUR

General Comment

A wide-ranging question, requiring the examinee to look at privilege from the angles of the House of Commons (by character prejudiced angles) and of the courts (by character independent angles). But assessment of those angles should take place in the context of the historical development of privilege, which at least gives a kind of rational basis to Parliament's exclusive claims in several important areas. Critical analysis should be supported by reference to appropriate academic research.

Key Points

- Definition of parliamentary privilege and problems of control
- Internal proceedings of the House and risk of abuse of collective power
- Roles of Speaker and Standards and Privileges Committee
- Manner of hearing for alleged contemnors
- Scope of privilege of free speech under art 9 Bill of Rights 1688
- Internal discipline and absence of judicial review
- Vagueness of concept of 'proceedings in Parliament' and case for and against codification
- Other reform proposals are considered at appropriate points during the solution

Suggested Answer

Parliamentary privilege is part of the common law which grants certain exemptions from the law to MPs in order that they may perform their functions. By its nature privilege is difficult to subject to normal processes of parliamentary and judicial review. There is the added complication that parliamentary privilege was won after an historic conflict between the legislature and an absolute monarchy (the latter at times supported by the judges). This explains the traditional sensitivity of the relationship between the legislature and the judiciary on the matter of privilege, raising fears for the rule of law.

Dicey argued for equality under the law, but the internal proceedings of the House of Commons are not subject to judicial review. Control, if any, must be exercised by the Commons itself, principally through the Speaker and the Select Committee on Standards and Privileges. The danger is that the House, collectively, may act as judge and jury in its own cause on a matter concerning an individual MP's rights to represent the constituency which elected him, eg as in the House's expulsion for political reasons of the radical Charles Bradlaugh: *Bradlaugh* v *Gossett* (1884). Since no judicial review is available over such a decision, the only remedy for an expelled member is to petition the House which expelled him: *Case of the Sheriff of Middlesex* (1840).

The House also claims exclusive rights to punish 'strangers' (non-MPs) for breaches of MPs' individual privileges and for contempt of the whole House. These are dealt with either by rulings from the Speaker or by reference to the Committee of Standards and Privileges, consisting of MPs from all parties chosen for their expertise in parliamentary law and their long experience of the life of the Commons. But MPs not on the Committee as well as academic observers, have expressed fears about the degree of discretion delegated to the Speaker and the Committee by the whole House. The methods used to deal with 'offenders' are far removed from 'due process of law'.

For example, the accused may be arrested by the Sergeant-at-Arms (the enforcement officer of the House) and brought before a private hearing of the Committee. The accused has no right to legal representation and may be cross-examined by a panel of QCs. The accused has no right to call evidence or to cross-examine the witnesses against him. The Committee reports to the whole House on whether the offence is proven and, if so, what penalty (including, in theory, imprisonment) should be imposed. There is no right of appeal to the courts against conviction or sentence and no opportunity for judicial review over the way the decision was reached.

It is not surprising that authorities such as the late Professor de Smith condemned privilege hearings as a 'travesty of justice' in which biased MPs acted as judges in their own cause. He argued cogently that, with a modern independent judiciary, such privileges were not necessary and that the House's jurisdiction over punishable contempts and breaches of privilege should be transferred to the courts so that these matters are subject to due process of law.

Similarly it has been argued that the House no longer needs the absolute rights to freedom of speech granted in respect of 'proceedings in Parliament' by art 9 Bill of Rights 1688. Such freedom has the potential to become a licence to defame, to be used irresponsibly by publicity-seeking members. Whilst the House, through the Speaker, has the power under its internal standing orders to discipline members who abuse the right, it appears that the House has been very reluctant to exercise such discipline, at least over an MP who criticises the conduct of outsiders. When an MP criticises the behaviour or integrity of a fellow MP this is usually taken more seriously and the speaker will demand a retraction and issue warnings about the need for 'parliamentary language in respect of the honourable members of this House'.

Patricia Leopold suggested that the House should introduce new safeguards on this matter, eg new conventions which oblige MPs to give advance notice to the person they intend to criticise, and to use all other methods to establish the truth of particular rumours/allegations before ventilating them under the cover of privilege: [1981] PL 30. Others have argued that the absolute privilege under art 9 should be replaced by the defence of qualified privilege, giving MPs the same degree of protection as given to everyone else by the law of defamation.

In the absence of such reform judicial control will be haphazard and uncertain, mainly because of the difficulty of defining precise limits to the concept of 'proceedings in Parliament': see the inability of the Judicial Committee of the Privy Council to reach a decided view on this point in the reference arising from the *Strauss Affair* (1957–58): *Re Parliamentary Privilege Act* (1958). Only a bold judge would feel able to give the benefit of any doubt to the citizen when faced with a claim to privilege, eg Popplewell J in declaring that the register of MPs' Interests was not privileged in *Rost* v *Edwards* (1990). Miss Leopold commended this 'robust' attitude but argued that the matter is too important to be left to haphazard development of the common law, contending that the area of privilege requires codification on lines of Australia's Parliamentary Proceedings Act 1987: [1990] PL 475. However, although codification might end the uncertainty of judicial review, a jealous and suspicious Parliament might also take the opportunity to define its privileges as widely as possible, leaving no chance for judges to give the kind of decision Popplewell J gave in *Rost* v *Edwards*.

Nevertheless the need for reform could be said to have increased as a result of Parliament's decision to allow MPs to waive their art 9 privilege in order to sue for defamation: s13 Defamation Act 1996. It seems unfair that MPs can choose whether or not to make use of absolute privilege, and the present position is offensive to the Diceyan concept of equality under the law.

5

The House of Lords

Introduction

This chapter is concerned with the role of the second chamber in the British Constitution. The need for a second chamber will be examined and then the arguments will be considered concerning the kind of second chamber most suitable in a modern parliamentary democracy. The peculiar nature of the House of Lords inevitably raises questions concerning the continuing suitability of its composition, but these questions cannot be considered in isolation from the functions it performs. Whilst there is a strong case for reform of the House of Lords, it should not be assumed that a representative body is essential to perform the basic functions of a second chamber.

The debate over the House of Lords has been raging for most of the twentieth century, yet attempts at fundamental reform have been tried but failed to obtain the support of the House of Commons - most notably in 1969, with the defeat of the Parliament (No 2) Bill. Hence, it is necessary to study the history of such attempts at reform in order to appreciate the complex nature of the problem, which involves not only the relationship between the two Houses but also the future of the House of Commons itself. There are those who argue that reform of the Commons is a necessary precondition to successful reform of the House of Lords.

For examination purposes it is essential to be familiar with the composition and functions of the House of Lords, particularly its ability to delay legislation. Consider whether the Parliament Acts 1911 and 1949 are a satisfactory compromise between the need to ensure the ultimate supremacy of the elected chamber and the need to ensure that a reasonable time for second thoughts on an issue is made available. A great deal of the controversy concerning the House of Lords is the result of the continuing influence of the hereditary peers. It is the policy of the Labour Government, elected in May 1997, to begin reform of the House of Lords by depriving the hereditary peers of their right to vote during the law-making process. Who, if anyone, should replace them? Elected members? Nominated members and, if so, nominated by whom?

Reform of the House of Lords has tended to be a hardy annual in typical examination papers in constitutional law and, with reform back on the political agenda, it can be reasonably expected that questions requiring critical analysis of current reform proposals will appear on a regular basis. The problem for the examination candidate is anticipating the 'slant' of a particular question since the issue can be approached in so many ways. Reference to research articles in the main law journals is a useful foundation upon which to develop themes for discussion. A recent example is an article by Shell [1997] PL 70.

Questions

INTERROGAMS

1 Outline the composition of the House of Lords.
2 Outline the main functions of the House of Lords.
3 What is the effect of the Parliament Acts 1911 and 1949?
4 Outline the principal arguments for and against reforms of the House of Lords.

QUESTION ONE

What contribution, if any, does the House of Lords make to the British Constitution?

London University LLB Examination
(for external students) Constitutional Law June 1987 Q4

QUESTION TWO

'The House of Lords is becoming more and more important in the legislative process. It is the House of Commons which really needs reform'

Discuss.

London University LLB Examination
(for external students) Constitutional Law June 1988 Q1

QUESTION THREE

Evaluate the statement that the Parliament Acts 1911 and 1949 represent an appropriate balance between the House of Commons and the House of Lords.

London University LLB Examination
(for external students) Constitutional Law June 1989 Q2

QUESTION FOUR

'With a perfect Lower House it is certain that an Upper House would be scarcely of any value. But … beside the actual House (of Commons) a revising and leisured legislative is extremely useful.' (Bagehot)

Discuss.

London University LLB Examination
(for external students) Constitutional Law June 1990 Q5

Answers

ANSWERS TO INTERROGRAMS

1 There are approximately 1,200 members of the House of Lords, of whom about 920 are eligible to vote (ineligible are minors, bishops and, by convention, Law Lords). Membership is not fixed at any particular number and all members are unelected.

There are 26 Lords Spiritual (senior clergy of the Church of England, including two Archbishops and 24 Bishops). The remaining peers are known as Lords Temporal and consist of hereditary peers and life peers. Hereditary peerages are held by approximately 770 persons. There are approximately 400 life peers, including 12 serving Law Lords, who, though legally entitled to vote, by convention do not do so. There are only about 20 female hereditary peers and only about 60 female life peers. Life peers are nominated by the Prime Minister - a tremendous power of patronage. Of the peers eligible to vote only approximately 360 attend on a regular basis. These are known as the 'working peers', the majority of whom are life peers. Hereditary peers who rarely attend are known as 'backwoodsmen' (because they remain at their country estates!).

2 The 1968 White Paper on reform of the House of Lords usefully identified seven functions of the House as follows:

a The appellate role as the supreme court of appeal. By convention only the Law Lords sit in the House's judicial capacity.

b The provision of a forum for free debate on matters of public interest. Wednesdays are traditionally reserved for special debates on a wide range of subjects. The diverse nature of the composition of the House often produces debates of high quality.

c The revision of public Bills from the House of Commons. In practice this is the most significant of the daily functions of the House. Since it tends to be a non-contentious function the question arises of whether it is necessary to be 'representative' in order to perform it.

d The initiation of public Bills. The House of Lords can be used by the government to introduce largely uncontroversial legislation as a way of efficiently managing its legislative timetable. Peers can also introduce Private Members' Bills.

e The consideration of subordinate legislation. This is an important additional check over the risks of abuse of power through government by regulation.

f The scrutiny of the activities of the executive. Question Time and debates are the main methods. There are no standing committees for public legislation but there are some select committees.

g The scrutiny of private legislation. This is usually done in committee. Consideration of private Bills helps ease the workload on the House of Commons.

3 The Parliament Act 1911 ensured that many Bills could become law without the consent of the House of Lords if not passed by the Lords without amendment within one month of being sent up by the Commons (at least one month before the end of the parliamentary session); that any other public Bill, except one for extending the life of a Parliament, could become law without the consent of the Lords after two years delay; and that the maximum duration of a Parliament should be five years (previously seven years).

The Parliament Act 1949, passed under the 1911 Act procedure without consent of the Lords, reduced the delaying powers on the non-money public Bills to one year. The War Crimes Act 1991 was passed under the 1949 Act procedure - the first time the 1949 Act had been used.

4 In favour of reform:

a To get rid of the hereditary element. It is simply unacceptable in a modern democracy for people to acquire law-making powers by accident of birth.

b To get rid of the patronage powers of the Prime Minister by ensuring that any system of nominating new life peers is done by a non-partisan body, perhaps chaired by the Speaker.

c To democratise the second chamber by having elected peers, perhaps through a system of proportional or regional representation.

d To increase the powers of the new chamber so that it can provide effective safeguards against abuse of power by the executive-dominated House of Commons.

Against reform:

a Altering its composition might lead to the loss of independent-minded contributors who speak for the national interest rather than party or constituency interests.

b Reform might simply produce another 'House of Commons' dominated by party loyalists who engage in political point-scoring rather than courteous and well-informed debates.

c Any rational system of choosing membership of the new second chamber would give it an equal claim to sovereignty. How would conflicts be resolved between the Commons and the new second chamber, assuming that use of the Parliament Acts 1911 and 1949 would no longer be acceptable?

d Traditionally the House of Lords has proved its value so far as the performance of its main functions is concerned. The very fact that it has survived for so long is an indication that nothing is seriously wrong with its contribution to the British Constitution.

SUGGESTED ANSWER TO QUESTION ONE

General Comment

The question involves discussion of the role of the House of Lords as the second chamber in our bicameral parliamentary system and the effects on the constitution which would arise if the lords were not there.

Key Points

- Introduction - general position of the House of Lords within the constitution
- The role of the House of Lords (the work of the Judicial Committee, role of the House as a revision chamber for public Bills and role of Lords as a check on the executive)
- Effects on the British constitution if the House of Lords abolished (need for change in House of Commons procedure and need for written constitution)
- Proposals of Labour Government on reform of House of Lords

Suggested Answer

The House of Lords is the second chamber in our bicameral parliamentary system. To its critics, the House of Lords as presently constituted is undemocratic, out-dated and unsuitable in a modern society. Many therefore favour reform, so that for example its composition becomes more democratic. Others, however, wish to go further still and see the total abolition of the House of Lords. Those in favour of abolition refuse to accept that the House of Lords makes a valuable contribution to the British Constitution. Despite the problems regarding its composition, the fact remains that the House of Lords does perform a valuable service within the present parliamentary system and if abolished many of its functions would still have to be performed by some other body, presumably the House of Commons. In 1968, the Government White Paper 'House of Lords Reform' referred to seven functions of the House of Lords. An examination of each of these functions serves to illustrate the contribution made by the House to the effective working of our constitution and highlight some of the problems that might result if the House of Lords ceased to exist.

Firstly, the House of Lords acts as the final court of appeal for the whole of the United Kingdom in civil cases and for England, Wales and Northern Ireland in criminal cases. The judicial work of the House is separate from its other functions and only involves the Judicial Committee, drawn from the Lord High Chancellor, the Lords of Appeal in Ordinary and Lords who hold or who have held high judicial office. It could be argued that the Court of Appeal could become the final appeal court for England and Wales.

Secondly, the House of Lords provides a forum for free debate on matters of public interest, Wednesday in particular being traditionally set aside for special debate on a wide range of subjects. Apart from the fact that these debates are usually of a very high standard, their loss would not pose any great constitutional problem.

Thirdly, and perhaps most importantly, the House acts as a revising chamber for public Bills brought from the House of Commons. About one half of the time of the House of Lords is devoted to the consideration of public Bills. The majority of this time is spent on revising Bills which have already passed the Commons, where the great majority of government legislation is introduced. The House of Commons does not have the time to fully debate all the legislation it has to pass each session and the use of procedures for the curtailment of debate, such as the guillotine, often means that Bills are passed by the Commons without really being considered at all. A second chamber is therefore required to examine and revise such Bills. This is the greatest contribution made by the House of Lords to the British Constitution and it is probably true to say that as far as this particular function is concerned, if the House of Lords did not exist then it would have to be invented. If the House ceased to exist then the procedures of the House of Commons for enacting legislation would have to be changed if the present standard and volume of legislation were to be maintained. This could be achieved by membership of the House of Commons becoming full-time and by making even more use of committees. However, even then the volume of legislation may still prove to be too great, necessitating either a shortening of the procedure by which a Bill is enacted or making more use of subordinate legislation, which some would argue is already overused as it is. Certainly some fundamental changes would have to be made to the procedures of the House of Commons.

Also it must be remembered that the House of Commons, because of the distortion produced by our electoral system, is largely controlled by a government which does not represent even 50 per cent of the electorate. A second chamber is thus required to at least delay substantially controversial legislation which may be unpopular with the majority of the people of the country. If the House of Lords were not there then the only way to control a government with an absolute majority in the House of Commons may be to have either a written constitution or a Bill of Rights containing entrenched clauses, perhaps requiring a referendum for amendment. Experience has shown that the House of Lords, with its independent membership, may be the only check that exists on the powerful executive and frequent defeats have been inflicted by their Lordships, thus helping to weaken executive control of the legislature.

The House of Lords also initiates public Bills. While the more controversial and important Bills almost invariably begin in the House of Commons, Bills which are relatively uncontroversial in party political terms are regularly introduced in the House of Lords. If the House did not exist these Bills would have to be dealt with by the Commons thus adding to its already overburdened workload. Similarly, the subordinate legislation and the private legislation at present dealt with by the House of Lords would also fall to be wholly dealt with by the Commons if the second chamber did not exist.

It can be seen therefore that the House of Lords makes a very great contribution to the effective and efficient working of the British constitution. Any proposal for reform of the House of Lords will need to take account of the special functions it performs. The Labour Government, elected on 1 May 1997, is pledged to abolish the voting rights of hereditary peers but is already coming under pressure from both Houses to propose reforms to Commons procedures as a necessary precondition to such reform.

SUGGESTED ANSWER TO QUESTION TWO

General Comment

Despite a first impression to the contrary this is not a question requiring in-depth consideration of reform of the Lords, but does require some consideration of the changes in the nature of the work done by the House of Lords. Detail needs to be provided of the contribution made by the House of Lords, and also proposals for reform of the House of Commons.

Key Points

- Brief history of House of Lords decline and rise
- Consider powers of the upper House
- Guillotine
- Amendment powers
- Reform of the House of Commons
- Accommodation
- Hours

- Proceedings
- Impact of election of Labour Government, May 1997
- Conclusion

Suggested Answer

The importance of the House of Lords as a constitutional institution has declined since the latter half of the nineteenth century, as the importance and dominance of the House of Commons has increased. The House of Lords has for centuries recognised the privileges of the House of Commons in respect of financial matters, and with the enactment of the Parliament Act 1911, its power to delay legislation passed by the House of Commons was effectively reduced to two years. The Parliament Act 1949 reduced this period even further to one year.

In the post war era the House of Lords came to be seen by many as something of an anachronism. Particular criticism was made of its hereditary membership, the absence of women, and its inherent Conservative bias. Reform was clearly necessary, and it came in the form of the Life Peerages Act 1958, and the Peerages Act 1963. The combined effect of these measures was to introduce life peers into the house (in addition to those who were already life peers appointed under the Appellate Jurisdiction Act 1876), and to increase significantly the number of women entitled to sit.

Many would contend that these measures went a long way towards revitalising the House of Lords as an important element in the constitution, giving it greater credibility as part of the legislative process, and broadening the range of expertise amongst the members of the house. Experience since 1958 has shown that it is from the ranks of 500 or so life peers who have been appointed, that the house has drawn its most valuable participants.

The importance of the House of Lords as regards the legislative process has undoubtedly grown since 1979. From May 1979 to May 1997 the country was governed by successive Conservative Governments, each of which enjoyed a majority in the House of Commons. The result was that the opposition parties were left somewhat impotent in their efforts to challenge, delay or amend government proposals for legislation. It thus fell to the House of Lords, since 1979, to provide really effective challenges to legislative proposals.

An impotent opposition in the House of Commons is one likely to resort to 'wrecking' or 'timewasting' tactics, with the result that the government is likely to impose a time allocation order, or guillotine, on a Bill in the House of Commons to ensure that it passes through all its stages in the lower house in good time. The problem with guillotine orders is that any part of a Bill not considered before the time allotted for its consideration expires, has to be voted upon as it is. Hence the Bill may not be properly scrutinised by the House of Commons, prior to its being sent up to the House of Lords. The guillotine motion was relied upon as many times between 1979–1985, as it had been in the preceding 20 years. There is no guillotine motion in the House of Lords, thus any matters not fully considered by the House of Commons can be scrutinised for as long as is necessary.

More generally, the House of Lords can use its powers to amend certain types of legislation sent up from the House of Commons, and to delay the passage of legislation to allow more time for debate outside Parliament. It would appear that the House of Lords has been more and more prepared to stand up to governments and reject legislative measures that are seen as going too far. As evidence of this it is worthy of note that between 1979 and October 1986, the House of Lords inflicted 100 defeats on successive Conservative governments.

As regards which House of Parliament is in the greater need of reform it is difficult to say. There have certainly been more attempts at reform of the House of Lords in recent years, but many of these might be seen as being politically motivated, rather that being based upon any pragmatic research. There are undoubtedly certain aspects of the work of the House of Commons that might be seen as ripe for reform.

The accommodation provided for backbench and Opposition MPs is frequently criticised as inadequate, with many having to share rooms. The use of nearby buildings to take the 'overflow' is not an ideal solution. The hours of work within the House of Commons are frequently criticised, with all-night sittings playing havoc not only with the health of members, but also their domestic lives. More could be done to provide better research facilities for MPs, particularly those involved in committee work on behalf of the House.

The reliance upon the whip system in debates in the Commons ensures that the outcome of debates is usually a forgone conclusion, forcing MPs to fire rhetoric and propaganda at each other, rather than using their oratorical skills to persuade others to agree with a particular viewpoint.

More generally the behaviour of MPs in the House of Commons does not always reach the levels of courtesy and politeness that one would wish to see in the nation's legislative chamber. In this respect the introduction of the televising of proceedings in the House of Commons has had a salutary effect on standards of behaviour.

In many of these matters listed above, the House of commons could usefully learn from the lead already shown by the House of Lords.

In conclusion, it can be said that whilst the House of Lords has undoubtedly become more important in the legislative process in recent years, whether it remains so will depend largely on the composition of the House of Commons in the future. The Labour Government, elected at the General Election on 1 May 1997, has a massive Commons majority of over 170, so the problems of 'impotent' opposition in the Commons, touched on above, will continue for the immediate future. However, whether the House of Lords will oppose the new Government with the same degree of determination shown against Conservative Governments during the period 1979-1997 remains to be seen, particularly as the Lords are threatened with reform in the shape of abolition of the voting rights of hereditary peers. The need for reform of Commons' procedures therefore seems even more urgent.

SUGGESTED ANSWER TO QUESTION THREE

General Comment

A detailed knowledge is required of the background to, and contents of, the Parliament Acts 1911 and 1949. A critical analysis should be given of the use and effects of the two Acts.

Key Points

- History prior to Parliament Act 1911 and relationship of Commons and Lords
- First state what the two Acts provide for
- Main result of the Acts in practice
- Reform/abolition of the upper house
- Likely impact of any reforms
- Conclusion

Suggested Answer

Before the Parliament Act 1911 there was widespread recognition that since the House of Commons was the elected chamber its will should override that of the House of Lords, which, in those days, was entirely hereditary in composition. In law the legislature, the Queen in Parliament, had three equally important constituent parts – the Commons, Lords and Monarch – but there were already in existence conventions to regulate the conduct of the House of Lords. It was the breach by the House of Lords of the convention that it would not interfere with the government's financial proposals passed by the Commons which gave rise to the 1911 Act. The Parliament Act 1949 was passed further to curtail the delaying powers of the House of Lords by a Labour Government which was attempting to prevent its post war nationalisation programme being delayed by the House of Lords. The preamble to the 1911 Act clearly reveals that its reforms were intended only as a stopgap measure until radical reform of the House of Lords was undertaken. However, such reforms of the Lords as there have been during the twentieth century cannot be classified as radical and have not removed the substantial influence of the hereditary peers.

The Parliament Acts 1911–1949 provide that, in certain circumstances, Bills may receive the Royal Assent after approval by the Commons alone. This may happen in the case of a money Bill if it has not been passed by the Lords within one month and in the case of a public Bill if it has not been passed by the Lords within one year, eg as happened with the War Crimes Act 1991.

The Parliament Acts do not apply to Bills which seek to extend the maximum duration of Parliament beyond five years. Also these Acts do not apply to local and private legislation nor to delegated legislation – in this case the power of the Lords depends on whether the parent Act expressly empowers the Lords to approve or disapprove of the delegated legislation in question.

The procedure provided by the Parliament Act 1911 with regard to a money Bill (which is, of course, also a public Bill) is as follows. A money Bill is defined as a Bill which deals with the imposition, repeal, remission, alteration or regulation of taxation or with the Consolidated Fund or the National Loans Fund and other financial matters including raising or guarantee or repayment of loans but Bills dealing with taxation, money or loans raised by local authorities or bodies for local purposes are not certifiable as money Bills. Under s2 of the 1911 Act any certificate of the Speaker (to certify that a Bill is a money Bill), 'shall be conclusive for all purposes, and shall not be questioned in any court of law'.

Once a Bill has been certified as a money Bill then if it is not passed by the Lords within one month of the Bill reaching that Chamber it may be passed direct to the Royal Assent and thus become law. In the case of all other public Bills (with the one exception noted above) if a Bill is not passed by the Lords after the Commons have sent it to them in two separate sessions (with a lapse of a year between the second reading by the Commons in the first session and the third reading in the second session) then it may be passed direct to the Royal Assent. Until the Parliament Act 1949 the delaying period was greater - three sessions spread over two years.

From an examination of the wording of these provisions it would be possible to draw the misleading impression that the Commons always has its legislative way. Although in the last resort the Commons can always, by operating the Parliament Acts, override the opposition of the Lords to its legislative proposals in fact the Parliament Act 1911 was operated only to pass the Welsh Church Act 1914, the Government of Ireland Act 1914 and the Parliament Act 1949. On several occasions in the 1970s the Lords utilised their delaying powers to hinder controversial legislation until policy was changed, and in the 1975-76 session the Labour Government commenced the 1949 Act procedure but this was later rendered unnecessary by compromises. The Acts therefore operate mainly as a deterrent, the psychological effect of which is normally to ensure that in case of conflict between Commons and Lords, the Lords give way. However, it may sometimes be the case that rather than face a delay of one year before legislative proposals become law, thereby disrupting the legislative timetable for later sessions, a government would rather compromise, modifying its Bill in some way so as to satisfy the Lords in order to gain a swift passage to the statute book. Thus in the 1983/4 session the Government suffered an amendment to its Local Government (Interim Provisions) Bill imposed by the Lords to ensure that pending abolition of the Greater London Council in March 1986 councillors, whose term of office would normally have expired in May 1985, would retain their seats rather than being replaced by representatives nominated by the London Boroughs, a Government proposal condemned by the Lords as essentially anti-democratic.

No assessment of the House of Lords' legislative role would be complete without consideration of its importance in relieving the burden on the Commons by its work in private legislation and by its initiation of non-controversial Bills, such as the Courts Act 1971. In addition, the Lords is extremely valuable in its role as a revising chamber. It provides an added opportunity for the government or private member promoting a public Bill to modify the Bill in response to criticism or unforeseen circumstances. An even more important point is that the House of Lords sits as a whole on the committee stage of Bills and there is therefore available a wider perspective on the Bill since the Lords is made up not only of hereditary peers but also life peers who may be Law Lords or those who have been successful in careers in industry or education etc. These Lords may be more clearly aware of the practical effect of proposed legislation on a particular industry than MPs in the Commons.

Reform of the House of Lords was envisaged in the preamble to the 1911 Act. A new second chamber based on a popular vote was to be set up and the old hereditary structure was to be abolished. The views of Viscount Bryce are interesting to note at this stage. Bryce saw the functions of a second chamber to be: (a) examination and revision of Bills brought from the Commons; (b) initiation and discussion of non-controversial Bills; (c) delay of Bills for a reasonable time in order only to alert public opinion; (d) and discussion of current issues of policy which the Commons had no time to discuss. No action was taken on reform however. In 1948 the question surfaced again and disagreement broke out. This led to the passing of the 1949 Act by the Labour Party. This did not settle the question - in 1967 another attempt at reform was made. Disagreement once more broke out leading to the Parliament (No 2) Bill 1968–69 which sought to eliminate the hereditary basis of the Lords. This, however, was not passed following a backbench rebellion in the Commons of MPs fearful of losing power to a reformed and strengthened second chamber.

Plainly the constant efforts at reform/abolition of the Lords show that 'an appropriate balance' has not been achieved. However, the relationship between Commons and Lords has an appropriate balance in the sense that the Commons holds basic power. Whether or not the Lords will remain as the second chamber, the 1911–1949 Acts were successful in confirming the Commons as the chief legislative chamber. Viewing the situation in this context one could say that a 'perfect' balance was not achieved and there is still room for reform of the second chamber. The Labour Government, elected on 1 May 1997, proposes the abolition of the voting rights of hereditary peers, but this will not affect the balance of power between the two Houses unless any replacement has a more 'democratic' character than the hereditary peerages. If, for example, reform involves an elected element or a better form of nomination than by the Prime Minister alone, as at present, then there may be pressure for reform of the Parliament Acts 1911 and 1949 to give the new second chamber a more positive partnership role with the Commons.

SUGGESTED ANSWER TO QUESTION FOUR

General Comment

The question calls for a critical analysis of the House of Lords as a second chamber, with the emphasis on the functions that it performs.

Key Points

- Nature of representative democracy
- Failings of the Commons
- Functions of a second chamber
- Problems with the composition of the House of Lords
- Does composition affect ability to discharge functions?
- Reform proposals

Suggested Answer

An instinctive answer to the present question is 'nothing is perfect'. The truth of this statement is not diminished by the context of the question. The Houses of Parliament are invested with supreme constitutional power to legislate on all matters, but with responsibility to represent the interests, not only of the electorate, but all members of society. This is obviously a grave responsibility and in terms of work load an arduous one. In the light of this it is certainly not difficult to support the implicit assertion of the question that a legislature consisting of two chambers (a bicameral legislature) is not only convenient, but extremely desirable from a practical and constitutional point of view.

Much has been said in criticism of the present membership of Parliament and these observations have given rise to consideration of reform by some of the major political parties, particularly of the Upper House. This synopsis has largely been derived from democratic concerns.

The principal objections to the current constitution of the Commons relate to the election of Members of Parliament in accordance with the 'first past the post' system which does not proportionately represent the various minorities that, taken as a whole, make up the electorate. Nor can it truthfully be said that the combined number of seats of both Houses provide an adequate forum in terms of manpower to represent these views. One way of achieving constitutional perfection (which of course is in the eyes of the beholder, or jurist, or politician) may be to compensate for the inadequacies of both Houses by a radical overhaul of just one. A strong argument for this is that the long standing traditions and complex conventions that provide for the, by and large, smooth running of the legislature would be disrupted intolerably by attempted reform of both Houses.

In essence this is in keeping with the ethos behind bicameralism; that having two chambers, with different constitutions, is desirable since each can complement and regulate the other. As it stands, there is much justification for the present system. This centres around the practical difficulties of coping with the legislative burden, and around the peculiar skills of the House of Lords.

In essence, the simplest of the arguments in favour of the bicameral system is that two Houses can cope with twice the amount of legislation. This means that non-controversial Bills that are unlikely to be rejected outright in the Commons stage may be introduced in the Lords, leaving the Commons to grapple with more contentious legislation that might be radically altered in the Lower House. By having two forums, opportunities for debating or quizzing government ministers are doubled. These popular assertions may, however, be countered by the contention that these ends might more easily be achieved by shortening the legislative process, reducing the parliamentary 'holidays' and delegating more of the routine legislation to departments and more of the scrutiny of government to the committee system. The democratic desirability of diverting business off the floor of the House, especially into the hands of the government, or of distracting busy members from their constituency duties, is debatable. The justification for such measures, as opposed to retaining extra politicians and an alternate venue, are largely of a financial nature, however, and do not diminish the fact that for practical purposes the bicameral system is still preferable.

A more serious function of any second chamber is as a constitutional safeguard against incompetence or imbalance in the first chamber. The Lords, as they stand, comprise a reservoir of expertise and talent in all manner of matters and as such can contribute considerably to the more technical aspects of the content of legislation. Moreover, in the present electoral system, where the 'first past the post' system can occasionally lead to the predominance of one political party in the Commons, the House of Lords provides a balance of membership that represents the long-term views of the country.

Much has been said in criticism of the methods of appointment of the Lords, based on the misconception that Lords are created predominantly in consequence of the hereditary system. The constitution of this chamber on the basis of merit has been ensured by the Life Peerages Act 1958 and the Peerage Act 1963. Although this creates a situation that may be termed as 'undemocratic', the membership of the upper House is more and more determined by the leaders of the main parties in the Commons. Thus, the appointees, although representing the views of the electorate over the years, albeit indirectly, are insulated from the less desirable side of democracy, the constant worry about the security of one's seat and the need to put forward 'popular' policies. This allows an objective view of legislative problems and a practical approach to their resolution. Given a situation where the second chamber is one with less constitutional power, then this provides the perfect situation where, providing the chamber contains a genuine cross-section of interests and experience, a pragmatic and informed base is given to the legislature which is not swayed by transitory movements in public opinion.

This reserve of informed and experienced ability may also initiate reform in areas that are perhaps not at the forefront of the minds of Commons members. This is well illustrated by the circumstances that led to the passing of the Sexual Offences Act 1967, which can honestly be said to have been originated as a backbench bill in the Lords.

Amendments to the Foreign Compensation Act 1969 and the Local Government Act 1972 illustrate how such expertise has proved, in hindsight, more than advantageous. This revising capacity coupled, in the present situation, with the power to remit bills for reconsideration, acts as an active filter of the Commons' output ensuring that both the practical substance and the political content is well considered. Although this has occasionally resulted in confrontation, which has been resolved in favour of the Lords (as with the Aircraft and Shipbuilding Bill in the mid 1970s) and in favour of the Commons (as with the Trade Union and Labour Relations Bill of the same era), usually a balance is struck. There is no doubt that this function, regardless of the politics of the government of the day, has enhanced the public's opinion of the Lords and is a strong recommendation for the retention of a second chamber. One must note that the Lords may be as wayward as they feel is necessary since the threat of deselection will not sway them from their resolve.

One cannot, however, disregard criticisms of the current second chamber. There is a genuine concern that there is an inbuilt Conservative majority in the Lords, although this can be easily rectified by a government with the right mandate and political will.

However, there is a more deep-seated mistrust of bodies that are not directly electorally accountable which has spawned the idea of an elected second chamber. To elect a second chamber on the same basis as the first would merely operate as an expansion of the Commons. To elect a second chamber in an alternative manner would necessarily lead to the question of which House truly represented the democratic will of the people and there would certainly be a power struggle of some description. The problems of such an upheaval, leaving aside the problems of electoral administration, more or less justify the general, if somewhat complacent, attitude of most jurists that we should let sleeping dogs lie. Irrespective of proposals, such as those of the Conservative Review Committee 1978, there have been no concerted efforts at reform since 1968.

Nevertheless, the Labour Government, elected at the General Election on 1 May 1997, is committed to a radical reform of the second chamber, which is likely to take the form of depriving the hereditary peers of their voting rights, though perhaps giving life peerages to deserving and hard-working hereditary peers who lose out under this reform. The problem with such reform is that it increases the patronage powers of the Prime Minister and the perception of party political manipulation of the composition of the second chamber may lead to a loss of confidence in its ability to act as a restraint on the Commons.

6

The Central Government and Prerogative Power

Introduction

This chapter is concerned with the role of the executive in the British Constitution, in particular the accountability of ministers for the administration of policies. Conventions play an important part in the Cabinet system of government and it is essential to understand the principles of individual and collective ministerial responsibility, as these are fundamental to the parliamentary democracy of the United Kingdom. In addition, the ability of ministers to use established powers under the Royal Prerogative has long been a source of controversy since important decisions can be taken under these powers without reference to Parliament. Dicey warned of the threat to the rule of law posed by the use of wide prerogative discretion, and the recent growth of judicial review of such discretion needs to be explored to establish whether the courts can provide sufficient protection for the rule of law in this area. The case for codification of the Royal Prerogative should also be examined: whilst on the one hand such reform might ensure better accountability to Parliament, would it run the risk of impeding the smooth operation of government and inhibit the ability of the central executive to respond quickly to certain kinds of emergency?

In a typical examination paper at least one essay-type question could be anticipated on the central executive. In recent years essay questions on individual responsibility have started to appear, probably because of the Scott Report (1996) and the controversial development of the doctrination between 'policy' errors (for which the minister must accept responsibility) and 'operational' errors (for which the minister accounts but does not accept personal blame). The extent to which behaviour in a minister's private life is part of his or her public responsibility is also an aspect requiring critical examination. Useful recent research on ministerial responsibility can be found in Turpin's essay, Chapter 5 of Jowell and Oliver's *The Changing Constitution* (1994, 3rd ed). See also recent articles by Woodhouse [1997] PL 262 and Scott [1996] PL 410.

Essay questions on judicial review of prerogative powers have been regular favourites since the seminal case of *Council of Civil Service Unions* v *Minister for the Civil Service* (the GCHQ Case) [1985] AC 374. There are several important subsequent decisions illustrating the extent of the breakthrough made in that case. Note, especially, *R* v *Secretary of State for the Home Department, ex parte Fire Brigades Union* [1995] 2 All ER 244 (HL) and *Reckley* v *Minister of Public Safety and Immigration (No 2)* [1996] 1 All ER 562 (PC). Recent articles examining these developments include: Allan [1995] CLJ 481, Barendt [1995] PL 357, Ganz (1996) 59 MLR 95, Thomas (1996) 112 LQR 177, Hare [1996] CLJ 401, Pannick [1996] PL 557 and Gelber (1997) 60 MLR 572.

Questions

INTERROGRAMS

1 Outline the scope and purpose of the convention of collective ministerial responsibility.
2 Outline the scope and purpose of the convention of individual ministerial responsibility.
3 Is there a case for codifying the Royal Prerogative?
4 Is judicial review available over the whole field of prerogative powers?

QUESTION ONE

'The principle of collective responsibility requires from each Minister a full and whole-hearted acceptance of the measures decided on by the Cabinet and of the policies underlying them' (Lord Wilson).

Discuss the purpose and nature of this rule.

London University LLB Examination
(for external students) Constitutional Law June 1988 Q3

QUESTION TWO

'If a mistake is made in a Government Department the Minister is responsible even if he knew nothing about it.' 'A Minister cannot be blamed for a mistake made if he did not make it himself.'

Consider these contrasting views.

London University LLB Examination
(for external students) Constitutional Law June 1989 Q4

QUESTION THREE

'Prerogative powers are essential to the smooth operation of government.'

Do you agree?

London University LLB Examination
(for external students) Constitutional Law June 1990 Q3

QUESTION FOUR

'The acts of the prerogative are as reviewable as any other executive acts.'

Discuss.

London University LLB Examination
(for external students) Constitutional Law June 1992 Q2

QUESTION FIVE

Critically assess the respective roles of the House of Commons and the courts in regulating the Royal Prerogative.

London University LLB Examination
(for external students) Constitutional Law June 1993 Q8a

QUESTION SIX

'The uncertainties surrounding the scope and exercise of the Royal Prerogative give rise to serious constitutional questions concerning the Rule of Law in a democratic society.'

Critically assess this statement

London University LLB Examination
(for external students) Constitutional Law June 1994 Q5

Answers

ANSWERS TO INTERROGRAMS

1 The convention of collective responsibility has three aspects:

- a the confidence rule (the whole government must resign if it loses a specific vote of confidence in the Commons);
- b the unanimity rule (a Cabinet minister should resign or be dismissed if he or she cannot publicly support a Cabinet decision); and
- c the confidentiality principle (all ministers must keep secret current Cabinet discussions, disagreements, etc).

The purpose of the convention is to secure uniformity of policy advice to the Monarch and complete accountability for that policy to Parliament.

2 The convention of individual responsibility has two aspects:

- a a minister must take responsibility for the political and administrative *competence* of his or her government department; and
- b a minister should take moral responsibility for upholding proper standards of behaviour in public life, which includes the minister's own behaviour as well as that of his or her officials.

Since the principle is based on convention it is not legally enforceable and hence its purpose (of ensuring personal responsibility for actions of the executive) is sometimes undermined, eg by use of the doctrine of collective responsibility to shield a minister from political attack, particularly from his or her own backbenchers. It is rare nowadays for a minister to resign as a matter of honour, though sometimes resignations occur after a prolonged period of criticism from the media.

3 Codification might help to clarify the precise scope of individual prerogative powers, particularly those surrounded by conventions, such as the Monarch's powers to appoint a Prime Minister. On the other hand the unpredictable nature of political

events makes it desirable for discretion to exist so as to produce a solution acceptable to the political actors involved, and it may not be possible to legislate for such solutions. A code would have the advantage of subjecting the exercise of its powers to normal parliamentary and judicial methods of review, but, again, this might hamper the ability of the executive to respond quickly to a crisis in which prompt use of discretionary powers might be essential.

4 In the leading case of *Council of Civil Service Unions* v *Minister for the Civil Service* [1985] AC 374 three of the five Law Lords indicated, obiter, that judicial review should in principle be available over prerogative powers, but that because of the intensely political character of many of these powers it might not be appropriate for all the normal grounds of judicial review to be applied. Lords Diplock and Scarman agreed that the scope of judicial review over individual prerogative powers should be decided on a case-by-case basis, and both Law Lords thought that national security issues would be factors excluding completely the possibility of a judicial review. Lord Roskill indicated that in his view non-justiciable prerogatives included the making of treaties, the granting of honours, the dissolution of Parliament, the appointment of ministers; national security, and the prerogative of mercy.

Subsequent cases have acknowledged the possibility of judicial review in areas such as the issuing of passports (*R* v *Secretary of State for Foreign and Commonwealth Affairs, ex parte Everett* [1989] 1 All ER 655), homosexuals in the military (*R* v *Ministry of Defence, ex parte Smith* [1996] 1 All ER 257) and the use of the prerogative to bypass existing statutory obligations (*R* v *Secretary of State for the Home Department, ex parte Fire Brigades Union* [1995] 2 All ER 244). Although judicial review was granted for error of law in a case involving the prerogative of mercy (*R* v *Secretary of State for the Home Department, ex parte Bentley* [1994] 2 WLR 101), it appears that judicial review of this prerogative is not available on any other ground: see view of Judicial Committee of Privy Council in *Reckley* v *Minister for Public Safety and Immigration (No 2)* [1996] 1 All ER 562.

SUGGESTED ANSWER TO QUESTION ONE

General Comment

Essentially a straightforward question requiring an explanation of what the doctrine of collective responsibility involves, an explanation of its purpose, and citation of relevant examples of ministerial practice to support the points made.

Key Points

- Collective responsibility
- Unanimity on policy
- Confidentiality
- Examples of its observance
- Examples of its breach
- Reference to *Jonathan Cape* decision
- Consideration of the need for the doctrine and its importance

Suggested Answer

As generally understood, the doctrine of collective responsibility is a constitutional convention whereby government ministers undertake to present a united front in public in support of government policy as formulated in Cabinet. If a minister is unable or unwilling to publicly support government policy the convention is that he or she should resign. The result is that a politician cannot, or at least should not, disown or criticise a policy which was being promulgated by a Cabinet from which he or she did not resign.

It can be argued that collective responsibility also embraces two other conventions. First, that a government which loses the support of the House of Commons should resign. Secondly that ministers must maintain the confidentiality of information received as a consequence of Cabinet membership.

If a government loses a vote of no confidence in the House of Commons, convention dictates that all its ministers should resign, thus indicating that they all accept responsibility for the government's record. Similarly a minister is expected to resign where he or she loses the confidence of fellow Cabinet members, as they cannot be expected to defend in public the position of a colleague which is plainly no longer tenable.

The need for confidentiality in respect of cabinet meetings is obvious. If differences of opinion which surface during Cabinet discussions are made public it will become extremely difficult for Cabinet members to put on a later show of public unanimity.

The difficulty with the general propositions considered above, is that they are not necessarily borne out by the evidence of ministerial practice in the post-war era. Certainly there is evidence that ministers have resigned as a result of irreconcilable differences with Cabinet colleagues. The resignation of Michael Heseltine over the handling of the 'Westland affair' within the Cabinet (1986) is one of many, but there are frequently other factors behind such decisions.

The clearest example of the doctrine of collective responsibility being placed under very considerable strain, arose in relation to the differences within the Labour Cabinet of 1975 on the issue of continued membership of the European Community. Following a vote within the Cabinet which revealed a majority of 16–7 in favour of continued membership, an 'agreement to differ' was arrived at whereby those Cabinet members who were opposed to EC membership were allowed to campaign against it outside Parliament but not within the House of Commons. Perhaps this is evidence of a convention that collective responsibility can be suspended at the discretion of the Prime Minister of the day in relation to selected issues? If this is correct it would certainly suggest that the description of collective responsibility as something requiring from ministers '... a full and whole-hearted acceptance of the measures decided on by the Cabinet and of the policies underlying them ...' goes too far.

More generally, it is widely acknowledged that there are always shades of opinion within any group of government ministers and that individual ministers can make speeches which involve veiled criticisms of government policy, provided they do not go too far. Again it is a matter ultimately to be resolved with reference to political expediency rather than legal principles. The key questions are the amount of freedom a particular Prime Minister is willing to give Cabinet members, and the extent to which views expressed find common support within the Cabinet. The level of resignations by so called 'wets' (non-monetarists) from successive Cabinets presided over by Mrs. Thatcher (May 1979–November 1990) indicates the way in which dissenting voices are steadily purged if the Prime Minister does not believe in a 'broad church' approach to Cabinet membership.

As to the confidentiality of Cabinet proceedings, whilst it is well known that Cabinet ministers, as Privy Councillors swear an oath of confidentiality, it is equally well known that there is a steady flow of information as to the nature of Cabinet decisions and discussions in the form of unofficial and unattributed 'leaks'. On occasion these leaks turn into floods when an ex-minister decides to publish his or her political memoirs complete with telling tales of Cabinet infighting. The matter was considered by Lord Widgery LCJ in *Attorney-General* v *Jonathan Cape Ltd* (1976).

The Attorney-General applied for an injunction to prevent publication of the diaries of the late Richard Crossman who had been a Labour minister during the mid 1960s. The Attorney-General had contended that the injunction was necessary to preserve the confidentiality of Cabinet proceedings, and also collective responsibility. The Lord Chief Justice recognised the importance of collective responsibility as a constitutional convention, but doubted whether the publication of details of Cabinet meetings that had taken place some 11 years previously would actually cause that much harm or embarrassment to those who had been involved. His Lordship doubted whether collective responsibility in itself was a sufficient basis for the granting of an injunction, preferring to rely on breach of confidence if a remedy was to be provided. Ultimately it was decided that an injunction would not be granted in this case, but might be if in a subsequent case the evidence of the harm caused by disclosures of Cabinet discussions was more compelling.

Does the doctrine of collective responsibility as it is understood within the British constitution serve any useful purpose? Much depends upon the way in which a Cabinet is run. If ministers discuss policies and consider a variety of proposals until they come up with a scheme that is agreeable to all because it is the best solution to a problem, then there is much to commend the idea that they should then present a united front on the subject in public. If, however, it is a case of policies being imposed on ministers with the ultimatum of 'support the measure or resign' it is a doctrine that is likely to dissuade freedom of thought within the Cabinet, and ensure that its membership represents a narrow band of opinion, which cannot be a healthy state of affairs. The doctrine undoubtedly places difficulties upon junior ministers who are not Cabinet members and thus not privy to Cabinet discussions, yet have to support decisions taken by the Cabinet.

On a broader level it can be said that the doctrine does help to encourage some degree of integrity on the part of ministers in that if they wish to accept the credit for the successes of the administration of which they are a part, they must also be prepared to accept the blame for the failures.

Ultimately, it is submitted, the difficulty with collective responsibility is that it is observed on an everyday basis by scores of ministers without the matter even being seen as worthy of comment. It is only when there is an apparent breach of the doctrine that it attracts publicity, with the inevitable cries that it is fast becoming a constitutional irrelevance. What is perhaps needed is a sense of proportion.

SUGGESTED ANSWER TO QUESTION TWO

General Comment

Discuss individual responsibility giving examples which are relevant. A lot depends on the attitude of the Prime Minister of the day.

Key Points

- Definitions of conventions of collective and individual ministerial responsibility
- Concept of accountability - not every failure of policy results in a resignation
- Examples of rare resignations due to individual responsibility
- Distinction between policy and operation of policy
- Political factors behind any decision whether or not to resign
- Conclusion

Suggested Answer

In any democratic state it is a requirement that the people who govern should be responsible to those whom they govern. In the UK, for instance, responsibility is collective ie the government as a whole is responsible to Parliament and responsibility is individual ie individual ministers are responsible to Parliament for decisions taken by them or their civil servants in their departments. The principle of individual ministerial responsibility developed historically before the doctrine of collective responsibility. Collective and individual responsibility are rules of convention and as such are flexible concepts since conventions are rules of political practice regarded as binding by those to whom they apply but everyone recognises that they are subject to exceptions. Neither of the two quotations is an accurate statement of the requirements of individual ministerial responsibility, which it is almost impossible to formulate in a way which indicates in every case what the outcome will be for a minister who has made a mistake or whose department has in some way failed.

A minister is responsible for his or her personal acts whether or not he or she is a member of the Cabinet. Responsibility will also include general conduct in the relevant department and any acts or omissions done in the name of the department. The responsibility may be legal or political or a combination of these. It seems that the meaning of responsibility and the persons or bodies to whom it is owed will vary according to the circumstances.

One of the practical expressions of individual ministerial responsibility is that a minister is required to answer questions in Parliament with regard to the conduct of officials in his department. It is true that a minister need not accept responsibility if an official has committed a dishonest act, exceeded his authority or disobeyed instructions. He cannot, however, totally absolve himself and he will be required to explain in public what has happened. In this sense the minister will - whether he is to blame or not -

have to account (ie explain what went wrong). The minister must also, of course, when required, explain government policy in relation to his department. In the event that the minister's replies fail to satisfy MPs or the Lords a motion to reduce the minister's salary or to censure him may result, but because of party discipline these are rare. In order to consider the truth or otherwise of the quotations it is now necessary to consider some precedents in detail categorising them, if possible, under one of the quotations.

Perhaps one of the clearest examples of a minister resigning because of a mistake is that of Sir Thomas Dugdale who resigned as Minister of Agriculture as a result of the Crichel Down Affair in 1954. In doing so he took responsibility for alleged maladministration by senior civil servants apparently committed without his knowledge. Some commentators have sought to explain this resignation on the basis that compulsory purchase was involved, (a matter about which the electorate were extremely sensitive at the time) but it certainly stands as a most stringent example of the 'rule' in force, particularly since the maladministration affected only one family and was a matter of embarrassment rather than one where severe loss either financial or in terms of physical wellbeing was concerned.

Lord Carrington's resignation in 1982 as Foreign Secretary, together with those of the other Foreign Office ministers who resigned with him, can also be seen as an example of the first quotation in that it could be argued that Lord Carrington was poorly advised during the negotiations with Argentina over the Falkland Islands but personally made no mistake. On the other hand one could argue that he himself was culpable in that the department's failure to predict the invasion was an indication that it was inefficient or ill run and that in his position he should himself have been better informed and better able to foresee the invasion.

In recent times a rather different attitude has been taken in relation to mistakes by civil servants; whereas formerly the minister maintained the anonymity of the civil servant and would take responsibility in certain cases the blame has been laid squarely at the feet of civil servants (who have sometimes been disciplined) whilst ministers have felt no compunction to resign. Examples of this include the prison breakouts which were followed by resignation or dismissal of civil servants but no ministerial departures, and the occasion when an intruder entered the Queen's bedroom and the Home Secretary, William Whitelaw, considered resigning but eventually did not do so.

These two examples illustrate the 'rule' set out in the second quotation, ie that a minister should be personally blamed only where personally involved in policy that turns out to be misjudged, and not where the fault lies at the 'operational' level of civil servants or others over whom the minister has no daily control.

If the first quotation is correct then it follows that it would be expected that any minister himself making a mistake would have to take responsibility for it and very likely resign. However, much depends on the power politics of the day. When the Conservative Government's economic policy collapsed in the autumn of 1992 following the suspension of the pound from the Exchange Rate Mechanism (ERM), neither the Prime Minister nor the Chancellor of the Exchequer resigned in the immediate aftermath, even though both were primarily associated in the public mind with the ERM policy.

The second quotation also tends to imply that a minister who personally makes a mistake will be 'blamed'; and the concomitant of this would very likely be resignation. If one examines recent cases one can see that there is no hard and fast rule. Some mistakes by ministers lead to resignations; others merely to calls by the opposition for resignation. Whether a minister survives a mistake seems to depend upon factors such as whether he nevertheless retains the confidence of the Prime Minister and the Cabinet, the view of the backbenchers of his own party and the level of public outcry. For instance, Sir Leon Brittan survived calls for his resignation as Secretary of State for Trade and Industry over allegations that he had misled the Commons about a letter from British Aerospace to the government during the Westland Helicopter Affair in 1986. His survival was due to the continued support of Prime Minister and Cabinet. However, when his behaviour (in authorising a leak to the press of a letter sent by the law officers to Michael Heseltine and then arguably covering up what had been done) came to light, several weeks later not even the Cabinet's support could protect his position when the Conservative backbenchers withdrew their support from him and he was forced to resign. In December 1988 Edwina Currie resigned as a Health Minister after over enthusiastic and somewhat misleading comments on the level of salmonella infection in poultry production. Her fault was to alienate poultry producers who had suffered severe financial loss and the government was forced to mount a costly compensation scheme. The remarks cost Mrs Currie her job but was she simply unlucky? Had there been some other important news story on the day of her remarks perhaps the media and the public would have overlooked them entirely - they would not then have been a 'mistake' and there would have been no resignation.

A lot depends, therefore, on the attitude of the Prime Minister of the day, the Cabinet and backbenchers and the attitude of the public to the particular mistake. The two contrasting views expressed in the question, are neither taken singly nor together a sufficient explanation of the difficult and subtle convention of individual ministerial responsibility.

SUGGESTED ANSWER TO QUESTION THREE

General Comment

A question requiring an historical analysis of the development of prerogative powers in order to demonstrate their purposes and the extent to which they become subject to external controls.

Key Points

- Historical developments and role of the courts
- Characteristics of modern prerogative powers
- Prerogatives regarded as essential for smooth operation of government
- Response of judges to exercises of wide prerogatives
- Prerogative in foreign affairs
- Conclusion

Suggested Answer

Prerogative powers stem from the historic rights and privileges of the monarch and as such represent a separate root of authority from that which devolves from the supremacy of Parliament. Although prerogatives can be traced even in the modern day to the sanction and approval of the monarch, vital prerogatives are largely exercised by central government. In addition they are now regarded as being subject to the scrutiny of Parliament and of the courts. Moreover any possibility of prerogative powers usurping the legislative supremacy of Parliament has long been disregarded. In fact statute may suspend or eliminate existing prerogatives and the courts have expressed unwillingness to recognise the existence or unnecessary extension of such powers: *Attorney-General* v *De Keyser's Royal Hotel* (1920), *R* v *Secretary of State for the Home Department, ex parte Fire Brigades Union* (1995).

As such it is hard to define precisely the nature of the modern prerogative; however certain elements may be clearly identified. Firstly the prerogative is residual to the will of Parliament as had been made clear by the Bill of Rights 1688 and the Crown Proceedings Act 1947. Secondly, prerogative powers derive from the common law and are therefore interpreted by the courts who may delineate the parameters within which they may be lawfully exercised. As a matter of practice most significant powers of this kind, by convention, are normally exercised by the government of the day. There are certain personal prerogatives of the Queen; however, conventionally even these are subject to scrutiny or veto. Prerogatives such as the giving of the Royal Assent or the appointment of Prime Ministers are regulated by convention and it is inconceivable in the modern constitutional framework that these conventions will be departed from. This is not to say however that prerogatives could be dispensed with even where they seem to be purely a matter of form. Their exercise contrary to convention, for example where the monarch uses her powers against the wishes of the government of the day, may be justified in circumstances where that government seeks to act unconstitutionally and all conventional methods of controlling central government powers are ineffectual. It is because this situation seems such an unlikelihood that Royal Prerogatives have the semblance of being ossified by the traditional mores of constitutional behaviour.

Thus, the application of these more formalised prerogatives are not essential for smooth government in routine circumstances, but relate to situations where there is serious constitutional conflict. However, there are a panoply of prerogative powers that, although they inhere in the Crown and are exercised in the name of the monarch, are principally at the disposal of the agencies of central government to facilitate the exercise of the executive function.

Certain of these relate to the fundamental administration of affairs of state. Matters such as disposition of armed forces which require swift and sometimes, for the purposes of national security, secret decisions are subject to prerogative powers. The defence of the realm, which is primarily the responsibility of the Crown, must be dealt with in a decisive manner and in consequence decisions relating to the armed forces, such as the extent to which protection of citizens must be provided, are subject to the exclusive privilege and cognisance of the Crown. This is illustrated by the decision in *China Navigation Company* v *Attorney-General* (1932) in which it was stated by Scrutton LJ:

'that the administration of the army is in the hands of the King who unless expressly controlled by an Act of Parliament cannot be controlled by the court'. To some extent this unquestioning view of privilege and the notion that the Crown may give conclusive certification of the needs of national security represents the old view of prerogative. It is clear from developments in legal thinking with regard to Crown privilege that the courts feel more able to scrutinise circumstances where national security is used to cloak arbitrary governmental action. Possibly the most significant developments in the sphere of judicial conceptions of prerogative are to be found in *Council of Civil Service Unions* v *Minister for Civil Service* (1985), where the House of Lords decided that simply because a decision making power derives from the common law as opposed to statute this did not exclude the possibility of judicial review on the grounds of illegality, irrationality or procedural impropriety. The attitude in this case follows closely the rationale of Lord Denning in *Laker Airways Ltd* v *Department of Trade* (1977) which identified the prerogative as being a discretionary power exerciseable on the basis of necessity in such situations where the law has made no alternative provision for decision making frameworks.

This attitude, it is submitted, represents a realistic assessment of the circumstances when these powers may be exercised legitimately and their role in facilitating smooth and efficient government. The parliamentary attitude to central government effecting vital decisions without the explicit approval of its members is a somewhat sceptical one for although a minister may, by convention, be accountable after the event this does not prevent such actions being taken. Since in constitutional theory statute is the supreme source of law which the courts must follow it is clear that where a prerogative power exists Parliament may either abolish it or place it in abeyance. Indeed the courts, when faced with conflicts between statute law and purported exercises of this privileged Crown capacity, have given precedents to the former and shown scant regard for contentions that the Crown may pick and choose which source of law to follow. Furthermore it was contended in *Malone* v *Metropolitan Police Commissioner* (1979) that even if such a claim succeeds the Crown may still be under a duty to compensate for lawful exercise of this decision making facility.

Less restrictions seem to attach to the exercise of Crown discretions in the sphere of foreign affairs, such as the making of treaties and matters relating to overseas interests generally. Where prerogatives are exercised for the purpose of foreign policy, judicial interference is less common, primarily because Parliament is regarded as the more appropriate and competent authority to scrutinise such matters, which seldom have full legal standing without parliamentary approval.

The exercises of modern prerogatives and their status in legal theory thus, to a great extent, reflect the practical need for executive power in circumstances and times where prompt execution of governmental decisions are required. The way in which these powers have devolved to the organs of central government mirror the general centralisation and development of the Executive function, necessitated by the complex and fast moving nature of modern society. Where possible, it is clear, the parliamentarians' dislike of wide executive discretion has stripped the Crown and its servants of prerogatives and this is as it should be within our constitutional framework.

The courts, also, have shown their disdain of the use of prerogative to execute policy decisions that lack the authority of statute, where the motive seems to be an arbitrary political one. In stressing the common law basis for prerogative powers, judges, such as Lord Denning, clearly recognised that this 'pre-eminence of the Crown' is to be regarded as a complement to the supreme authority of Parliament, as a governmental weapon of last resort. Having said this, however, it would be hard to conceive of Parliament and the courts allowing the continued existence of certain elements of the prerogative if they did not genuinely believe them to be vital for the efficient administration of the country. One need only look at governmental action concerning the Gulf War (1990–1991) to understand the proper place of prerogative powers. By virtue of statutory instrument, sanctions were imposed, and using prerogative powers and following the responsibilities placed by treaties, created in pursuance of the prerogative, the government was able to implement emergency measures to deal with this situation. However, it is significant that Parliament was recalled to examine the steps taken, even in this emergency situation.

SUGGESTED ANSWER TO QUESTION FOUR

General Comment

This question requires a good knowledge of the GCHQ case in particular and of the courts' attitude to the prerogative generally. Recent case law suggests conflicting judicial attitudes in this area and these attitudes need to be explored.

Key Points

- Definition
- Example - traditional approach of the courts
- Lord Denning's dicta in *Laker*
- GCHQ
- Cases post-GCHQ (*ex parte Everett, Bentley, ex parte P, ex parte Fire Brigades Union*)
- Conclusion

Suggested Answer

The prerogative is that collection of powers and immunities of the Crown which is residual and which is now largely exercised by the Government. Since the prerogative derives from the common law, it can be abolished or restricted by statute. However, its review by the courts is a comparatively recent development.

Traditionally, the courts did not review purported prerogative acts but could determine the existence and extent of prerogative powers. For example, in *BBC* v *Johns* (1965), it was reaffirmed that only those powers recognised at common law would be upheld, Diplock LJ holding that it was '350 years and a civil war too late for the Queen's courts to broaden the prerogative'. Another example is *Malone* v *Metropolitan Police Commissioner* (1979), where the courts recognised that the Crown had the right, under the prerogative, to intercept postal telecommunications and then went on to consider whether this extended to phone tapping.

Once it was established that the act complained of was an exercise of the prerogative, the courts would not challenge its use. However, this traditional approach has shifted in favour of allowing judicial review of the exercise of the prerogative, although only in certain circumstances. To some extent, Lord Denning paved the way. In *Gouriet* v *Union of Post Office Workers* (1978) the House of Lords rejected his view - expressed in the Court of Appeal - that the Attorney General's decision not to lend his name to proceedings against the union could be challenged in court, despite being an exercise of prerogative power. In *Laker Airways Ltd* v *Department of Trade* (1977) Lord Denning argued that the law could interfere if the executive exercised their discretionary prerogative powers improperly.

This view was considered by the House of Lords in the leading case of *Council for Civil Service Unions* v *Minister for the Civil Service* (1985) - better known as the GCHQ case. It concerned the ban by the Prime Minister, without any prior consultation, on trade union membership at Government Communications Headquarters. The applicant union sought judicial review on the grounds of failure to consult, despite the ban being issued under the Government's prerogative powers.

Their Lordships held that because a power exercised in the sphere of public law was derived from the common law, that did not mean it should be immune from review. Lord Diplock felt that judicial review had developed to the extent where one could classify under three heads the grounds for review: illegality, irrationality, procedural impropriety. Reviewing a prerogative power for procedural impropriety was, in his Lordship's view, acceptable. To put it another way, it was 'justiciable'.

However, this right to challenge was qualified. Where the prerogative power related to the defence of the realm, for example, it was not reviewable. Of course, this judicial deference to national security is not confined only to consideration of the prerogative and it can be argued that it reflects the courts' attitude to acts of the executive generally (eg *R* v *Secretary of State for the Home Department, ex parte Hosenball* (1977)). Therefore, to the extent that the prerogative can - with some qualification - be reviewed, it is similar to executive acts based upon statutory sources.

Post-GCHQ cases illustrate conflicting judicial attitudes to what are justiciable prerogative powers. The issue and revocation of passports, once non-reviewable, are matters declared suitable for review by the Court of Appeal in *R* v *Secretary of State for Foreign and Commonwealth Affairs, ex parte Everett* (1989). In the GCHQ case Lord Roskill had opined that the prerogative of mercy remained non-justiciable, but it has been reviewed on the narrow ground of error of law in *R* v *Secretary of State for the Home Department, ex parte Bentley* (1994). In *R* v *Criminal Injuries Compensation Board, ex parte P* (1995) the Court of Appeal was divided two to one on the issue of whether prerogative changes to the compensation scheme were justiciable. Evans and Peter Gibson LJJ opined that they were justiciable but Neill LJ thought that such high level policy decisions were a 'judicial no-man's land'.

Finally, in *R* v *Secretary of State for the Home Department, ex parte Fire Brigades Union* (1995), the House of Lords were divided three to two on the issue of whether the Home Secretary could use his prerogative powers to introduce a new compensation scheme when a scheme already existed under a statute which had not yet been brought into force. The majority held that the use of the prerogative in such circumstances was unlawful, but Lords Keith and Mustill delivered strong dissenting judgments warning against the use of judicial review in an area best controlled by Parliament.

These conflicting views illustrate the uncertainties created by the GCHQ case and tend to refute the proposition under discussion, since the peculiar character of many prerogative powers inevitably means that they may be subject to unusual treatment by the courts of law.

SUGGESTED ANSWER TO QUESTION FIVE

General Comment

Questions on the Royal Prerogative have become familiar in recent years and almost predictable as far as judicial review is concerned. However, this question places equal emphasis on the role of the Commons in regulating the Prerogative, so it is important that a balanced approach is adopted. There is the opportunity to use examples from the field of government and politics and also to make use of recent cases and academic research.

Key Points

- Definition and scope of the Royal Prerogative
- The threat to the rule of law
- Examples and effect of the Prerogative in domestic affairs
- Examples and effect in foreign affairs
- Problems of weak Commons scrutiny and control
- Scope and development of judicial review culminating in the breakthrough in the GCHQ case
- Limited scope of that breakthrough
- Critical conclusions

Suggested Answer

The Royal Prerogative covers the residue of discretionary executive powers left to the monarch after the establishment of the constitutional monarchy in the period 1688-9. Most of the powers concern matters of state and government policy and these are exercised by the monarch, by convention, on the advice of her ministers. A few powers may be exercised at the monarch's personal discretion.

The essential character of the Royal Prerogative is such as to make parliamentary and judicial control almost impossible. Hence the Diceyan view that the Prerogative, like all wide discretionary power, is a threat to the rule of law. Reformers like Tony Benn MP wish to see a codification of the Prerogative which, whilst allowing the monarchy to remain, would strip the monarch and her government of the ability to take fundamentally important decisions without prior approval of Parliament. Such codification would also make it easier to obtain judicial review, which is a system much more appropriate to the construction of statutes to discover whether delegates have exceeded the statutory discretions conferred on them.

In domestic affairs of state the Royal Prerogative covers such areas as the regulation of the armed forces; the administration of justice through the supervision of public prosecutions and 'public interest' civil actions; the release of prisoners under the prerogative of mercy; the regulation of the civil service; the granting of honours such as peerages; the issue and revocation of passports; and there are others. Many of the powers (eg over the civil service and peerages) are exercisable by the Prime Minister, giving the Prime Minister a position of special authority within the Constitution and raising fears that, from time to time, a Prime Minister is able to enjoy an almost presidential type of authority. Indeed Tony Benn, when presenting his Commonwealth of Britain Bill to the Commons a few years ago, argued that a British Prime Minister enjoys more power to act unilaterally in many fields than an American President, who is confined by a written constitution, a rigid system of checks and balances in his relationship with Congress, and vigorous judicial review from the Supreme Court.

In foreign affairs the Royal Prerogative covers even more far-reaching decisions such as the power to declare war and peace or other hostilities (fleets were sent to the Falklands and the Gulf under prerogative power: parliamentary consent was sought only after the fleets had been despatched); the power to sign international treaties so as to bind the United Kingdom in international law; the power to recognise foreign states and their diplomats; and to commit hostile acts on foreign soil under protection of 'Act of State', which protects the Crown from civil action in domestic courts.

Commons control over such decisions is comparatively weak because of the absence of normal methods of parliamentary scrutiny found in the processing of legislation. Nevertheless political pressures are normally sufficient to ensure that at least a debate is held on the exercise of particularly important decisions, although at one point in recent times (in 1993, during the passage of the legislation to ratify the Maastricht Treaty), the Prime Minister had indicated a readiness to use the Prerogative if he lost the vote on the Social Chapter element, provoking accusations of unconstitutional and undemocratic behaviour from the Opposition (and some of his own backbenchers). He did not lose the vote so the threat did not materialise but the ability of the executive to bypass Parliament or ignore a parliamentary vote is still there.

Until the late 1970s and the 1980s judicial review of the Royal Prerogative appeared to be confined to ensuring that decisions were taken under established prerogatives and not in conflict with statutes: *BBC* v *Johns* (1965), *Attorney-General* v *De Keyser's Royal Hotel* (1920). It appeared to be well established that judges could not investigate the manner of prerogative-decision-making or the policy wisdom of such decisions: *Chandler* v *DPP* (1964). Then, in *Laker Airways Ltd* v *Department of Trade* (1977), Lord Denning MR suggested, obiter, that the prerogative is a discretionary power exercisable for the public good and that judges could intervene if it is exercised 'improperly or mistakenly'. Hence he was suggesting that the 'ultra vires' concept, used in relation to statutory powers, was capable of extension to prerogative powers. Indeed, Lord Denning applied the concept to the exercise of the Attorney-General's prerogative powers in *Gouriet* v *Union of Post Office Workers* (1977). Although the Denning views were rejected by the House of Lords on the appeal in *Gouriet*, they were revitalised when the Law Lords reviewed the development of administrative law in the GCHQ case (*Council of Civil Service Unions* v *Minister for the Civil Service* (1985)), where a majority suggested, obiter, that judicial review should depend not on the source of executive power but on the subject matter, so that if the latter was of a justiciable kind, judges would have the power of review.

Although this was a major breakthrough in extending a form of control over what previously had been almost uncontrollable power, it has been argued that the traditional, natural reluctance of judges to involve themselves in political decisions has resulted in very limited use of the review power, which has been confined either to non-contentious political decisions, such as the revocation of a passport (*R* v *Secretary of State for Foreign and Commonwealth Affairs, ex parte Everett* (1989)) or clear errors of law involving the administration of justice, such as the exercise of the prerogative of mercy (*R* v *Secretary of State for the Home Department, ex parte Bentley* (1994)). It is doubtful whether judges in the United Kingdom will be tempted to review prerogative decisions relating to defence and foreign policy in the way Canadian judges have been prepared to do: see analysis by Walker ([1987] PL 62). In cricketing terms it is up to Parliament to assert itself as the wicket-keeper; the courts can only be a long stop and may be unable to catch executive hits which offend democratic principles and the rule of law.

SUGGESTED ANSWER TO QUESTION SIX

General Comment

A question that illustrates the dangers in question-spotting, since it requires knowledge of both the rule of law and of the Royal Prerogative. A tricky question, too, since both these areas must be discussed - and linked - in the context of the quote. However, given this overlap and that it is not an easy question, candidates familiar with the areas should not be dissuaded from an attempt; a good answer to a difficult question should gain a good mark. As ever, the success of the attempt depends largely on actually answering the question - critically assessing the statement; and to do this, the introduction is crucial.

Key Points

- Definitions of the rule of law, the Royal Prerogative and their relationship
- Prerogative and statute (Bill of Rights, *Attorney-General* v *De Keyser's*, *Northumbria Police Authority* and *BBC* v *Johns*)
- Political control - ministerial responsibility
- Judicial control (GCHQ, *Bentley, Reckley* and *Everett*)
- Conclusions

Suggested Answer

It is doubtful whether Dicey's traditional exposition of the rule of law, focusing on government in accordance with law and equality before the law, remains wholly adequate. In a modern democratic society the rule of law means more: it requires, inter alia, clarity and certainty in law, so that individuals know what it is they can and cannot do. To the extent, therefore, that there are 'uncertainties surrounding the scope and exercise of the Royal Prerogative', it would be hard to disagree with the statement in the quote. But it will be argued below that the scope of the Prerogative today is relatively well-defined and that recent developments, particularly in judicial review of the Prerogative, have clarified many of the uncertainties surrounding its exercise.

Blackstone defined the Prerogative in terms of the special pre-eminence enjoyed by the King over and above all others, so that prerogative powers were those enjoyed by the King alone and not shared with the ordinary subject: Blackstone's *Commentaries*. Such a definition does seem to offend the requirement of equality before the law, but it is important to recognise the justification for the existence of prerogative powers - that they are necessary to enable the Crown to perform its function of governing the country. Some inequality may thus be tolerable, provided adequate controls exist to prevent abuse of power. It is submitted that the controls available, both political and legal, are indeed adequate to ensure that the government, in exercising prerogative powers, is subject to the rule of law.

Certain propositions about the Prerogative are, in modern law, quite clear: it has been settled law since the Bill of Rights 1688 that the Prerogative is subordinate to statute; Parliament may thus abolish prerogative powers. Even when Parliament has not chosen to abolish a prerogative, *Attorney-General* v *De Keyser's Royal Hotel* (1920) establishes that, where prerogative and statutory powers co-exist, the Crown is precluded from relying on the former and must act under its statutory powers. While it is arguable that the *application* of this principle may give rise to some uncertainties - see, eg, *R* v *Secretary of State for the Home Department, ex parte Northumbria Police Authority* (1989) - the principle itself is clear. Similarly, prerogative powers are residual: in Diplock LJ's memorable phrase, 'It is 350 years and a civil war too late ... to broaden the prerogative'; its limits 'are now well settled and incapable of extension': *BBC* v *Johns* (1965).

That government is carried out in accordance with law is also ensured, at least in theory, through political controls; although in law prerogative powers vest in the Monarch, they are by convention exercised on her behalf by ministers of the Crown. Those ministers are, by convention, responsible to Parliament in respect of any exercise of prerogative powers. Should ministers abuse their powers, Parliament may remove those powers by statute. It is, however, arguable that the ability of Parliament adequately to control ministers is, at least in modern law, something of a fiction. To this extent it is true that the dominance of Parliament by the executive does pose serious questions concerning the rule of law in a democratic society - and not merely in the context of the Prerogative.

It is perhaps in recognition of this 'democratic deficit' that recent years have seen remarkable developments in judicial control of the Prerogative. The traditional rule was that the courts exercised jurisdiction to determine the existence of a prerogative power - they could thus decide that a claimed prerogative did not exist - but once its existence was established, they would not rule on the manner of its exercise. This traditional approach was abandoned in the GCHQ case (*Council of Civil Service Unions* v *Minister for the Civil Service* (1985)), where the House of Lords held that, in principle, the exercise of prerogative powers was subject to judicial review, although their Lordships did add that not all prerogative powers were reviewable: in particular, where the exercise of the power gave rise to a 'non-justiciable issue', it would still be immune from review.

It is noteworthy, however, that in *R* v *Secretary of State for the Home Department, ex parte Bentley* (1993), the Court of Appeal was willing to review the exercise of the prerogative of mercy, treating as obiter its inclusion in the list of non-justiciable issues given in the GCHQ case. However, review was granted on a very narrow basis (error of law) and later the Judicial Committee of the Privy Council gave its views that the prerogative of mercy remained non-reviewable under the broader grounds of judicial review: *Reckley* v *Minister of Public Safety and Immigration (No 2)* (1996). In *R* v *Secretary of State for Foreign and Commonwealth Affairs, ex parte Everett* (1989), the Court was prepared to review the prerogative power to issue passports on the basis that its exercise involved 'administrative decisions affecting individuals'.

In conclusion, it remains true to say that, in so far as the exercise of some prerogative powers remains unreviewable, primarily those that operate in the sphere of foreign affairs, serious constitutional questions concerning the rule of law do still arise - although it is, of course, always open to Parliament to intervene in case of abuse. It is however submitted that recent years have seen considerable clarification of the uncertainties surrounding the scope and exercise of the Prerogative and, while some do remain, the existence of the Royal Prerogative does not, in general, offend against the rule of law.

7

Local Government

Introduction

This chapter is concerned with the organisation and powers of local authorities and their relationship to central government and the courts. All local authorities are public corporations and are elected and accountable bodies. All of their powers are derived from statutes and hence are subject to the ultra vires principle of judicial review. There is also a considerable network of controls emanating from central government, and one of the important constitutional issues considered in this chapter is the balance of power existing between central and local government. During the 1980s there was a considerable attack on the autonomy of local authorities through policies such as the privatisation of some services and the creation of new unelected 'quangos' to run other services. Severe financial controls were imposed through the administration of central government grants to local authorities and though the 'capping' of (putting an upper ceiling upon) the amount of money which local authorities could raise through local taxation such as the 'poll tax', which later became the council tax.

Traditionally, the division between central and local government has been one of the few areas of the British Constitution in which respect has been paid to the concept of the separation of powers and the need to devolve powers to an appropriate local level so as to bring government nearer to the communities it serves. The reforms of the 1980s might be portrayed as undermining this traditional arrangement. However, the election of the Labour Government in May 1997 has witnessed a change of mood in central government, with a greater willingness to tolerate strong systems of local self-government. The devolution of powers to a Scottish Parliament and a Welsh Assembly (scheduled for 1999) are the principle means by which this will be achieved, though there remain long-term plans for setting up regional assemblies in England. It is also intended to introduce a system of elected mayors for the major cities along the lines of the American system, starting with a mayor for London. Recent reorganisation of some local authorities into larger, unitary bodies may also be evidence of a return to stronger, more vibrant local self-government.

Examination emphasis will usually be on the relationship between central and local government within the general context of the doctrine of the separation of powers. Some syllabuses, for example, University of London LLB External, have examined this topic regularly, so that at least one essay question can be expected on it each year. Others may not examine it at all, preferring to test it in other subjects such as administrative law at second/third-year level. Hence, it is important to check a syllabus to ascertain whether local government is examinable in first year constitutional law.

A useful recent article on local authority powers and the controls which exist over them is by Sir Robert Carnwath: [1996] PL 244.

Questions

INTERROGRAMS

1 Outline the main financial controls exercised by central government over local government.
2 Outline the main non-financial controls or influences exercised by ministers over local authorities.
3 Outline some of the reforms of local government which occurred during the 1980s.
4 What is the likely future of local government - continuing decline or regeneration?

QUESTION ONE

One of the most difficult constitutional problems today is striking a balance between central government control and local government autonomy.

Discuss.

London University LLB Examination
(for external students) Constitutional Law June 1987 Q5

QUESTION TWO

'Since we have no written constitution which fixes the boundary between central and local government, it can be shifted by the actions of successive governments.'

Discuss.

London University LLB Examination
(for external students) Constitutional Law June 1988 Q5

QUESTION THREE

To what extent can the relationship between central and local government be described as a partnership?

London University LLB Examination
(for external students) Constitutional Law June 1990 Q2

QUESTION FOUR

Although local authorities derive their powers directly from statute and so are legally enabled to act by the conferment of direct authority, their relations with central government departments shape and affect every important decision they make.' (Hartley & Griffith).

Discuss.

London University LLB Examination
(for external students) Constitutional Law June 1992 Q3

QUESTION FIVE

In what respects, if any, has the constitutional role of local government changed in recent years?

London University LLB Examination
(for external students) Constitutional Law June 1993 Q4

QUESTION SIX

'One result of the legal reforms in the period May 1979 to April 1997 is that local government, once the most responsive form of democracy, has been relegated to the position of manager of local services with little or no residual autonomy.'

Critically assess this statement.

Adapted from London University LLB Examination
(for external students) Constitutional Law June 1994 Q8

Answers

ANSWERS TO INTERROGRAMS

1 Central government has the power to determine how resources are to be provided to local authorities and, in particular, what method of local taxation is to be used to raise revenue for local authority functions (currently the council tax). The raising of loans by local authorities must obtain the approval of the Secretary of State for the Environment. Central government also provides either specific grants for approved local authority functions or money as part of the general support grant which relates to approval of an authority's overall spending. Many statutory controls exist in all the above areas. According to Wade, *Administrative Law* (1994, 7th ed), at p139: '... the Local Government Finance Acts 1982–1992 have given the central government a stranglehold on local authority revenue and expenditure'.

2 Ministers can exercise control and influence over the actions of local authorities by statutory and non-statutory methods. Under the Local Government Act 1972 ministers enjoy wide powers to issue statutory orders regulating local authority functions.

In certain fields, such as town and country planning, it is common practice for a minister to issue circulars to local authorities indicating the view of central government as to how a scheme should be administered or certain cases be dealt with. Many individual statutes, such as the Housing Finance Act 1972, provide ministers with default powers so as to take over specific functions if it appears that a local authority has unreasonably refused to perform its duties under the Act. Certain services, such as the police and education, are subject to central government inspection. Ministers also have the power to confirm or refuse to confirm by-laws, compulsory purchase orders, and educational schemes, and to hear appeals in respect of some local authority decisions, such as refusals of planning permission.

3 During the 1980s there was a radical shake-up in the organisation of local government, notably through the abolition of an 'upper tier' comprising the Greater

London Council and six metropolitan borough councils. There was also a fundamental reform of local authority powers. Examples include: the Local Government, Planning and Land Act 1980, which transferred urban development powers to new, unelected corporations; the Local Government Act 1988, which compelled local authorities to put out the provision of many basic services (eg refuse collection) to competitive private tender; the Housing Act 1988, which allowed council tenants to switch their tenancies to housing associations or co-operatives, and which also established housing action trusts to redevelop poor quality council estates; and the Education Reform Act 1988, which gave schools and further education colleges the right to opt out of local authority control, introduced a national curriculum for what could be taught in schools, and removed local government control over the former polytechnics and other major colleges.

4 As a result of the 1980 reforms (above) many commentators took a gloomy view as to the future of local government. For example, Loughlin concluded that local government has been reduced to the status of an agency responsible for ensuring the provision of a range of discrete services which the market cannot directly provide: essay on local government in Jowell and Oliver's *The Changing Constitution* (1994, 3rd ed). De Smith's *Constitutional and Administrative Law* (1989) likened the relationship between central and local government to that of rider and horse (with presumably central government holding the whip hand!). With the re-election of the Conservative Government in April 1992 it appeared that the future of local government remained bleak, but all of this may change following the victory of 'New Labour' at the May 1997 General Election. The Labour Government has pledged itself to a policy of regeneration of the regions in which local self-government will be encouraged. The devolution of powers to a Scottish Parliament, a Welsh Assembly and city mayors is part of a new commitment by central government for a 'fresh start' in central-local government relations.

SUGGESTED ANSWER TO QUESTION ONE

General Comment

A critical analysis is required, exploring the nature of the relationship between central and local government and the inevitable tensions that arise in that relationship.

Key Points

- Introduction (unitary nature of the United Kingdom and the role of local government)
- Central government control of local authorities (finance, regulations, inspection, default powers and abolition)
- The reasons for conflict (maintenance of national standards and national economic policy)
- Relationship between central and local government (partnership or central dominance and problem of conflict of democracies)

Suggested Answer

Although the United Kingdom is a unitary state there is a highly developed system of local government. The organs of local government serve two broad purposes. Firstly, they enable many public services to be administered at a level nearer the people for the benefit of whom the service is provided. Secondly, they enable local political opinion to be organised and expressed. Local authorities, however, although representative bodies chosen by popular election, have not the autonomy of Parliament; indeed they are dependent upon Parliament for their powers.

The powers of local authorities derive either expressly or by implication from statute and they are exercised subject to the doctrine of ultra vires. The application of these rules in disputed cases is a matter for the courts and no local authority can determine the extent of its own powers. But within the limits of its powers, and subject to the performance of any statutory duties laid upon it, a local authority has a discretion in deciding how it is to administer the services for which it is responsible. In practice, however, this discretion is subject to many forms of direct and indirect pressure from central government and during the 1980s there was a tendency for central government to restrict the freedom of local authorities to decide their own policies.

The array of local authority controls available to central government is formidable. Perhaps some of the most effective are those concerned with local authority finance. The services provided by local government will of course require expenditure and the two main sources of local authority finance to meet this expenditure are council taxes and grants from central government. But central government departments not only have the power to make grants but also to withhold them. They also have the power to control borrowing for capital projects.

As well as these powers over local authority finance, central government departments also have powers to prescribe rules for the conduct of local services. This may be achieved directly by regulations, or indirectly by the introduction of parliamentary legislation. Certain services, for example the police and education, are subject to central government inspection. Relevant central government departments also have the power to confirm or refuse to confirm by-laws, compulsory purchase orders, educational schemes, senior appointments etc, to conduct local inquiries under certain statutory powers and to entertain appeals in respect of certain local authority decisions, for example refusals of planning permission. Central government departments may also exercise default powers, by removing responsibility for the conduct of a service from one authority to another or by taking over responsibility for the service centrally or by issuing a mandatory order or obtaining from the courts an order of mandamus to compel the authority to carry out its statutory duties.

By its very nature therefore local government implies a measure of local self government. Local authorities do not operate as mere agents of central departments subject to the latter's full direction and control. But, because of central government's responsibility for national policies some of which, for example education and housing, depend completely upon local implementation, it is inevitable that claims have to be made by central government departments to supervise or control local authority activities, both for the overall maintenance of standards of service and reasons of national economic policy.

This relationship which results from these claims of central government and from the desire of local authorities for some autonomy is sometimes described as a partnership. However in reality it is central government that dominates the relationship. This is inevitable. Increasingly party politics is infiltrating local government and where the political composition of a local authority differs from that of the central government there is great scope for conflict. Local authorities are still responsible for the exercise of many powers and duties and spend vast sums of public money. They can therefore seriously frustrate the plans of the central government. But in any conflict it is usually the central government that wins. Central government controls Parliament and Parliament is supreme. Legislation may be enacted to control the functions of local authorities or even abolish authorities in some cases (as happened during the 1980s). Local authorities must not stand in the way of central government policy. But the problem is of course that local authorities are elected just as central government is elected and they too have their mandate. The great problem is striking a balance between these two conflicts of democracy.

SUGGESTED ANSWER TO QUESTION TWO

General Comment

A question that proceeds on the assumption that the United Kingdom does not have a written constitution, so perhaps some thought should be given to that at the outset. It then proceeds to suggest that this accounts for the nature of the relationship between central and local government, an assertion that certainly needs careful analysis. Some examples of the distribution of responsibilities between central and local government will obviously be needed, as well as an examination of the extent to which the introduction of a written constitution would alter the situation.

Key Points

- Explain relationship between central and local government
- Give examples of allocation of functions
- Reservation of powers to central government
- Consider the operation of a written constitution
- Cite problem of express repeal
- Implied repeal
- Higher law argument
- Supreme court
- Implications of reform proposals on devolution of Labour Government, elected 1 May 1997

Suggested Answer

Any statement to the effect that the United Kingdom does not possess a written constitution has to be considered very carefully. Whilst all would accept that there is no one constitutional document embodying the framework of government, not even the Bill of Rights 1688 coming near to this, it should equally be accepted that many important aspects of constitutional law are ascertainable in a written form, either as common law, or legislation. The Crown Proceedings Act 1947, the Parliament Acts 1911-1949, the Representation of the People Act 1983, and the House of Commons Disqualification Act 1975, are all examples of legislation dealing with matters that can broadly referred to as 'constitutional'. As regards the relationship between central and local government there is no shortage of 'black letter' law. The main piece of legislation is still the Local Government Act 1972, but in recent years nearly every parliamentary session has seen the enactment of additional legislation on the topic.

It is submitted that the statement under consideration really prompts two questions. First, whether the boundary between central and local government really can be shifted by the actions of successive governments, and if so, secondly whether a written constitution could prevent this from happening.

Local government is generally seen as a 'good thing' on the ground that it enables locally elected persons to determine the provision of local services and amenities. Traditionally, the matters entrusted to local government have included education, planning, housing, and environmental protection. All of these are areas where political differences are likely to be sharp, resulting in an uneasy relationship between central and local government, especially where central government is of a markedly different political persuasion to that of a particular local authority.

On the one hand government ministers will not be unhappy that these functions are the responsibility of local authorities, since it means that ministers will not be answerable to parliament for the day to day activities of local authorities; on the other there is a need for ministers to retain a considerable degree of ultimate control in order for at least minimum standards to be observed nationally in respect of matters such as education. In extreme cases ministers may be vested with default powers whereby the functions of a local authority can be taken over completely by the relevant minister.

Examples of the boundary between central and local government being shifted as regards the allocation of powers and duties are not difficult to find. The Education Act 1944 placed a broad duty upon local education authorities to provide adequate education for their inhabitants. The Education Reform Act 1988, however, proposed that all schools should follow a national curriculum to be determined by central government, thus restoring to central government a good deal of the discretion that formerly rested with local government. By virtue of the Housing Act 1957, local authorities are under a duty to provide for homeless persons within their areas, but since the enactment of the Housing Act 1980, council tenants have had the right to buy the council accommodation in which they are living. Where a local authority appears to be 'dragging its feet' in implementing the right to buy, the Secretary of State can intervene to take over the 'right to buy' scheme in any local authority's area. Further, under the Town and Country Planning Act 1990, the Secretary of State for the Environment can 'call in' a planning application and institute a public inquiry, rather than leave the matter to be determined by the local planning authority.

In addition to legislation empowering central government to take over the functions of local authorities, there has, in recent years, been a marked increase in the volume of legislation introducing extra controls over local government. Many of these measures have been aimed at constraining local government expenditure, but others have dealt with a wide range of matters, from prohibitions upon political advertising, the introduction of competitive tendering, and the publication of the minutes of council meetings, to the prohibition upon the promotion of homosexuality, and limitations upon 'creative accounting'. To what extent would a written constitution affect any of the above? Implicit in the statement under consideration is the suggestion that a written constitution would clearly delineate the boundary between local government and central government. This could certainly be achieved with some precision, but its long term effectiveness would depend upon other constitutional reforms being introduced. If a written constitution were introduced in the form of a general Act of Parliament, it could be repealed by any subsequent parliament. Even if some attempt were made to entrench such an Act, perhaps by requiring a two thirds majority in both the Commons and the Lords before it could be altered or repealed, it is submitted that a future Parliament could still repeal it on the basis of a simple majority vote. The reason for this is the adherence to the doctrine of parliamentary sovereignty, and its continued recognition by the courts: see *Pickin* v *British Railways Board* (1974).

Further, under the doctrine of implied repeal as it is currently understood, any later Act of Parliament which appeared to conflict directly with the 'written constitution' legislation, would be applied in preference: see *Vauxhall Estates Ltd* v *Liverpool Corporation* (1932). Hence even if an Act were passed which appeared to enshrine the rights and independence of local government, there would be nothing to prevent a subsequent parliament enacting legislation to abolish a specific local authority, or even a whole tier of local government, as was the fate of the Greater London Council and other metropolitan county councils.

For a written constitution to prevent local government being at the mercy of central government, therefore, a fundamental change would have to be made in the framework of government, amounting to a new constitutional settlement. The written constitution, enshrining the rights of local authorities, would have to be regarded as a kind of 'higher' law to which all other legislation was subordinate and with which all subsequent legislation was required to comply: see *Harris* v *Minister of Interior* (1952). This would also involve the creation of a constitutional court empowered to invalidate legislation which purported to conflict with the provisions of the written constitution.

In conclusion, it is submitted that local government will continue to be treated as a political football for as long as central government has the power to do so. The constitutional reforms necessary to prevent this being the case are so fundamental and far reaching that it seems most unlikely that the situation is going to change in the foreseeable future. The only hopeful sign on the horizon for those who believe in vigorous local government is the proposed devolution of powers to a Scottish Parliament and Welsh Assembly. The Labour Government, elected on 1 May 1997, is committed to this form of devolution, though it has postponed plans for regional English assemblies. There is also to be a special 25-member elected assembly for London, with an elected mayor who will enjoy considerable financial spending powers for the regeneration of the city. Such developments may be the start of a new era in central-local governmennt relationships, one in which the central government may be prepared to take a more tolerant view of local democracy.

SUGGESTED ANSWER TO QUESTION THREE

General Comment

A question requiring a historical survey of the way central government has conferred powers on local authorities, diluted them, abolished them, and re-invented them!

Key Points

- Historical developments
- Examples of central government controls
- Restructuring of local government by central government
- Likely impact of new devolution proposals
- Impact of 'opting out' policies
- Conclusion

Suggested Answer

The relationship between central and local government is often expressed in terms of a partnership, but as de Smith commented, if it is 'it is a partnership between a rider and a horse'. The measure of autonomy once enjoyed by local authorities has been somewhat eroded over recent years, particularly by the effects of government spending restrictions, the new form of finance for local authorities and by the legitimisation of 'opting out' by services whose control had been the cornerstone of their power.

However, it must be appreciated that since the rise of the Liberal Party under Joseph Chamberlain, central government has come to depend on a more 'grass roots' attitude towards politics, developing local issues and using pilot schemes organised and administered by local authorities as role models to illustrate not only the way in which a government appreciates the needs of the electorate, but, more recently, to prove ideological points.

The dependency of central government on local government is illustrated by the great weight afforded to local government representations when, as often happens, a government department will consult on a local issue. Frequently, local authorities will be instrumental in the instigation of legislation.

However, a vast array of central controls are in place to promote effective and cost efficient services. The change in methods of funding away from the rates which were payable direct into local government coffers to the council tax which is distributed by the Treasury according to central government perception of need effectively robs regional authorities of control of expenditure. This is so even though council taxes are set locally since the controversial use of 'capping' denies true freedom in the determination of financial goals.

The true power of local authorities has traditionally stemmed from their powers to administer and control the essential services. However ultimate control must of necessity lie with central government to ensure the maintenance of minimum standards nationwide. In matters such as planning and environmental issues there is always a final veto or appeal direct to the Secretary of State for the Environment. As de Smith observed: 'No one reading through two years' output of Town and Country Planning Regulations will doubt the reality of central control over matters of procedure and substance'.

Executive control by ministers and their departments acting in a supervisory or judicial function is a primary technique applied to ensure compliance with statutory obligations. Generally, no power of a local authority exists or may be exercised without Parliament's implicit sanction. This will usually be found in the form of specific statutory enactments or the interpretation of Acts of Parliament by the courts with regard to the vires of a local authority's exercise of powers. In pursuance of the maintenance of standards in the provision of services within the control of a local authority, inspection either generally by the National Audit Office with regard to expenditure or consequent to a specific statute may be carried out. Normally such functions of inspectors are accompanied by the power to make formal or informal compliance orders.

The appointment and dismissal of certain local authority officers also is subject to the sanction of central government. The Local Government and Housing Act 1988 put effective restrictions on those who can hold such offices when they seek regional political appointments. Even the qualified legislative power to create by-laws is subject to the confirmation and approval of the appropriate minister, as are any schemes, proposals or plans where statute places the requirement of ministerial assent.

Ultimately, the Local Government Act 1972 provides the machinery for a review of local government areas in the form of boundary commissions. In recent years governments have shown more than a willingness to 'reform' certain problematic or overpowerful councils. Perhaps most significant of all was the abolition of the Greater London Council by the Local Government Act 1985. However, the Labour Government elected at the General Election on 1 May 1997 is committed to introduce the office of a city mayor who would enjoy the sort of powers exercised by some mayors in the big cities in America. Such reform might witness a resurgence in the influence of local power over central government. Similarly, the setting up of the Scottish Parliament and the Welsh Assembly under the Labour Government's devolution plans will see a redistribution of powers which should tilt the balance back towards a strong system of local self-government.

A more serious and insidious erosion of the independent power of regional government stems from the newly created concept of 'opting out'. Hospitals, formerly under the control of local health authorities, may now create self governing trusts, taking the administration and funding decisions away from regional authorities substituting direct accountability to the Department of Health. In a similar vein, schools may establish their own individual control, again accountable direct to the Department. Although the uptake of this option has not been great, the potential for usurpation of these traditional powers is significant.

Thus, in conclusion we must relate our review of central government's relationship with local authorities to the concept of partnership suggested by the question. Partnership intimates an equality of status and a degree of mutuality. There can be no doubt that the administrative burden, practical requirements for good government and the appreciation of local needs dictate that there will always be a demand for some kind of local executive function. However, the term government must be viewed in the context of a degree of executive freedom that the encroaching controls and fetters stemming from Whitehall and Westminster would seek to prevent.

SUGGESTED ANSWER TO QUESTION FOUR

General Comment

This is a fairly standard question on the relationship between local and central government. It would be difficult to argue against the view expressed in the quotation.

Key Points

- Derivation of powers
- Function of local authorities
- Financial controls
- Regulations, appointments and approval
- Appeals to Secretary of State
- Supervisory role
- Conclusion

Suggested Answer

Local authorities are entirely creatures of statute. Their powers are derived from either public or private Acts of Parliament. However, while these powers may be exercised with varying degrees of independence, local authorities remain subject to control by central government.

Local authorities are involved in virtually every aspect of local life - for example, education, housing, planning. Yet all of these functions are not only allocated and prescribed by statute, they may also be taken away if Parliament chooses, as, for example, through thc 'opting out' schemes for hospitals and schools. Similarly, the very structure of local government can be altered as when the Local Government Act 1985 abolished the Greater London Council, transferring its functions to the London borough councils.

The relationship between central and local government has been likened to that of rider and horse, although one might qualify the metaphor by adding that this horse cannot throw its rider. If it is a partnership, it is not one of equals although that does not deny a measure of mutual dependence.

The relationship with central government departments allows comprehensive and effective control of local authority activity. This relationship takes several forms. Firstly - and perhaps most effectively - there are controls through finance. While the method of raising income locally through the council tax is determined by central government, other sources of income are controlled by government departments. Thus, capital expenditure, which is largely financed by borrowing, is subject to the approval of the Secretary of State; grants from the national exchequer are either specific to an approved function or part of the support grant which relates to approval of an authority's overall spending. There is an array of statutory control to cover these, such as the Local Government Act 1972 and the Local Government, Planning and Land Act 1980.

Secondly, many Acts conferring powers or ascribing duties to a local authority allow the relevant minister to control the way the particular function or service is performed or provided. This may be through regulations contained in subordinate legislation or through approval of plans submitted by the local authority. Similarly, there are statutory powers of inspection by the relevant department for education, police and fire services. There are powers of appointment, either directly or by establishing the methods to be followed in making appointments, as, for example, under the Fire Services Act 1947 or the Local Government and Housing Act 1988. Even local byelaws are ineffective until confirmed by the appropriate minister.

Thirdly, at times there is contained within a statute the right of appeal to the Secretary of State by the aggrieved party against the local authority's decision. For example, the Town and Country Planning Act 1990 allows appeal to the Secretary of State for the Environment against refusal to grant planning permission.

Fourthly - and embracing all of the above - is the supervisory role of the central government department. This recognises the national importance of many of a local authority's functions. For example, the National Curriculum operates to standardise education and reflects the Secretary of State's statutory duty 'to promote the education of the people of England and Wales'. It also reflects the source of a local authority's power and the central government department's role in ensuring compliance with statutory obligations.

In conclusion, therefore, what emerges is a one-sided picture and one must agree with the view expressed by Hartley and Griffith. What is more, the continued erosion of the local authority's role in certain areas of local life through opting out means that important decisions will not only be subject to central government departments' approval but will increasingly be taken by the department with no reference to the local authority.

SUGGESTED ANSWER TO QUESTION FIVE

General Comment

The question requires a detailed narrative of legislative changes affecting the role of local government in recent years. General waffle must be avoided, because the examiner is looking for a catalogue of precise changes, along with their impact. Few students do well on this sort of question because they have never given the topic of local government the kind of specialist in-depth study which a question of this kind requires. There is a wealth of material and one must be selective; the suggested solution concentrates on changes to the structure and functions of local government, but alternative approaches could include material on finance (the impact of the community charge/poll tax and its replacement by the council tax) and the effect of the European Single Market of 1992 on trading standards, consumer protection, free movement of labour, education, health and safety, and environment so far as it affects the provision of local government services. Hence there is an opportunity for each student to demonstrate an area of specialist study. Try to avoid regurgitating general narratives from the main textbooks, most of which are too vague and some of which are bound to be out-of-date because of the rapidity of change in this area. Make use of one or more of the specialist texts on local government.

Key Points

- Widdicombe Report 1986
- Values of local democracy
- Changes to urban development functions
- Changes to the structure of local government and their political background
- Introduction of competitive tendering of services
- Education changes
- Housing, health and police reforms
- Impact of Citizen's Charter
- Setting up of the Banham Commission
- Remaining role of local government and likely future

Suggested Answer

The Widdicombe Report on Local Government (1986) identified the value of local government as stemming from three essential attributes:

1 pluralism, through which it contributes to the national political system;
2 participation, through which it contributes to local democracy; and
3 responsiveness, through which it contributes to the provision of local needs through the delivery of services.

Each of the three attributes has come under threat in recent years, mainly from central government. The 1980s witnessed a stream of legislation altering both the role and functions of local government and crucially changing the balance of power existing between central and local government.

The Local Government, Planning and Land Act 1980 removed local authorities' lead role in urban development, passing the ownership and control of inner city land in a number of areas to government appointed urban development corporations (UDCs), themselves closely modelled on the bodies which built the New Towns in 1946. This was followed by legislation abolishing the 'upper tier' of local government, namely the six metropolitan borough councils and the Greater London Council (1984). As *The Times* commented in an editorial ((1993) The Times 6 May):

> 'For Margaret Thatcher, the destruction of municipal socialism and abolition of the six metropolitan borough councils was a necessary assault on the "last vestiges of feudal power". Never again would a pretender like Ken Livingstone be able to declare his

> intention "to use the council machinery as part of a political campaign both against the government and in defence of socialist policies".'

(Ken Livingstone was the leader of the Greater London Council.)

The 'Thatcher Years' (1979–1990) continued with reforms which radically altered the scope, provision and management of many local authority services. The Local Government Act 1988 compelled all local authorities to put out the provision of many basic services (eg refuse collection) to competitive tender. The Education Reform Act 1988 gave schools and most further education colleges the right to opt out of local authority control and to become grant maintained, funded and managed directly by the Department of Education and Science. The Act also introduced a 'national curriculum' which meant that for the first time in England and Wales the central government was responsible for what is taught in schools. The control of the former polytechnics and other major colleges was also removed from local government.

The Housing Act 1988 allowed council tenants to switch their tenancy from their council to control by housing associations, approved landlords or cooperatives. The Act also established housing action trusts which were charged with taking over poor quality council estates in run-down areas in order to redevelop them. Under other legislation elected councillors have been excluded from health authorities and will in future play only a small role in the new police authorities.

The reforms of local government continued under John Major's administration (1992–1997). The Local Government Act 1992 applies provisions of the Citizen's Charter to local government to ensure greater openness about decision-making and more sensitive 'customer care'. The Act also established a Local Government Commission (under the chairmanship of Sir John Banham) to conduct a boundary review and to recommend structural and electoral changes. The Commission took over the functions of the Local Government Boundary Commission, which was abolished by the Act. The Banham Commission embarked on a review to decide whether district and county councils, which often find themselves in conflict, should be replaced by unitary authorities. It is expected that the eventual result should be a substantial reduction in the number of councillors.

So what is left to the role of local government? It will continue to spend more than £70 billion a year and may spend more when it assumes new duties under health legislation for general community care. But, even so, some have ventured to think that local authorities might eventually wither away, with their powers gradually being transferred to 'Care Associations' staffed by vigorous citizens: views, John Patten, Education Secretary (spring 1993). *The Times* editorial (above) commented:

> 'His vision of democratically elected councillors replaced by self-appointed civic activists is still a remote prospect. But it should encourage the public to ask how much more power it is prepared to sign away to quangos and unelected groups, and what sort of local governance it wants.'

However, the election of the Labour Government at the General Election on 1 May 1997 may signal a new era in which claims to more local self-government are treated with sympathy by the central government. Devolution of powers to a Scottish

Parliament, a Welsh Assembly and a city mayor for London will be evidence of a major constitutional resettlement.

SUGGESTED SOLUTION TO QUESTION SIX

General Comment

As with all questions on the constitutional role and position of local government, a good answer requires a fairly detailed knowledge of rather a technical area. However, if the candidate has such knowledge, it should be possible to produce just such a good answer. But, as ever, the most important thing to do is to answer the question: by discussing the statement quoted.

Key Points

- Historical development
- Local government (representative role)
- Financial control
- Functional control (education, housing and police)
- Fresh start on 1 May 1997

Suggested Answer

It is hard to deny that the period from May 1979 to April 1997 saw considerable legislative activity by Parliament in the sphere of central-local government relations. No doubt, such is inevitable where the political complexion of central government remained unchanged during that period, so that the almost inevitable tension between central and local government, where the two are of different political persuasions, has been exacerbated. However, the question in essence rests upon two assumptions: first, that local government was 'once the most responsive form of democracy' and, second, that the result of the reforms has been to relegate local government to the position of a 'manager of local services with little or no residual autonomy'. In discussing the quote, it is necessary to consider whether these are valid assumptions.

English law has long recognised a functional division of powers between local and central government, at least as long ago as the Justices of the Peace Act 1361; moreover, it is clear that a considerable degree of local autonomy was enjoyed by local officials such as sheriffs and constables prior to that date. The 1361 Act might well be seen as an early attempt at centralisation. By the seventeenth century, however, central control of the justices was much reduced. 'For the next 200 years', as Hood Phillips noted, 'local government was, subject to the legislative power of Parliament, almost autonomous': *Constitutional and Administrative Law* (1987, 7th ed), p583. Since the main reforms of the nineteenth century, establishing the modern framework of local government, the central-local relationship has been well-recognised as an essential part of the constitutional system in England.

It was in these nineteenth century reforms that local government first acquired its representative function. Several Acts were enacted to provide for locally elected councils. Loughlin has pointed out that, at least until the advent of direct elections to the European Parliament, 'Local councils are the only governmental institutions outside of Parliament which are subject to direct periodic election': essay on local government in Jowell and Oliver's *The Changing Constitution* (1994, 3rd ed), p264. The basic legal framework of local government elections is now contained in the Representation of the People Act 1983. As elected bodies, they thus enjoy a democratic legitimacy unmatched by any other institution of the constitution, save the House of Commons itself.

Indeed, it may be argued that in some respects local government enjoys more legitimacy than its central counterpart. Thus, unlike a prospective Westminister candidate, an intending councillor, to qualify as a candidate, must have some connection with the area in which the election is fought, either as an elector for the area, or as having resided, worked or occupied land there during the previous year; similarly, a local authority's term of office is fixed by statute: Local Government Act 1972; see, generally, Wade, *Administrative Law* (1994, 7th ed), p122 et seq. In these senses, then, it is possible to argue that local authorities are a highly responsive form of democracy, where the links between represented and representative are much closer than at the national level. However, it should be pointed out that the turn-out of voters at local elections is generally far poorer than that for general elections, which tends to undermine their legitimacy and, hence, the claim that they are the 'most' responsive form of democracy.

Nevertheless, it might seem, given that they enjoy considerable democratic legitimacy, to be appropriate that they enjoy a degree of local autonomy in the conduct of those aspects of the executive function that may properly be carried out at local level. It is somewhat ironic, no doubt, that the central government should put such faith in the principle of subsidiarity as the 'local' authority vis-à-vis the 'central' European Community, and yet was unwilling to concede a similar sphere of competence to local authorities in England. Yet it seems true that reforms in the period May 1979 to April 1997 have tended to reduce local government to the status of a 'manager of local services with little or no residual autonomy'.

Central government has always exercised ultimate control over the structure of local government, culminating in the enactment of the 1972 Act. This process is certain to continue under the Local Government Act 1992 with the establishment of the Local Government Commission empowered to make recommendations to the Secretary of State for structural, boundary or electoral changes in local government: s13 Local Government Act 1992. In terms of finance, central government exerts the power of the purse-string, since local government relies primarily on government grants for the revenue to carry out its tasks: it may not therefore be too surprising that central government might wish to exercise greater control over how this money is spent, but it is certainly arguable that party political considerations have been to the fore of late. Further, although the alterations in the system empowering local authorities to tax - the community charge and its replacement the council tax - were intended to make local government more responsive to its electors, they have instead proved highly controversial and led to considerable friction over the issue of central governmental controls 'capping' local expenditure. As Wade says, 'the Local Government Finance Acts 1982–92 have given the central government a stranglehold on local authority revenue and expenditure': *Administrative Law* (1994, 7th ed), p139.

The period since May 1979 has also seen considerable legislative action by central government encroaching on the functions of local government. In matters such as education and housing, for example, historically typical areas of local control, changes have seen further centralisation.

Hence, there is much force in the assertion in the quote that local government, a responsive form of democracy, has been reduced to the status of agent of central government, deprived of much of the autonomy that it enjoyed in practice, if not strict law, in earlier years. However, the election of the Labour Government on 1 May 1997 may be the start of a new era of resurgent local government since the new Government is committed to a constitutional resettlement involving a Scottish Parliament, a Welsh Assembly and a city mayor and assembly for London. The effect may be to reverse some of the centralising measures that took place in the period up to 1 May 1997.

8

Judicial Review of Administrative Action

Introduction

This chapter is concerned with the fundamental principles of administrative law. Judicial review has been a growth area of English law over the past 40 years and is still developing. It is essential to understand the scope of the three main grounds for judicial review, namely, procedural impropriety, illegality and irrationality. In addition, the potential development of a fourth ground, namely, proportionality, also deserves critical analysis. Judicial review ought to be concerned with the manner in which administrative decisions are taken, rather than with the substantive merits of such decisions. However, it has been argued that some of the existing grounds for review have been used so as to place artificial common law limits on the exercise of legitimate executive discretion. This raises important constitutional questions as to the extent to which judges may be undermining sovereignty, since Parliament delegated discretionary powers to an accountable executive rather than to an unaccountable judiciary. On the other hand, vigorous judicial review is an essential safeguard in upholding the rule of law against the risks of arbitrary and unfair decision-making.

In addition to the grounds of review, it will be necessary to understand the basic procedural rules governing an application for judicial review. These are special rules requiring that the application concerns public issues and public authorities, that the application is made promptly and within a time limit of three months, and that the applicant has locus standi, that is, sufficient interest in the matter to which the application relates, since the court will not listen to a 'mere busybody' interfering in things that do not concern him!

An outline knowledge of the remedies available for a judicial review is also required. Sometimes Parliament attempts to make particular powers 'judge-proof' by asserting that they 'cannot be questioned in any legal proceedings' or by stating that a minister's decisions on a matter are 'final'. These ouster clauses are deserving of detailed study because they represent real challenges to the rule of law and the judges have usually found ways of interpreting them so as to preserve access to the courts.

Judicial review is a vast and complex topic and it is only possible to study it at a fairly superficial level in first year constitutional law. At least one question on it can be expected every year in a typical examination paper and it will usually take the form of a problem-type question in which it is necessary to identify the grounds for judicial review relevant to particular factual situations. Sometimes an essay-type question will require critical analysis of the purpose and scope of the ultra vires doctrine (which embraces the three grounds for judicial review) and its value in the general context of the separation of powers and the rule of law. There is a vast amount of case law which can be used to illustrate various aspects of judicial review, but in practice it is enough to know one or two leading cases on each of these aspects. Since there are many angles from which an examiner can set a question on judicial review, the opportunity has been taken to include a considerable range of past examination questions and answers in this chapter so as to try to cover as many of these angles as possible.

Important recent cases include: *R* v *Secretary of State for the Home Department, ex parte Fayed* [1997] 1 All ER 228 (jurisdictional error, breach of natural justice and ouster clauses); *R* v *Secretary of State for the Home Department, ex parte Hargreaves* [1997] 1 All ER 397 (doctrine of legitimate expectation - whether procedural or substantive); *R* v *Secretary of State for the Environment, ex parte Kirkstall Valley Campaign Ltd* [1996] 3 All ER 304 ('real danger of bias' text applied to purely administrative decisions); *Percy* v *Hall* [1996] 4 All ER 523 (invalidity of bye-laws; concepts of void and voidable in public law); *R* v *Ministry of Defence, ex parte Smith and Others* [1996] 1 All ER 257 (scope of the irrationality ground for review in cases involving human rights); *Pierson* v *Secretary of State for the Home Department* [1997] 3 All ER 577 (abuse of power, substantive fairness and the rule of law); *R* v *Secretary of State for the Home Department, ex parte Venables and Thompson* [1997] 3 All ER 97 (procedural fairness, irrelevant considerations, fettering discretion); *R* v *Gloucestershire County Council, ex parte Barry* [1997] 2 All ER 1 (relevancy of considerations); *O'Rourke* v *Camden London Borough Council* [1997] 3 All ER 23 (the 'public/private' divide for the purpose of making a judicial review application); *Trustees of the Dennis Rye Pension Fund* v *Sheffield City Council* [1997] 4 All ER 747 (public/private divide).

The *Public Law Journal* is the specialist law journal for students of Administrative Law and it is useful, though not essential, to consult the 1996–1998 issues for articles examining the recent developments in public law and judicial review.

Questions

INTERROGRAMS

1 What is meant by the 'exclusivity principle' in relation to applications for judicial review?

2 What is the locus standi test for the purpose of making an application for judicial review?

3 What is the doctrine of legitimate expectation?

4 What is the rule on bias as applied to administrative decision-making?

5 What is meant by 'total unreasonableness'? Is proportionality part of total unreasonableness or a separate ground for review?

6 What is the effect of a total ouster clause on the potential for judicial review of administrative tribunals?

QUESTION ONE

'Judicial review is concerned, not with the decision, but with the decision-making process' (*R* v *Chief Constable of North Wales Police, ex parte Evans* [1982] 1 WLR 1155 per Lord Brightman at 1174).

Discuss.

London University LLB Examination
(for external students) Constitutional Law June 1985 Q6

QUESTION TWO

When, and in what circumstances, will judges quash administrative decisions?

London University LLB Examination
(for external students) Constitutional Law June 1987 Q7

QUESTION THREE

Discuss, giving examples, the extent to which the courts distinguish between statutory and prerogative powers in judicial review of administrative action.

London University LLB Examination
(for external students) Constitutional Law June 1995 Q5

QUESTION FOUR

In what manner and to what extent does judicial review of administrative action uphold the sovereignty of Parliament?

London University LLB Examination
(for external students) Constitutional Law June 1993 Q7

QUESTION FIVE

'The Courts will rarely be deterred by attempts to exclude their power to review decisions of administrative bodies, whether made directly by ouster clauses in one form or another, or indirectly by statutory provisions' conferring wide discretionary powers formulated in subjective terms.'

Explain and discuss with reference to relevant authorities.

London University LLB Examination
(for external students) Constitutional Law June 1989 Q6

QUESTION SIX

'In making sense of the inconsistencies in the application of the rules of natural justice, it should never be forgotten that natural justice is not intended to be a precise and uniform code of procedure' (de Smith).

Discuss.

London University LLB Examination
(for external students) Constitutional Law June 1992 Q9

QUESTION SEVEN

The Rural Mini-Buses Act provides that each District Council shall have the duty to subsidise such mini-bus services within its area as it shall consider necessary in the interests of the community.

The Redvale District Council decides to subsidise:

a a mini-bus service running from Redvale to Blacktown (which is outside Redvale District);

b a daily coach service within Redvale provided by Henry, the brother of Ivan, the Chairman of the Council;

c a weekly mini-bus service to the shopping centre in Redvale which is used almost exclusively by senior citizens who are Ivan's constituents.

John, a mini-bus owner and Redvale council tax payer, has offered to provide a cheaper mini-bus service within Redvale (see (b) above) but his offer was rejected without reasons being given. He wishes to attack the legality of the decisions in (a), (b) and (c) above, and seeks your advice.

Adapted from London University LLB Examination
(for external students) Constitutional Law June 1986 Q8

QUESTION EIGHT

A University Law Faculty has 100 places for its LLB course but receives 2,000 applications. The Sub-Dean for Admissions asks her secretary to choose the 100 candidates with the best 'O' level results. The secretary does this by looking at the application forms. The Sub-Dean then writes to the unsuccessful applicants saying that 'after the most careful consideration, we have reluctantly decided not to offer you a place. If you would like to discuss this with me, please arrange an appointment through my secretary.' All 1,900 disappointed applicants try to arrange appointments. The Sub-Dean writes again to withdraw her offer to meet applicants because of 'pressure of work'. She adds that 'applicants have no right to a hearing before or after a decision to refuse them admission'.

Have there been any breaches of the principles of administrative law?

London University LLB Examination
(for external students) Constitutional Law June 1988 Q7

QUESTION NINE

The (fictitious) University Complaints Commission was set up under the Education Act 1997 to receive and investigate complaints from students on 'academic matters'.

In May this year Jane, a final-year student reading History at the New World University, was accused of removing legal articles from the library, contrary to University regulations. Following internal disciplinary proceedings, at which Jane was not represented, Jane was expelled from the University.

Jane complained to the UCC requesting an investigation. The Commission wrote to Jane stating that it did not have jurisdiction to investigate her complaint, as her expulsion from the University related to a disciplinary rather than academic matter.

Jane wishes to apply for judicial review of the decision of the University to expel her and the decision of the University Complaints Commission.

Advise her.

Adapted from London University LLB Examination (for external students) Constitutional Law June 1994 Q6

QUESTION TEN

The Highways and Byways Act 1996 (a fictitious Act) s12 provides that:

1 A local authority must protect and maintain existing public rights of way within its area.

2 Where the closure of a public right of way is necessary in the interests of promoting the efficiency of road traffic, a local authority may:

  a close that right of way and redevelop the land as a road for motor traffic, provided that:

    i public notice has been given in the local press for a period of not less than three months; and

    ii all local residents have been informed by written notice, and have been given an opportunity to make representations.

3 The decision to close the right of way and redevelop the land must be made by the Planning Committee of the local authority.

In December last year the Kingshire County Council Planning Committee decided to exercise its power under the Act to provide routes for cyclists and motor-cyclists only. The Committee invited Mr Fitt, Secretary of the Blankshire Two Wheel Club, to attend the meeting and investigate and report on the matter. Mr Fitt recommended that the towpath alongside the River Thames should be developed for this purpose, and further, that part of the adjacent recreation ground should be developed as a training and racing track for cyclists and motor-cyclists.

In February this year Mr Fitt reported his findings to the Committee, but unfortunately, because of the bad weather conditions only the Chairman and Mr Fitt were present at the meeting. They agreed to the plan and the Chairman asked Mr Fitt to proceed.

Mr Fitt requested his secretary, Miss Able, to prepare the necessary notices for the press, and the mailing to local residents. Miss Able did this, but failed to write to several families who were living in the caravans at the side of the towpath. Mr and Mrs Jones, who live in a caravan, have hears of the plans and wish to challenge the legality of the Kingshire Council's action.

Advise Mr and Mrs Jones.

Adapted from London University LLB External Examination (for external students) Constitutional Law June 1991 Q6

Answers

ANSWERS TO INTERROGAMS

1 The 'exclusivity' principle comes from the speech of Lord Diplock in *O'Reilly* v *Mackman* [1983] 2 AC 237. Lord Diplock explained that the procedure for obtaining judicial review was reserved for public law cases, ie where it was contended that a public authority had acted in an ultra vires manner. Special safeguards were built into the procedure designed to protect public bodies from tardy or unmeritorious harassment, and hence it would be an abuse of process for a citizen to bypass these safeguards by using private law procedures (eg by writ) if his or her case was entirely or predominantly one of public law.

Unfortunately the distinction between public and private law issues is not an easy one to make in many factual situations and the rigidity of the exclusivity principle came to be seen as a source of hardship for many genuine plaintiffs who might find themselves penalised for making an honest and reasonable mistake as to choice of procedures. In recent case law there has been a tendency to apply the exclusivity principle in a more flexible, pragmatic way, having regard to the realities of litigation: see *Mercury Communications Ltd* v *Director-General of Telecommunications* [1996] 1 WLR 48 and *Trustees of the Dennis Rye Pension Fund* v *Sheffield City Council* [1997] 4 All ER 747.

2 For the purpose of making an application for judicial review the applicant must show a 'sufficient interest in the matter to which the application relates': O.53 r3(7) RSC. At one time the test was applied strictly so as to limit the number of challenges being made in the courts and also to discourage the concept of 'public interest' litigation. However, today the courts have developed a more liberal attitude and recognise the need to permit sincere citizens or reputable pressure groups to bring applications for review by representing local or national interests: see especially *R* v *Secretary of State for Foreign and Commonwealth Affairs, ex parte Rees-Mogg* [1994] 2 WLR 115 and *R* v *Inspectorate of Pollution, ex parte Greenpeace Ltd (No 2)* [1994] 4 All ER 329. As Lord Diplock remarked in *IRC* v *National Federation of Self-Employed and Small Businesses* [1981] 2 WLR 722 at 740: 'it would be a grave lacuna in our system of public law if a pressure group ... or even a single public spirited taxpayer were prevented by outdated technical rules of locus standi from bringing the matter to the attention of the courts to vindicate the rule of law and to get the unlawful conduct stopped'.

3 In *Council of Civil Service Unions* v *Minister for the Civil Service* (the GCHQ Case) [1985] AC 374 at 408 Lord Diplock defined a legitimate expectation as some kind of established right or benefit of which it would be unfair to deprive the holder without first giving the holder a fair hearing. In subsequent cases attempts were made to give this procedural concept a substantive character by holding, for example, that a public body which had conferred the right or benefit in question might be unable to resile from its publicly stated position unless it was clearly in the public interest to do so: eg, see *R* v *Secretary of State for the Home Department, ex parte Ruddock* [1987] 2 All ER 518. This came to be known as the doctrine of 'substantive' or 'reasonable' expectation, sometimes referred to as 'substantive fairness'. It was a controversial development because it appeared to conflict with the well-established principle that a public body cannot fetter the exercise of its discretionary powers by making promises or representations to individual citizens. In a recent case the Court of Appeal appeared to retreat from this progressive trend by emphasising the purely procedural character of doctrine: *R* v *Secretary of State for the Home Department, ex parte Hargreaves* [1997] 1 All ER 397.

4 In *R* v *Gough* [1993] 2 All ER 724 the House of Lords held that in regard to judicial or quasi-judicial decision-making a decision would be vitiated upon proof of a 'real danger of bias' in the way the decision had been taken. This has been interpreted as requiring proof of a real risk or a real possibility of bias: *R* v *Inner West London Coroner, ex parte Dallaglio* [1994] 4 All ER 139. Traditionally, a different approach has been adopted to test the fairness of administrative decision-making. In this context the courts preferred to examine whether the financial or other interest held by the public body in question unlawfully fettered the exercise of its discretion on a matter in which that interest might be affected: *Steeples* v *Derbyshire County Council* [1984] 3 All ER 468. However, in a recent case Sedley J explained that the fettering of discretion was a conceptually distinct ground for review from bias and that it was an important safeguard for a citizen to be able to contend that there was a real danger of bias in administrative decision-making. Consequently Sedley J applied *R* v *Gough*, above, to such decision-making: *R* v *Secretary of State for the Environment, ex parte Kirkshall Valley Campaign Ltd* [1996] 3 All ER 304.

5 The concept of 'total unreasonableness' comes from the judgment of Lord Greene, MR, in *Associated Provincial Picture Houses Ltd* v *Wednesbury Corporation* [1948] 1 KB 223 at 228. Lord Greene said: 'if a decision on a competent matter is so unreasonable that no reasonable authority could ever come to it, then the courts can interfere'. Since this concept was often criticised for being opaque and tautologous, a new concept of 'irrationality' was suggested to replace it: see per Lord Diplock in *Council of Civil Service Unions* v *Minister for the Civil Service* (the GCHQ case) [1985] AC 374 at 410: an irrational (or totally unreasonable) decision would be 'a decision so outrageous in its defiance of logic or of accepted moral standards that no sensible person who had applied his mind to the question to be decided could have arrived at it'.

Whilst a disproportionate penalty could be classified as an irrational one (see *R* v *Barnsley Metropolitan Borough Council, ex parte Hook* [1976] 3 All ER 452), it is clear that the doctrine of proportionality is itself a separate ground for review not yet recognised by English law because it involves judges too closely in examining the merits of executive decisions: see per Lord Diplock in the GCHQ case, above, and the dicta of Lords Ackner and Lowry in *R* v *Secretary of State for the Home Department, ex parte Brind* [1991] 1 AC 696. It may be that the incorporation of the European Convention on Human Rights into English law (expected to take place during 1998) will give judges the authority to apply proportionality as an additional ground of judicial review.

6 Many statutes contain provisions which, on a literal interpretation, would appear to oust the jurisdiction of the courts and protect the executive from judicial review. A typical example was a clause providing that a minister's decision was 'final'. Such clauses were described by Lord Denning as threats to the rule of law and he refused to apply a literal interpretation to them, holding instead that 'final' meant final as to the facts but not as to the law: *R* v *Medical Appeal Tribunal, ex parte Gilmore* [1957] 1 QB 574. In *Anisminic Ltd* v *Foreign Compensation Commission* [1969] 1 All ER 208 Lord Reid said that a clause providing that 'determinations' of the Commission could not be challenged in any legal proceedings could operate only as to valid determinations since Parliament would not have intended an administrative tribunal unreviewable opportunities to make errors of law and thereby exceed its jurisdiction or otherwise abuse its powers. The *Anisminic* principle was applied recently to quash a decision of the Home Secretary for procedural unfairness despite a statutory provision that his decisions on the matter in question were not to be subject to appeal or review in any court: *R* v *Secretary of State for the Home Department, ex parte Fayed* [1997] 1 All ER 228. It appears, therefore, that the existence of a total ouster clause will not deter the courts from applying the ultra vires doctrine to decisions of administrative tribunals apparently covered by such clauses.

SUGGESTED ANSWER TO QUESTION ONE

General Comment

A relatively straightforward question, concerning judicial review of administrative action. Students should generally argue that Lord Brightman is correct in his statement and support the argument with appropriate examples drawn from the doctrine of ultra vires. The distinction between appeals and judicial review must also be stressed, together with the effects of the public law remedies available under judicial review, in particular that of certiorari.

Key Points

- Nature of administrative law - purpose of judicial review
- The distinction between an appeal and judicial review
- Examples to illustrate that judicial review is concerned with the decision-making process (ultra vires - substantive and procedural; natural justice - procedural nature of audi alteram partem and nemo judex in causa sua)

- Public law remedies as an illustration of judicial review being concerned with the decision making process - the effect of an order of certiorari
- Conclusion

Suggested Answer

Administrative law is the law relating to the control of governmental power, and in particular with the legal controls upon the exercise of those powers by subordinate administrative authorities. Judicial review is the means whereby the courts achieve this control, and as Lord Brightman points out, in reviewing administrative action the court is not so much concerned with the merits of an actual decision, but rather with the process by which that decision was reached.

Judicial review must therefore be distinguished from an appeal. An appeal is concerned with the merits of a decision. A superior court is thus called upon to determine whether the decision of a lower court is right or wrong. With judicial review, however, the Divisional Court of the Queen's Bench Division is called upon to consider the legality of an act or order of a subordinate body. It must determine whether that act or order is lawful or unlawful. Instead of substituting its own decision for that of some other body, as on appeal, the court on review is concerned only with the question whether the act or order under attack should be allowed to stand or not.

The grounds upon which judicial review will lie illustrate the fact that it is the decision-making process rather than the actual decision which is the subject of the review. Ultra vires for example is based upon the fundamental principle of English law that no person or body should be permitted to exceed its lawful powers. When considering the question of ultra vires therefore the courts are not concerned with the merits of a particular decision, but rather with discovering whether or not the administrative authority in question has acted in excess of its statutory powers (see, for example, *Attorney-General* v *Fulham Corporation* (1921)) or acted in excess of its jurisdiction (see *Anisminic Ltd* v *Foreign Compensation Commission* (1969)), or whether or not the authority in the performance of its functions has followed the procedures prescribed by the parent Act: for example, *Grunwick Processing Laboratories Ltd* v *ACAS* (1978). The point is illustrated by the power of the court to declare an excess of jurisdiction on the part of an administrative authority to be ultra vires. All administrative authorities have limited jurisdiction. Where an authority acts in excess of its jurisdiction as laid down in the parent Act, its acts will be ultra vires and void. But where an authority makes a mistake, the traditional view (*R* v *Fulham, Hammersmith and Kensington Rent Tribunal, ex parte Zerek* (1951)) has been that so long as the authority is acting within its jurisdiction to hear an applicant, it does not lose its jurisdiction and thereby act ultra vires, by coming to a wrong conclusion, whether it was wrong in law or in fact. Therefore, the fact that an administrative authority makes a mistake in the exercise of a power does not necessarily render its decision ultra vires, and thereby subject to judicial review, so long as the error was committed within its jurisdiction. In recent times all errors of law have been treated as jurisdictional errors: *R* v *Lord President of the Council, ex parte Page* (1993).

Similarly with procedural ultra vires, when, for example, the courts are determining whether or not there has been an unreasonable use of a discretion the courts are concerned with the legality of the process by which the discretion was exercised and not with its merits. The requirements of reasonableness summarised by Lord Greene in *Associated Provincial Picture Houses Ltd* v *Wednesbury Corporation* (1948) illustrates this by being wholly and exclusively concerned with the decision-making process viz has the person entrusted with a discretion directed himself properly in law, called to his attention those matters which he is bound to consider and excluded from his consideration matters which are irrelevant. So long as these procedural requirements have been satisfied the decision reached will stand and will not be subject to review.

The requirements of natural justice also illustrate the point that judicial review is concerned solely with the decision-making process. The right to a fair hearing, audi alteram partem, in practice means that a person or body taking a decision must consider both sides of the case before taking that decision. No man is to be condemned without a hearing. Where a decision is one to which natural justice applies, or where the decision involves the duty to act fairly, then the person or body taking that decision must observe certain procedural requirements: see, generally, *Selvarajan* v *Race Relations Board* (1976). Basically, the right to a fair hearing requires that a person who stands to be affected by the decision of an administrative authority should be given notice of the case he has to meet and a fair opportunity to answer the case against him and to present his own side of the case. The risk against bias, nemo judex in causa sua, is also purely procedural in providing that no man should be a judge in his own cause (see *Dimes* v *Grand Junction Canal Proprietors* (1852)), ie justice must be seen to be done.

The public law remedies available under an application for judicial review also illustrate the fact that judicial review is concerned not with the decisions but with the decision-making process. The effect of an order of certiorari for example is to quash the decision of an inferior body, thus rendering it null and void. However, in quashing a decision by way of certiorari the reviewing court does not substitute its own decision for that of the inferior body, but usually simply refers the case back to the authority concerned to decide against this time observing the rules of natural justice or acting intra vires.

The aim of judicial review therefore is to ensure that public bodies act within the law. It is not aimed at compensating the individual for what he has lost because of the ultra vires in question: *Dunlop* v *Woollahra Municipal Council* (1981). Consequently the courts are only concerned with the legality of a decision, not with its merits. The court is not there to substitute its own value judgments for those of the inferior body. Judicial review must therefore be contrasted with a statutory right of appeal where a decision can be overruled and a new decision taken on the merits of the case. With judicial review a decision may simply be quashed and remitted to the inferior body to take again. By exercising their powers of judicial review the courts hope to indicate to administrative bodies the way in which they should act in future, and through this the courts can provide fairer and more efficient administrative practices.

SUGGESTED ANSWER TO QUESTION TWO

General Comment

A rather general question concerning judicial review of administrative action.

Key Point

- Introduction
- Rules of the Supreme Court O.53
- Grounds for judicial review
- Illegality
- Irrationality
- Procedural impropriety

Suggested Answer

An application for an order of certiorari to quash an administrative decision is made by way of an application to the High Court for judicial review under O.53 Rules of the Supreme Court. The applicant must obtain leave of the court for his application to be heard and must establish the necessary locus standi, that is he must be shown to have a sufficient interest in the matter to which the application relates. If the court is satisfied as to the merits of the applicant's case and providing that the locus standi requirement is satisfied, it may then consider the substantive grounds on which judicial review may be exercised.

Generally speaking executive action will be the subject of judicial review on three separate grounds. The first is where the authority concerned has been guilty of an error of law in its action, as for example purporting to exercise a power which in law it does not possess. The second is where it exercises a power in so unreasonable a manner that the exercise becomes open to review under the principles set out by Lord Greene MR in the case of *Associated Provincial Picture Houses Ltd* v *Wednesbury Corporation* (1948). The third is where it has acted contrary to what are often called the principles of natural justice. In the case of *Council of Civil Service Unions* v *Minister for the Civil Service* (1984) Lord Diplock devised a new nomenclature for each of these three grounds, calling them respectively 'illegality', 'irrationality' and 'procedural impropriety'.

By illegality as a ground for judicial review is meant that the decision maker must understand correctly the law that regulates his decision-making powers and must give effect to it. According to Lord Diplock, whether he has or not is a justiciable question to be decided, in the event of dispute, by those persons, the judges, by whom the judicial power of the state is exercisable. It is a fundamental principle of English law that no person or body should be permitted to exceed its lawful powers. The starting point for judicial review of administrative action therefore is the doctrine of ultra vires founded upon the doctrine of parliamentary sovereignty. Administrative authorities must be restrained from exceeding their powers and inferior tribunals must be prevented from exceeding the limits of their jurisdiction.

Ultra vires may be classified as being either substantive or procedural. Substantive ultra vires occurs where an administrative authority acts in excess of its statutory powers or in excess of its jurisdiction. As regards excess of power, it is the role of the court, by examining the parent Act, to determine the extent of the specific powers conferred upon the administrative authority by Parliament and ensure that those powers are not exceeded, an example being the case of *Attorney-General* v *Fulham Corporation* (1921). As for excess of jurisdiction, all administrative authorities have limited jurisdictions. Where an authority acts in excess of its jurisdiction as laid down in the parent Act, its acts will be ultra vires and void.

Procedural ultra vires occurs where a statute not only creates a body to perform some task on behalf of the executive but in so doing also lays down a procedure that the body should follow in performing its functions. Where a procedural requirement is laid down in the parent Act, for example consultation with interested parties or the giving of notice, failure on the part of the administrative authority to follow that prescribed procedure may, depending upon the nature of the requirement, result in its decision being ultra vires.

The second ground for judicial review envisaged by Lord Diplock, that of 'irrationality', applies in his Lordship's view to a decision which is so outrageous in its defiance of logic or of accepted moral standards that no sensible person who had applied his mind to the question to be decided could have arrived at it. It is of course implied by the courts as a matter of statutory construction that Parliament did not intend the powers it has conferred upon an administrative authority to be abused and in particular the courts will always imply that Parliament did not intend the administrative authority to act unreasonably and will therefore render administrative action ultra vires. However, unreasonableness is a subjective concept and opinions can vary as to whether a particular decision is reasonable or not. Judicial review is concerned with the legality of decisions not their merits. The courts therefore have given the word 'unreasonable' a somewhat specialised meaning in the context of administrative law. According to Lord Greene MR in the case of *Associated Provincial Picture Houses Ltd* v *Wednesbury Corporation* (above) a decision may be ultra vires if it can be proved to be unreasonable in the sense that the court considers it to be a decision which no reasonable body could take. He said that a decision would be unreasonable if it failed to observe certain principles. A person entrusted with a discretion must direct himself properly in law. He must call his attention to the matters which he is bound to consider. Finally he must exclude from his consideration matters which are irrelevant to what he has to consider.

A growing number of decisions seem to illustrate that the courts are now willing to invalidate administrative action on the grounds that there is an absence of evidence to justify it. Also if a power is granted to an administrative authority for one purpose, it cannot be used to fulfil another purpose, the case of *Congreve* v *Home Office* (1976) being an example. The failure to exercise a discretionary power will also be ground for review. If an administrative authority upon which a power has been conferred delegates the right to exercise that power to another body, or fetters itself in the free exercise of that power, then its actions will be construed by the court as ultra vires and void. Fraud or bad faith will also render a decision open to review.

Lord Diplock described his third head on which administrative action is subject to control by judicial review as 'procedural impropriety'. His Lordship includes in this not only the failure to observe basic rules of natural justice but also the failure by an administrative tribunal to observe procedural rules that are expressly laid down in the legislative instrument by which its jurisdiction is conferred.

The rule that certain powers must be exercised in accordance with natural justice is one of the most important principles of judicial review of administrative action. The traditional view of natural justice is that it comprises two procedural rules. Firstly the rule that no man is to be condemned without a hearing. A person is entitled to notice of the case he has to meet and must be afforded a fair opportunity to answer the case against him and to present his own cause. People affected by judicial and administrative decisions have a right that the decision-maker should be impartial. Natural justice will therefore be breached where the person taking a decision has an interest in the case or where the person taking the decision is biased. Recently a third limb of natural justice has appeared, the so-called duty to act fairly. In many respects this duty encompasses both of the traditional rules, but it may possibly apply to a wider range of decisions. The precise requirements of natural justice will vary with the circumstances of each case, such as the nature of the decision being taken, the status and interest of the applicant, etc.

SUGGESTED ANSWER TO QUESTION THREE

General Comment

This question requires detailed knowledge of the way in which judicial review cases have operated to distinguish between these differing forms of powers. A general discussion of judicial review will not be perceived as answering the question accurately. The student must be careful to structure the answer between the two sides to the question and to introduce some detailed discussion of case law.

Key Points

- Prerogative powers
  - *CCSU* v *Minister for the Civil Service*
  - *BBC* v *Johns*
  - *Malone* v *Metropolitan Police Commissioner*
- Statute
  - *Ridge* v *Baldwin*
  - *Wednesbury* case
- Non-justiciable prerogatiove powers - *Rees-Mogg* case

Suggested Answer

The prerogative is that body of powers and immunities of the Crown which is residual and which is now largely exercised by the government. The prerogative itself derives from the common law and therefore can be fettered or abolished by statute. The review of the prerogative power is, however, comparatively recent.

Before the decision in *Council of Civil Service Unions* v *Minister for the Civil Service* (1984) (the GCHQ case), the courts restricted their review of the prerogative powers to the existence and extent of prerogative. However, the modern approach is to review the validity of purported prerogative powers. In *BBC* v *Johns* (1965) it was confirmed that only those powers recognised by the common law would be upheld in the courts. Famously, Diplock LJ held that 'it was 350 years and a civil war too late for the Queen's courts to broaden the prerogative'. In *Malone* v *Metropolitan Police Commissioner* (1979), the court recognised the right of the Crown to intercept postal communications as part of the prerogative.

The traditional view would consider first whether or not the act complained of was an exercise of the prerogative. If the act was found to be such an exercise of power, the courts would decline the jurisdiction to challenge its use. The modern view permits review of an exercise of prerogative power in certain circumstances.

The House of Lords in *Gouriet* v *Union of Post Office Workers* (1978) rejected a contention that a decision of the Attorney-General not to lend his name to proceedings against a trade union could be reviewed by the courts. In so doing, the House of Lords overturned a decision of Lord Denning in the Court of Appeal which had found the court competent to review that decision. In *Laker Airways Ltd* v *Department of Trade* (1977) Lord Denning argued similarly that the courts could interfere where the executive exercised prerogative powers improperly.

Subsequently, the GCHQ case came before the House of Lords. The facts of the case arose from a decision by the Prime Minister to ban trade unions from the Government Communication Headquarters at Cheltenham. This decision was taken without any prior consultation. The applicant trade union sought judicial review of the decision as an exercise of the government's prerogative powers.

The House of Lords decided that because a power exercised in the sphere of public law was derived from the common law, that did not mean it should be immune from review. Lord Diplock held that judicial review had developed to the extent where one could classify the grounds for review under three heads: illegality, irrationality, procedural impropriety.

The right to review the power, however, was qualified. Where the decision was made with reference to the defence of the realm, it would not be reviewable. Therefore, the extent to which the prerogative can be reviewed by the courts is similar to executive acts based upon statutory sources. As in *R* v *Secretary of State for the Home Department, ex parte Hosenball* (1977), there are principles of public policy which will be applied to the review of a power exercised by the executive, whether that is a statutory or a prerogative power.

Where the courts are considering issues of statutory interpretation, the scope of the decision will be governed more specifically by the terms of the statute itself. In *Ridge* v *Baldwin* (1964) the Brighton police committee had dismissed their chief constable after he faced conspiracy charges. The Police Act 1964 laid down a procedure for dismissal in these circumstances. The House of Lords considered the extent of this statutory power, finding that 'inasmuch as the decision was arrived at in complete disregard of the regulations it must be disregarded as void and of no effect'.

In addition to statutory construction, common law requires that statutory powers are exercised 'reasonably' in the sense of lawfully, fairly and rationally: *Associated Provincial Picture Houses Ltd* v *Wednesbury Corporation* (1948). It may be that such review is more difficult to undertake in regard to some types of prerogative decisions, which may involve high level policy judgments more suitable for challenge in the political arena of Parliament that in the courts of law, eg the signing of the Maastricht Treaty: *R* v *Secretary of State for Foreign and Commonwealth Affairs, ex parte Rees-Mogg* (1994).

Therefore, the difference between the review of the two types of power is contained in the approach of the court to the nature of the subject-matter of the power.

SUGGESTED ANSWER TO QUESTION FOUR

General Comment

Essentially the question requires detailed conceptual analysis of judicial review. Do the grounds for review undermine sovereignty and legitimate executive discretion? There is a wealth of case law available to illustrate the discussion, but it is probably sensible to concentrate on two or three leading cases in order to demonstrate depth of knowledge and research. This is an area which requires specialist study and a student will fail if he or she indulges in general waffle or superficial analysis. Reference should be made in the solution to specialist texts or articles in order to satisfy the examiner that the student has looked at appropriate sources.

Key Points

- The 'red light' and 'green light' concepts of judicial review explained and defined
- Reasons for the predominance of the green light approach among the judiciary
- The established grounds of review and their emphasis on procedure rather than substance
- Lord Denning's attempts to broaden the scope of judicial review in defence of individuals
- Jurisdictional error
- Proportionality
- Conclusions

Suggested Answer

The rapid development of the principles of judicial review over the last 40 years has been marked by a continuing debate as to how far judges should go in controlling the exercise of administrative discretion and in protecting the rights of citizens against the ever-growing power of the state. Those who subscribe to the 'red light' theory of judicial review contend that judges must become activist in putting a stop to the misuse of executive power, so that grounds of judicial review should be drawn liberally and widely to encompass not only all sources of state or public power but also to permit examination of the content and manner of public decision-making. Those who subscribe to the 'green light' theory argue that judges must respect parliamentary delegation of executive discretion even where it is couched in very wide terms; in this way judges would be giving the go-ahead to the executive to provide community services in an efficient and effective manner. (The 'red light' and 'green light' theories are propounded by Harlow and Rawlings, *Law and Administration* (1997, 2nd ed).)

When one examines judgments in some of the leading cases of judicial review in the last four decades it is apparent that the majority of judges have followed a 'green light' approach and consequently adopted a carefully restricted role for judicial review, probably because of their sensitivity to the delicate constitutional relationship between Parliament, the executive and the judiciary. Respect for parliamentary sovereignty and the separate functions of administrator and judge have deterred judges from entangling themselves in what in essence are political or administrative decisions dressed up in legal clothing. Such an approach has been criticised as too timid in defence of individual rights by red light theorists, but it has been applauded by Diceyan followers of the Rule of Law, sovereignty and the traditional constitutional boundaries between law and politics.

Typical of the green light approach is Lord Brightman's dictum that 'judicial review is concerned not with the decision but with the decision-making process ... unless that restriction on the power of the court is observed, the court will ... under the guise of preventing the abuse of power be itself guilty of usurping power': *R* v *Chief Constable of North Wales Police, ex parte Evans* (1982).

The established classification of the grounds of judicial review (procedural impropriety, illegality and irrationality: per Lord Diplock in the GCHQ case - *Council of Civil Service Unions* v *Minister for the Civil Service* (1984)) therefore puts the emphasis on review of procedural decision-making rather than the merits, policy or wisdom of the decisions themselves. As one distinguished lawyer commented:

> '... "substance" may be said to be "hands off"; "procedure" is definitely "hands on". This distinction reflects a constitutional awareness that the power and responsibility of making decisions on their merits is given by Parliament not to the courts but to the Executive ... Interference with substantive decisions usurps the democratic element in our constitution': John Laws [1989] PL 27 at 29.

Such an approach can be further supported by the argument that other checks exist on the exercise of political and executive power which may be more appropriate than the formal judicial process, eg MPs and the Select Committee system; Ombudsmen; tribunals and inquiries, etc. However, red light theorists contend that there can be no substitute for independent judicial review as a safeguard for the citizen against misuse of public power and discretion, and among the minority of judges who subscribed to this view probably the most famous was Lord Denning when Master of the Rolls in the period 1962–82. Some of his judgments became landmarks for their attempts to widen the scope of judicial review into (from some perspectives) almost an appellate process. Some of the landmarks did not stand for long, eg his attempt to abolish the distinction between jurisdictional error of law and error of fact made by courts of law, such as the High Court and county courts: rebuffed by the House of Lords in *Re Racal*

Communications Ltd (1980), which restated and explained the law on excess of jurisdiction laid down by *Anisminic Ltd* v *Foreign Compensation Commission* (1969).

Other Denning judgments lasted longer, eg his use of the concept of proportionality as part of the traditional test of total unreasonableness to strike down a grossly excessive penalty imposed on a market trader in *R* v *Barnsley Metropolitan Borough Council, ex parte Hook* (1976). In the GCHQ case Lord Diplock, in reformulating the test of unreasonableness under the test of irrationality, had doubts as to whether a test of proportionality would one day become part of English law. Those doubts were dispelled to some degree by some robust judgments in *R* v *Secretary of State for the Home Department, ex parte Brind* (1991), which upheld reporting restrictions imposed by the Government on media interviews with supporters of the Irish Republican Army. Lords Ackner and Lowry rejected a test of proportionality because it would transform judicial review into an appellate process: judges were not equipped by training, experience or expert knowledge to determine whether a Minister or other public official had stuck a proper balance, unless the decision was so grossly out of balance as to be irrational. But red light critics of such reasoning would point to the risks to freedom of the press created in the *Brind* case by apparent judicial reluctance to test the quality of the decision against, for example, the international standards set by the European Convention on Human Rights. The two Law Lords had taken, perhaps, an unduly restrictive approach to use of the Convention in the area of executive discretion that compares unfavourably to their more liberal use of the Convention in the areas of ambiguous statutory construction or ambiguous common law. The other three Law Lords were less hostile to the possible future introduction of proportionality as a test for review.

So, until Parliament incorporates the European Convention into English law (likely in 1998), it seems as if judges will continue to use judicial review as a process in which they may blow the whistle when the ball goes out of play but desist from taking part in the game or from telling the players how to play when the game restarts: per Lawton LJ in *Laker Airways Ltd* v *Department of Trade* (1977).

SUGGESTED ANSWER TO QUESTION FIVE

General Comment

Give an introduction as to the development and purpose of administrative law (use as much case law as possible). Comment on the areas where administrative law will not enter.

Key Points

- Introduction (administrative law, explanation of ouster clauses)
- Subjectively worded powers (*Padfield* v *Minister of Agriculture*)
- Time limit ouster clauses (*R* v *Secretary of State for the Environment, ex parte Ostler*)
- *Anisminic* type clauses (*Anisminic* and *Re Racal Communications Ltd*)
- Conclusion

Suggested Answer

Administrative law is the law relating to the control of governmental power, and in particular with the legal controls upon the exercise of those powers by subordinate administrative authorities. Judicial review is the means whereby the courts achieve this control. In reviewing administrative action the court is not so much concerned with the merits of an actual decision but rather with the process by which that decision was reached.

At one stage the court's control could, it was thought, be avoided by the use either of subjectively worded powers in a statute or by the insertion of an ouster or privative clause removing the courts' jurisdiction. Nowadays the courts apply various principles where a subjectively worded power is at issue in order to assess whether the power has been used correctly and the various types of ouster clauses have generally been interpreted narrowly by the courts.

An example of a subjectively worded power would be one where 'if the minister thinks fit ...' he may carry out an action or 'in the minister's discretion' he may .... Nowadays there is no doubt that in such cases the courts will review the exercise of such a power by a minister or other public authority to ensure that he has acted reasonably. They will consider, inter alia, such factors as the following – whether the statute is being used for the correct or merely an ulterior purpose, whether the relevant matters have been taken into account in making a decision and the irrelevant ones discounted, whether there has been bad faith, whether the rules of natural justice (if applicable) have been applied, whether the authority has reached a decision that no reasonable authority could make. There is no exhaustive list of these rules and many cases could equally well be explained as falling foul of several of the rules enumerated above.

In *Padfield* v *Minister of Agriculture* (1968) a subjectively worded power that a committee of investigation would investigate 'if the minister in any case so directs' was at issue. The minister's refusal to place a complaint by milk producers before such a committee was reviewed by the court because the minister had failed to carry out the purposes of the Act.

This modern view of the law can be contrasted with older cases such as *Liversidge* v *Anderson* (1942) where the court refused to intervene in the detention of a person under a power given to the Home Secretary during the Second World War to detain persons he believed to be of hostile origins or associations.

Ouster clauses may be found in several main forms. First clauses which impose a time limit (usually six weeks) outside which no appeal or application for review may be made and second clauses which provide that the decision of a body 'shall be final and shall not be called in question in any court of law'. These clauses are treated differently.

The time limit clauses are frequently used in statutes in areas such as compulsory purchase and town and country planning where many are affected by a decision. In these circumstances it is obviously important that a decision is rapidly reached and cannot after many months be set aside and therefore the courts have taken the view that the time limit clause should stand and no challenge be allowed at a later date, even where the complainant at the time time of the decision could not have known of the factor which, it is alleged, has tainted the decision. In *R* v *Secretary of State for the Environment ex parte Ostler* (1977), Ostler discovered that a decision taken many months before had been made by giving undisclosed assurances to certain objectors which affected his interests. He attempted to challenge the decision outside the six week limit. He failed, the court upholding the time limit.

The second type of ouster clause, commonly called an *Anisminic* clause, has caused much controversy in its treatment by the courts. In *Anisminic Ltd* v *Foreign Compensation Commission* (1969) the Foreign Compensation Act 1950 provided that the decision of the Commission (a tribunal) should be final and should not be called into question in any court of law. When the Commission under a mistake of law withheld compensation from Anisminic, Anisminic applied for judicial review. Anisminic was successful in the House of Lords. The Lords took the view that a clause of this type could prevent review by the court where the decision making body had remained within its jurisdiction but where it had exceeded its jurisdiction the clause would not prevent review. Since the tribunal was a lay body it would not have been intended by Parliament that they should decide the legal effect of words and actions, therefore a mistake of law took the Commission beyond its jurisdiction and the ouster clause did not operate to prevent review.

During the early part of the 1970s the Court of Appeal seemed to be taking the view that any mistake of law made by a decision making body of any type, which led it to reach a decision wrong in the eyes of the court, would take the body beyond its jurisdiction so that a clause attempting to oust review would fail to work. However this attitude was dealt a decisive blow by the House of Lords in *Re Racal Communications Ltd* (1981). In that case a High Court judge was empowered under the Companies Act 1948 to order the production of management accounts etc upon certain conditions being shown. There was in the Act a provision to the effect that his decision was 'not appealable'. He refused to order the production owing to what was alleged was a mistake of law and the Court of Appeal allowed an appeal but the House of Lords reversed the Court of Appeal.

Effectively the clear wording of this type of ouster clause prevented any challenge. Further, it could be presumed that Parliament intended this result in view of the status of a High Court judge.

To summarise the effect of these decisions one can state that an Anisminic ouster clause prevents review of a decision made within jurisdiction but not of one made outside jurisdiction. It may be very difficult to decide what mistake is jurisdictional in effect but where one is dealing with lay bodies, such as tribunals the courts seem to be prepared to treat any mistakes of law as taking them outside jurisdiction whereas, should the decision maker be a judge, his mistakes of law may, or may not, take him beyond his jurisdiction depending upon their gravity: see further *R* v *Lord President of the Council, ex parte Page* (1993).

SUGGESTED ANSWER TO QUESTION SIX

General Comment

This question allows a review of natural justice authorities, with a fairly general discussion.

Key Points

- Definition
- The development of natural justice
- Duty to act fairly
- Audi alteram partem
- Nemo iudex in causa sua
- Different tests: 'reasonable suspicion', 'real likelihood' and 'real danger'

Suggested Answer

Natural justice is an aspect of procedural impropriety. It is one of the principles of administrative law that certain powers must be exercised in accordance with natural justice. However, as with the curate's egg, it depends how you look at the problem with which you are dealing. There are too many variables to allow a precise and uniform code of procedure and this has led to inconsistencies in approach. Whether that is inevitable is another matter.

While natural justice has a long history, its modern development stems from the case of *Ridge* v *Baldwin* (1964) that the House of Lords applied the rules of natural justice to administrative functions, rather than judicial ones, the test being what was at stake for the individual whose rights were being affected by the decision. It is significant - in terms of this discussion - that Lord Reid made the point that the application of the rules varied, depending upon the nature of the dispute in question.

The emphasis upon an overriding principle of natural justice as opposed to a precise code is shown in the case of *Re HK (An Infant)* (1967). While the rules - discussed below - may be applied in certain situations, there is also a duty to act fairly. While this duty may be implied in subsequent judgments rather than expressed, it might explain inconsistent application of the rules.

The first of the rules is the right to a fair hearing: audi alteram partem. There are various aspects of this rule, so one might take two areas as examples. Firstly, a person has the right to notice of the case against them. For example, in *Glynn* v *Keele University* (1971), a student was fined for breaching university rules without being told why or being given a hearing. This was a breach of the rule, although for other reasons, no remedy was given - a reminder of the discretionary nature of remedies. Secondly, there is the right to make representations. This is a more difficult area, because the court may be dealing with a body that determines its own procedures or be in a situation where representations will be futile. For example, in *Cinnamond* v *British Airports Authority* (1980), car-hire drivers who had been flouting the law received little sympathy from the court. However, a reluctance to apply the rules of natural justice, rather than to apply them but find other reasons for denying a remedy - while it may amount to the same thing - weakens the principle.

The other rule of natural justice is that no man should be a judge in his own cause: nemo iudex in causa sua. The clearest statement of the dangers when someone sitting in judgment has an interest is in *Dimes* v *Grand Junction Canal Proprietors* (1852), where the Lord Chancellor's involvement as a shareholder and trustee in the canal company led to his decrees in the case being set aside. No allegation of partiality was made, but the existence of the interest was sufficient. This is a more straightforward breach for the courts to consider and allows the courts to be more consistent.

Another aspect of this rule - and a harder one for the courts - is the question of bias. In *R* v *Sussex Justices, ex parte McCarthy* (1924), Hewart LCJ said, 'Nothing is to be done which creates even a suspicion that there has been an improper interference with the course of justice'. The test has been seen in two ways: either that there is a reasonable suspicion of bias or that there is a real likelihood of bias. The reasonable suspicion test was easier to establish than the real likelihood test. The latter has now been preferred for all kinds of judicial decision-making and has been re-labelled 'the real danger of bias' test: *R* v *Gough* (1993). The test also extends to administrative decision-making: *R* v *Secretary of State for the Environment, ex parte Kirkstall Valley Campaign Ltd* (1996).

In conclusion, this brief survey of natural justice shows the difficulties that the courts face. The nature of the cases leads to an uneven application of the rules, but that is because concepts such as fairness and bias are harder to apply evenly. However, the principles are long-established and it is doubtful if they could ever be applied uniformly, given the diversity of the subject matter.

SUGGESTED ANSWER TO QUESTION SEVEN

General Comment

A relatively simple and straightforward problem question concerning judicial review of administrative action. As with all problem questions the relevant issues should be identified. Then simply work through the problem logically discussing each point in the light of the relevant authorities.

Key Points

- Introduction: public law remedy - application for judicial review under O.53; the requirement of locus standi.
- The mini-bus service running from Redvale to Blacktown: possibility of substantive ultra vires; whether necessarily incidental to achieving the main purpose of the statute.
- The daily coach service within Redvale provided by Henry: possibility of a breach of natural justice; the rule against bias; whether family relationship amounts to an interest; the right to be told the reasons for a decision.
- The weekly mini-bus service to a shopping centre in Redvale: possibility of a breach

of natural justice; whether procedural ultra vires; improper purpose or unreasonable exercise of discretion.

Suggested Answer

As this case concerns the public law functions of a public law body, John must, if he wishes to attack the legality of the decisions to grant the subsidies, apply for judicial review under O.53 Rules of the Supreme Court: *O'Reilly* v *Mackman* (1982). Firstly, however, John will have to obtain leave of the court to apply for judicial review. Accordingly his application must, generally speaking, be made promptly, and in any event within three months from the date when grounds for the application first arose and he must establish the necessary locus standi. In this respect the order provides that the court shall not grant leave unless it considers that the applicant has a sufficient interest in the matter to which the application relates.

Regarding locus standi, the courts have been careful not to give restrictive interpretations to the meaning of sufficient interest. It remains in each case a question of fact and law to be determined in the light of all the circumstances of the case and should usually be considered together with the substantive legal merit of the applicant's case: see *IRC* v *National Federation of Self-Employed and Small Business* (1982). The fact that John is a council tax payer may give him a sufficient interest in the granting of subsidies. Also the fact that he is a mini-bus owner who applied unsuccessfully to provide a service within Redvale may also give him a suffient interest to challenge the award of subsidies to those operators who were successful in their applications.

With regard to the mini-bus service running from Redvale to Blacktown, John may be able to challenge this on the grounds that in providing the subsidy for this service the authority is acting ultra vires.

It is a fundamental principle of English law that no person or body should be permitted to exceed its lawful powers. Parliament, by statute, confers powers upon subordinate administrative authorities and these subordinate authorities can only do that which Parliament has authorised them to do in the parent statute. All acts of administrative authorities must therefore, in general, be justified by reference to some statutory power. Accordingly the courts must ensure that subordinate administrative authorities only do that which Parliament, in the relevant Act, has authorised them to do. If an authority exceeds its statutory powers, then the courts must declare its actions to be ultra vires. Where, for example, an administrative authority has acted in excess of its statutory powers or in excess of its jurisdiction this may amount to substantive ultra vires. In such cases it is the role of the court, by examining the parent Act, to determine the extent of the specific powers conferred upon the administrative authority by Parliament and ensure that those powers are not exceeded. If they are, then the actions of the authority will be ultra vires: *Attorney-General* v *Fulham Corporation* (1921).

In the present case for consideration the Rural Mini-Buses Act provides that each District Council shall have the duty to subsidise such mini-bus services *within its area* as it shall consider necessary in the interests of the community. The parent statute therefore authorises the Council to subsidise mini-bus services within Redvale District. Prima facie therefore, in subsidising a minibus service to Blacktown, which is outside

Redvale District, the Council is exceeding its statutory powers and acting ultra vires. However in such cases the courts do have a discretion and may allow acts which although themselves are not directly authorised in the parent statute are nevertheless considered to be necessarily incidental to achieving that which is authorised in the Act: see *Westminster Corporation* v *London and North Western Railway* (1905). The subsidy of the service to Blacktown may fall into this class. Blacktown may for example be a major local shopping centre used by the people of Redvale and the provision of the subsidy for what may be an important local service may be considered an integral part of the Council's public transport policy for Redvale. However it can also be argued that as all District Councils are under a duty to provide such subsidies, the District Council for Blacktown should also contribute to the service if it is considered to be necessary in the interests of the community.

Regarding the daily coach service within Redvale provided by Henry, this may also be ultra vires. Although the service is provided within Redvale it involves a coach and the Act specifically refers to mini-buses. This particular subsidy may also be challenged on the ground that it was granted in breach of natural justice as Henry is the brother of Ivan, the Chairman of the Council. It is one of the most important principles of judicial review of administrative action that certain powers must be exercised in accordance with natural justice. Traditionally natural justice comprises two procedural rules; firstly the rule that no man is to be condemned without a hearing and, secondly, that no man should sit as a judge in his own cause. Since *Ridge* v *Baldwin* (1964) a third limb of natural justice has appeared, the so-called duty to act fairly.

The rule that no man should be a judge in his own cause requires that people affected by judicial and administrative decisions have a right that the decision maker should be impartial. No one should be a judge in a matter in which he is interested. The rule is not limited to pecuniary interest. As in the case of *Metropolitan Properties Ltd* v *Lannon* (1969) other interests, such as professional or family interests, may also invalidate a determination. It is necessary to show a 'real danger of bias': *R* v *Gough* (1993).

Although *R* v *Gough* was concerned with judicial decisions the 'real danger of bias' test also applies to purely administrative decisions: *R* v *Secretary of State for the Environment, ex parte Kirkstall Valley Campaign Ltd* (1996).

We are not told what part, if any, Ivan played in the award of the subsidy to the coach service operated by his brother Henry. If he did not participate at all, then all well and good. But if, as Chairman of the Council, Ivan did participate in the decision to award the subsidy, his relationship with Henry undoubtedly amounts to an interest of a kind likely to raise a 'real danger of bias' in the mind of the reasonable man. The suspicion of irregularity in the award of this subsidy is further aroused by the fact that John's offer was cheaper than that of Henry. In such circumstances the decision to award the subsidy to Henry may be ultra vires.

As regards the failure to give a reason for this rejection, generally speaking the right to be heard does not require the giving of reasons to a mere applicant, but under the circumstances because John's livelihood may be affected by the decision he may have a legitimate expectation that reasons be given for the decision. In view of John's interest the failure to give reasons may also be a breach of the requirement of fairness. This also therefore may amount to a breach of natural justice: *McInnes* v *Onslow-Fane* (1978).

Similarly, the decision to subsidise a weekly mini-bus service to a shopping centre in Redvale which is used almost exclusively by senior citizens who are Ivan's constituents may also breach natural justice. If Ivan participated in the decision to award this subsidy, the fact that it benefits a section of the community on whom Ivan relies for his continuance in office may breach the rule against bias. It is doubtful however that this particular subsidy is ultra vires. The parent statute places the Council under a duty to subsidise certain mini-bus services within its district but it has a discretion in that it need only make a subsidy where it is considered necessary to do so in the interests of the community. Where such a discretion is conferred on an authority the courts require, inter alia, that the discretion will be exercised for its proper purpose, ie that purpose envisaged by Parliament when it passed the parent Act, and that the discretion will be exercised reasonably.

In the present case whatever Ivan's real motive may be it is almost certain that the provision of transport to take old people shopping is one envisaged by Parliament as being in the interests of the community and it is also reasonable in the sense that it is a decision which a reasonable body would have taken: *Associated Provincial Picture Houses Ltd* v *Wednesbury Corporation* (1948).

SUGGESTED ANSWER TO QUESTION EIGHT

General Comment

A question requiring consideration of four aspects of the ultra vires principle, the rule against delegation, irrational selection policy, estoppel, and natural justice. The rubric accompanying the question does not specifically invite discussion of whether the matters in question should be challenged by way of writ or an application for judicial review, so it is suggested that a discussion of the public/private dichotomy is not required here.

Key Points

- The rule against delegation
- No abdication of power
- Irrational basis for selection
- Extent to which the University is bound by the unilateral undertaking
- Whether any breaches of natural justice have occurred

Suggested Answer

It is submitted that there are four grounds upon which the proceedings outlined in the above question might have involved a breach of the principles of English administrative law. Each will be considered in turn.

The rule against delegation

The rule against delegation, or the rule against sub-delegation as it should perhaps be described, operates to ensure that power is exercised by the body in whom it has been vested.

If, for example, a tribunal has been empowered under statute to determine claims for a benefit of some sort, and in the absence of any express power to do so it delegates this function to some other organisation, a violation of the ultra vires principle will occur, since a body which has not been properly empowered to act will in fact be taking the decisions. Prima facie the delegation of the task of selecting students, by the Sub-Dean for Admissions, to a secretary, would appear to be a violation of the rule against delegation, since it involves a sub-delegation of powers vested in the Sub-Dean by the University.

However, it could be contended that the facts under consideration do not involve delegation of a decision making function, but merely the use of an agent ie the secretary, by the Sub-Dean. Such an argument might meet with approval in the courts provided the ultimate decision making power still rests with the Sub-Dean, and also the responsibility for the decisions made; compare *Ellis* v *Dubowski* (1921) with *Mills* v *LCC* (1925)

Generally, it is submitted that the key question is not whether the Sub-Dean can delegate tasks to her secretary, but whether this particular type of task can be delegated. As suggested above, the act of delegation itself, might be more properly challenged on the ground of irrationality (considered below).

Irrational basis of selection

The decision of the Sub-Dean to select university entrants on the basis of their 'O' Level grades could be impugned upon the ground that it involves the over-rigid application of an irrational policy. Administrative agencies are permitted to exercise discretion according to policies, in order to achieve fairness and consistency, but this must not result in the exercise of discretion becoming 'straight-jacketed' by the policy, and the policy itself must be sound. The facts of the question suggest that the policy of referring to applicant's 'O' Level grades is being applied with considerable rigidity. This could be challenged on the basis that the university has 'shut its ears' to applicants who, despite poor 'O' Level grades, might have 'something new to say'; see *R* v *Port of London Authority, ex parte Kynoch* (1919). Against this, it has to be recognised that the Sub-Dean is dealing with a large number of applications, and in such circumstances the House of Lords has recognised that the adoption of a policy may be desirable, so that the administrative machinery can operate more efficiently; see *British Oxygen Ltd* v *Minister of Technology* (1971). Perhaps a stronger ground of challenge is that the policy itself is unreasonable or irrational. A complainant would have to show that the basis of selection was one that no reasonable university admissions tutor would have adopted; see *Associated Provincial Picture Houses Ltd* v *Wednesbury Corporation* (1948). Alternatively, the selection process could be described as 'irrational' in the sense outlined by Lord Diplock in *Council of Civil Service Unions* v *Minister for the Civil Service* (1984), wherein his Lordship spoke of a decision being challengeable because of its defiance of logic and moral standards, being one that no sensible person who had applied his mind to the matter in issue could have arrived at.

Given that most of those applying to university will not yet have their 'A' level grades, reference to 'O' level grades may be perfectly sensible, but it is perhaps irrational to ignore such matters as references from head teachers, and the work experience of mature applicants.

Estoppel
Can the Sub-Dean lawfully withdraw her offer to deal with enquiries from all the unsuccessful applicants? It might be contended that she is estopped from going back on her unilateral undertaking, see for example *Lever Finance Ltd* v *Westminster City Council* (1971). It should be borne in mind, however, that estoppel is 'a shield not a sword', and that any party wishing to raise the issue must show that they have acted in reliance upon the undertaking. It is submitted that a better approach would be to suggest that the undertaking of the Sub-Dean to deal with disappointed applicants gave rise to a legitimate expectation on their part that they would be given a hearing, and that the refusal of any such hearing amounts to a breach of natural justice; see *Attorney-General of Hong Kong* v *Ng Yuen Shiu* (1983). In that decision the Privy Council held that where a public body makes a unilateral public statement as to the way in which it intends to act, those likely to be affected have a legitimate expectation that the undertaking will be observed, unless it would involve the public body in acting contrary to its public law powers and duties. In principle there is no reason why the sub-Dean should not be required to act according to her original undertaking, but it might be pointed out that a hearing would be unlikely to achieve any result for those applicants who have not been successful.

Breach of natural justice.
Should all 2000 applicants have been given a hearing? Natural justice does not require that an oral hearing should be given to every person whose interests are to be affected by a decision. Broad guidelines as to the treatment that should be given are provided by the decision in *McInnes* v *Onslow-Fane* (1978), wherein Megarry VC identified three types of case. First there is the 'forfeiture' case where the individual in respect of whom the decision is being made, stands to lose some existing right or privilege. Secondly, the 'legitimate expectation' case, where the individual expects to receive some benefit because of passed conduct or treatment. Thirdly there are the cases concerning 'mere applicants' who, in the words of the Vice-Chancellor, do not have any right to heard as such, but who can expect their cases to be handled in good faith, without bias or caprice. It is submitted that the present question is concerned with this latter category. Applicants are entitled to be told of information unfavourable to their case: *R* v *Gaming Board for Great Britain, ex parte Benaim and Khaida* (1970).

The failure to interview all applicants does not, therefore, constitute a breach of natural justice, especially as the rejection of an application does not cast any particular slur on the reputation of the applicant, bearing in mind that there are other institutions of higher education to which the applicants can apply. This view is further supported by *Central Council for Training in Social Work* v *Edwards* (1978), wherein it was held that an applicant for a place at a polytechnic does not have a right to an interview prior to any decision being made, but if an interview is granted it should be conducted in accordance with the rules of natural justice.

SUGGESTED ANSWER TO QUESTION NINE

General Comment

A reasonably straightforward problem question on judicial review. Such difficulty as there is lies in separating Jane's two possible challenges although there is a considerable overlap between the two. As ever, it is important in the answer to make it clear that Jane is actually being advised; do not, therefore, treat the question as a general essay. Structurally, the approach taken here is, it is submitted, appropriate for most problem questions on judicial review.

Key Points

- Public law or private law?
- Procedural matters (leave, delay and sufficient interest)
- Grounds for challenge - GCHQ (illegality, irrationality and procedural impropriety)
- Remedies
- Relevant case law (*ex parte The Aga Khan, ex parte Datafin, R* v *Lord President of the Council, ex parte Page* and *ex parte Brind*)

Suggested Answer

Jane has a number of hurdles to cross before she can apply for judicial review of the decisions of the New World University (NWU) and the University Complaints Commission (UCC). In the first place, she will need to establish that, in respect of both, her claim lies in public, rather than private, law. Second, assuming this requirement is satisfied, she will need to ensure that she satisfies the various procedural requirements. She will then have to establish the grounds on which she may challenge the decisions; and, finally, she will need to consider what remedies she seeks. It is proposed to examine each of these in their turn.

With respect, first, to the NWU, it might seem that Jane's relationship to the University is primarily contractual. Jane would have to consider whether the NWU is established by Royal Charter, rather than statute, in which case her claim would normally arise in private law under contract. If the charter provided for the resolution of disputes by a Visitor, these would probably fall within the Visitor's exclusive jurisdiction. There is insufficient information given in the problem to be certain, but on the assumption that the NWU and its disciplinary powers find their source in statute then, as a public body discharging public functions, this could be enough to establish that Jane's claim arose in public law. With respect to the UCC, established under statute, it seems clear that, whether one adopts a 'source of power' (see, for example, *R* v *Disciplinary Committee of the Jockey Club, ex parte The Aga Khan* (1993)) or functional test (see, for example, *R* v *Panel on Take-overs and Mergers, ex parta Datafin plc* (1987)) decisions of the UCC may be said to impact on the realm of public law. It would seem, therefore, that she may apply to challenge both decisions.

Jane must be advised of the importance of compliance with procedural requirements. Thus, Jane must act without delay, since a court can refuse to grant leave to apply for judicial review, or any relief sought, if there has been undue delay in making the application; the period is three months. Second, Jane must establish that she has locus standi to challenge either or both decisions since a 'court shall not grant leave to make ... an application [for judicial review] unless it considers that the applicant has a sufficient interest in the matter to which the application relates': RSC O.53 r3(7).

Generally, whether the applicant does have sufficient interest is a matter of common sense - does the decision affect her? Some interests will be more sufficient than others - eg a financial interest in the decision taken, but no test is definitive, and it is always a matter of all the facts and circumstances. Here, it would seem that Jane clearly has the requisite sufficient interest. Finally, it is important to note that the court has a discretion whether to grant leave or not. Jane may yet fall foul of this requirement, though it would seem on the facts that her claim is not without merit.

The grounds on which a challenge to the decision of a public body may be made were conveniently laid down by Lord Diplock in *Council of Civil Service Unions* v *Minister for the Civil Service* (1985): these are illegality, irrationality and procedural impropriety. It seems from the facts that Jane's grounds of challenge are different for the two bodies and it is thus necessary to consider them separately.

With respect to the decision of the NWU, there is a suggestion here of procedural impropriety, in the sense that Jane was not represented at the hearing of her case. Under the rules of natural justice, there is a right to a fair hearing (audi alteram partem). There is a variety of matters of which courts take account in deciding whether a hearing is fair, including adequate notice, oral hearings, a right to legal representation and the requirement of reasons. It always depends on all the facts and circumstances whether a hearing is fair. Given that we are told Jane was 'not represented' (which may mean either she was not actually present or, while present, she was denied legal representation), it would seem arguable that either constitutes a breach of the rules of natural justice. In *R* v *Lord President of the Council, ex parte Page* (1993) the House of Lords held that, even in the case of a university established under charter, a Visitor's decisions could be challenged by way of judicial review for procedural impropriety.

It is also possible that a challenge might lie in the sense that the punishment imposed - expulsion - was disproportionate to the nature of the alleged offence. While it is unlikely following the decision of the House of Lords in *R* v *Secretary of State for the Home Department, ex parte Brind* (1991) that proportionality is a separate head of review, it is still arguable that the decision could be categorised as irrational in the sense of *Wednesbury* unreasonableness: *Associated Provincial Picture Houses Ltd* v *Wednesbury Corporation* (1948).

A challenge to the decision of the UCC refusing to investigate Jane's claim could lie on the grounds that in misinterpreting the phrase 'academic matters' in the Education Act 1997, the UCC has made an error of law in deciding that it does not have jurisdiction. In *Page* (above), the House of Lords explained that, where Parliament has conferred a decision-making function on a public body, this could only have been done 'on the basis that it was to be exercised on the correct legal basis: a misdirection in law in making the decision therefore rendered the decision ultra vires'. Whether or not Jane may succeed on this ground will depend on whether or not disciplinary matters fall within the meaning of 'academic matters' in the Act. It is impossible to say what a court might decide here, but Jane has at least an arguable case.

Finally, it remains to consider the remedies that might be available to Jane. The most appropriate remedies would be certiorari to quash the decision of the NWU expelling Jane. Certiorari would also seem to be the most appropriate remedy vis-à-vis the UCC, requiring it to reconsider Jane's complaint.

In conclusion, Jane may well be able to challenge the decisions of both the NWU and the UCC. Whether or not she will be successful in her challenge will depend on all the facts and circumstances of her case.

SUGGESTED ANSWER TO QUESTION TEN

General Comment

A detailed question requiring reference to several different grounds for review. It is suggested that the procedural matters be mentioned at the outset, and the possible grounds of review considered in turn. It is important to use case law to illustrate the points made.

Key Points

- Procedural matters
- Abuse of power
- Delegation
- Bias
- Fettering discretion
- Failure to give press notice
- Failure to notify residents
- Improperly constituted meeting
- Intermingling of functions

Suggested Answer

Mr and Mrs Jones would be advised to seek judicial review of the local authority's decision to adopt the Fitt recommendations.

Under O.53 RSC they would be regarded as having sufficient interest in the matter to which the application relates, and thus should be regarded as having locus standi. They should ensure that they make their application without delay, and in any event within three months of the impugned decision. The following outlines the grounds upon which they could seek review of the decision, and request an order of certiorari which if granted would have the effect of quashing it.

a The power under the Act is to close a right of way to develop the land for motor traffic. On this basis can the power be used to develop routes for two-wheeled traffic only? Even if it can, is it a reasonable decision to make? The discretion must be exercised with regard to the duty imposed upon the authority by s1 of the Act to protect and maintain existing rights of way. A general ground of challenge might be that the authority is failing to have regard to the aims and objects of the legislation under which it purports to act: *Padfield* v *Minister of Agriculture* (1968).

b The planning committee delegated the function of investigating the feasibility of the cycle route scheme to Mr Fitt. Local authorities do have the power to delegate functions under s101 Local Government Act 1972, provided they reserve to themselves the right to exercise those functions if they so wish. The problem with appointing Mr Fitt to exercise this function is that he has a vested interest in the proposed routes being approved. It may be alleged that there is an appearance of bias. Given that the function in question is classified as administrative, the test to be applied, on the basis of *Steeples* v *Derbyshire County Council* (1985), would be to ask whether the interest in the matter amounted to an unlawful fetter on the exercise of discretion by the local authority. If the answer were in the affirmative, the subsequent proceedings may have been vitiated. It had been thought that the additional test for bias was not appropriate for this kind of administrative decision-making, but in *R* v *Secretary of State for the Environment, ex parte Kirkstall Valley Campaign Ltd* (1996) Sedley J said that the unlawful fettering of discretion was a distinct and separate ground of review and should not be a substitute for a test of bias in this area. Accordingly, he extended the 'real danger of bias' test laid down for judicial decisions (*R* v *Gough* (1993)) to administer decisions. This would strengthen the challenge in the present case since Mr Fitt's involvement would appear to give rise to a real danger of bias.

c The statute requires three months notice to be given in the local press. This seems not to have been complied with.

In *R* v *Swansea City Council, ex parte Quietlynn* (1983) the local authority was required to give notice in the local press of the introduction of a licensing scheme for sex shops. Notice had to be given at least 28 days before the scheme was to come into effect. Certiorari was granted to quash the scheme when the local authority conceded that the time limit had not been complied with. The time limits were regarded as mandatory, as they were designed to give users of premises the opportunity of avoiding the commission of a criminal offence by applying for a licence. Relief was granted even though no prejudice had been suffered by the applicants in that case.

It is submitted that the failure of Kingshire County Council to comply with this requirement would of itself be sufficient to invalidate the whole process.

d The statute requires local residents to be consulted. This requirement has not been fully complied with. A statutory requirement of consultation is normally regarded as mandatory. Failure to comply invalidates any subsequent decision making; see *Grunwick Processing Laboratories Ltd* v *ACAS* (1978). An exception will be made where the decision making body has acted in good faith in trying to notify all those likely to be affected, and those not notified are unable to point to any prejudice suffered as a result of non-notification. In *Coney* v *Choyce* (1975), regulations required the posting of notices in the vicinity of schools which were to be re-organised under a policy of comprehensivisation. In the case of two schools, the requisite notices were not posted. It was held that the procedural requirement of giving notice had been substantially complied with, and there was no evidence of anyone suffering substantial prejudice as a result, hence the Secretary of State's action (in approving the scheme for reorganisation) was lawful.

The applicants in the present case have not been prejudiced by the failure to notify as they have heard of the decision anyway; thus normally the court might be minded to condone the authority's failure to comply with the requirement of notification. It should be remembered, however, that the authority has also failed to comply with the requirement of notice in the press, and in such circumstances the court may feel that there is not enough evidence that it was acting in good faith in trying to discharge its statutory duties.

e The decision of the planning committee appears to have been taken by the chairman acting alone. There are a number of challenges that could be brought in respect of this procedure. First, it is likely to be a breach of the authority's standing orders to proceed without a quorum of members. The lowest figure for a quorum is normally three. Secondly, the facts state that the Chairman and Mr Fitt agreed to the plan. Mr Fitt is not, on the evidence given, a member of the committee, thus should not have taken any part in its processes. Thirdly, Mr Fitt's presence at the meeting may also give rise to a real danger of bias. As the investigator and reporter he should not also be involved in the decision making process, notwithstanding that he may not even be a member of the committee; see *R* v *Barnsley Metropolitan Borough Council, ex parte Hook* (1976) .

In conclusion it is submitted that there are several grounds upon which the applicants would succeed in persuading the court to quash the decision.

9

Civil Liberties I: Freedom of Assembly and Association; Freedom of Expression; Police Powers of Arrest, Search, Seizure and Interrogation

Introduction

This chapter is concerned with certain aspects of civil liberties law, in particular those rights regarded as fundamental in a liberal, democratic society - such as the right to demonstrate peacefully, to express opinion, and not to be subjected to unreasonable or oppressive use of the powers of the state. Since this covers a very wide area it is usual for examinations in constitutional law to concentrate on freedom of speech and assembly in the context of public order law and/or national security law. Some syllabuses will also include police powers as an examinable topic, though other syllabuses, eg London University LLB External, may examine police powers in another subject such as English legal system.

Public order law is found in statutory provisions and the common law. It is essential to be familiar with ss1-5, 11-14 and 18-19 Public Order Act 1986 and with ss61-65, 68-71 and 154 Criminal Justice and Public Order Act 1994. A useful analysis of the 1986 Act can be found in an article by Bonner and Stone ([1987] PL 202) and a useful critique of the 1994 Act is given by Allen and Cooper: (1995) 58 MLR 364 at 378-389. In a typical examination paper it would be reasonable to expect at least one problem-type question testing knowledge of these statutory provisions. In addition, it may be necessary to know the scope of the offence of obstruction of the highway under s137 Highways Act 1980; the scope of the Protection from Harassment Act 1997; and the common law offences of breach of the peace and public nuisance. If an essay question is set on this area it will usually require a critical analysis of the failure of English law to give special positive protection to peaceful political demonstrators. The recent decision in *DPP* v *Jones* [1997] 2 All ER 119 (QBD) illustrates how, under s70 Criminal Justice and Public Order Act 1994, there is no legal right to hold a peaceful, non-obstructive assembly on the public highway. This decision may be said to confirm the fears held by many civil libertarians that the 1994 Act constitutes a further erosion of an already limited freedom: see Fitzpatrick and Taylor [1997] NLJ 338.

In addition to the wide range of public order laws there also exist a number of special state powers designed to deal with threats to national security. Although such questions do not appear as regularly as ones on public order law it is sensible to make a study of such statutes as the Official Secrets Acts 1911 and 1989, the Interception of Communications Act 1985 and the Prevention of Terrorism Act 1989, as well as the attitude of judges to the balancing of national security and individual rights, eg *R* v *Secretary of State for the Home Department, ex parte Hosenball* [1977] 1 WLR 766.

Whilst it is customary to test the law on freedom of expression in the context of political protests and public order law, some university syllabuses may require familiarity with common law and equitable principles regulating confidentiality of information and rights of privacy: see further Markesinis [1986] PL 67 and Wilson (1990) 53 MLR 43.

Finally, where the Constitutional Law syllabuses includes police powers, it will be reasonable to expect at least one problem-type question involving analysis of the particular powers of stop and search of persons, arrest, search and seizure on premises, interrogations of suspects (including scope of the right of silence), and the admissibility of evidence obtained illegally or unlawfully, including the special exclusionary rules on confessions. It is essential to be familiar with the provisions of the Police and Criminal Evidence Act (PACE) 1984 and the Codes of Practice issued under it. Important recent cases include: *O'Hara* v *Chief Constable of the Royal Ulster Constabulary* [1997] 1 All ER 129 (reasonable suspicion for making an arrest); *R* v *Khan (Sultan)* [1996] 3 All ER 289 (admissibility of evidence obtained by listening devices attached to a private home without owner's consent: the area is now regulated by ss91–108 Police Act 1997).

Useful recent articles include: Hunt (1997) 113 LQR 548 (discussing *O'Hara*), Carter (1997) 113 LQR 468 (discussing *Khan*), and Grevling (1997) 113 LQR 667 (discussing the admissibility of evidence under s78 PACE 1984).

Questions

INTERROGRAMS

1 Outline the scope of police powers to regulate public demonstrations under ss12 and 13 Public Order Act 1986.
2 Outline the scope of police powers to regulate public assemblies under s14 Public Order Act 1986, as amended by ss70 and 71 Criminal Justice and Public Order Act 1994.
3 Summarise the effect of the Official Secrets Act 1989 on freedom of information.
4 Outline the main safeguards for a suspect who has been arrested and taken to a police station for interrogation.
5 To what extent can illegally or unfairly obtained evidence be excluded from a trial at the discretion of the presiding judge?

QUESTION ONE

The Peace in Britain campaign organises a march to a Royal Air Force base. The marchers surround the base and in doing so block all the roads to the vicinity. They refuse to move when asked to do so by the police. Travellers, angry at the disruption to traffic, threaten to attack the marchers and to run them down.

Advise the local Chief Constable as to his powers and duties.

London University LLB Examination
(for external students) Constitutional Law June 1985 Q7

QUESTION TWO

Article 11 of the European Convention on Human Rights provides that 'Everyone has the right to peaceful assembly'.

How is this human right guaranteed in English law?

London University LLB Examination
(for external students) Constitutional Law June 1996 Q5

QUESTION THREE

To what extent, if at all, have changes to the law relating to state security curtailed freedom of expression?

London University LLB Examination
(for external students) Constitutional Law June 1989 Q7

QUESTION FOUR

'The Police and Criminal Evidence Act 1984 achieves a satisfactory balance between the interests of the community and the rights and liberties of suspects.'

Say how far you agree with this statement and support your argument by reference to the provisions of PACE and recent case law.

London University LLB Examination
(for external students) English Legal System June 1995 Q8

QUESTION FIVE

Angelo is a student of very scruffy appearance. In his spare time he is renovating an old car and yesterday bought some tools and cans of spray paint for this purpose. He was returning to his lodgings when he was stopped by Police Constable Hurd, who asked what was in his carrier bag. Despite Angelo's explanation PC Hurd took the bag and on examining its contents told Angelo that he was under arrest on suspicion of being 'connected' with a raid on Angelo's college by 'Animal Liberation' protesters who had caused considerable damage to laboratories and sprayed slogans on the buildings. PC Hurd then searched Angelo's bedroom, and found another student's lecture notes which Angelo had stolen. When he proposed to search the room of Angelo's best friend Bertie the latter pushed him away, using highly offensive language, before locking the door and refusing him entry.

Angelo has now been charged with the theft of the lecture notes and Bertie with obstructing the police.

Advise Angelo and Bertie.

London University LLB Examination
(for external students) English Legal System June 1989 Q4

QUESTION SIX

The police have been informed by London Underground security officers that two youths, Terence (aged 15) and Jonathan (aged 19) have been observed travelling on the underground system for several hours getting off at crowded stations and re-entering the system shortly afterwards. The police begin to follow Terence and Jonathan but Jonathan runs off when he sees that he is being followed.

Terence is searched and a quantity of money and a wallet with credit cards in the name of Williams are found in a bag he was carrying. A police officer tells him, 'It's obvious what you've been up to. Now you know we have to take you in and that anything you say can be used against you.'

Terence is taken to the nearest police station and is questioned for two hours. The police officer conducting the questioning tells him: 'If you simply tell us where your partner lives we will not charge you with anything serious, and you can go home.' Terence then says: 'It was all Jonathan's doing. I just carried the bag and looked out for likely people. He lifted their wallets.' The police obtain a warrant to search Jonathan's home. When they search it they find large quantities of money.

Assess the procedures involved and whether the police can offer Terence's statement in evidence.

London University LLB Examination
(for external students) English Legal System June 1994 Q8

QUESTION SEVEN

Jonathan and Trevor Bailey (two black youths aged 14 and 17) are jogging down a street with Orville Locks, a black youth association worker and keen athlete, dressed in a tracksuit. A police car pulls up and two police officers, PC Spotter and PC Quick Draw, stop them and demand to search the pack which Orville is carrying. Finding a length of lead piping and four wallets, PC Quick Draw exclaims 'Got you! No more steaming for you lot!' (Steaming is a version of mugging carried out by groups of young people dressed in training/jogging gear who run past individuals and grab their bags. Recent research known to the police had shown that 90 per cent of the individuals arrested for mugging in the past two years were black.)

Orville is taken away in a police van while Jonathan and Trevor are taken to a local police station.

After being cautioned, Jonathan and Trevor are questioned in separate rooms, with tape recorders operating. Trevor asks for a solicitor, but his request is refused. He is questioned for two hours and released. Jonathan is kept for two days and questioned extensively. Jonathan said he did not need a solicitor as that meant one more person would be present to ask him questions! On the second day the police discover that Jonathan is only 14 and bring a police typist into the room to act as an appropriate adult. Jonathan, who is crying and obviously distressed, now claims that Orville is 'always saying that he knows how to make quick money', and that 'sometimes we run into people on the street and Orville grabs their bags while we make lots of noise'.

Assess the effect of the procedures followed and whether Jonathan's statements amount to a valid confession.

London University LLB Examination
(for external students) English Legal System June 1992 Q8

Answers

ANSWERS TO INTERROGRAMS

1 By s12 Public Order Act 1986 a senior police officer may impose conditions as to the time, place or route of a public procession if he believes that serious public disorder or serious damage to property or serious disruption to the life of the community will result if the conditions are not imposed. He may also impose conditions if he believes that the purpose of the procession is to intimidate sections of the local community.

By s13 of the 1986 Act the Chief Constable for the area in question may apply to his local authority (in London, the Home Secretary) for an order prohibiting all public processions for a period up to three months. Where a local authority agrees to impose a ban the approval of the Home Secretary must also be obtained. The grounds for imposing a ban are the same as those for imposing conditions under s12, save that the Chief Constable must believe that the conditions will not be sufficient to prevent serious public disorder and that a ban on marches is therefore necessary. It is not possible to ban a specific march or type of march so that many innocent, peaceful processions might be caught by a blanket ban under s13.

2 Section 14 Public Order Act 1986 permits conditions to be imposed on public assemblies (defined as groups of at least 20 persons in places wholly or partly open to the air) on the same grounds as for imposing conditions on processions under s12 (above). In addition, the insertion of ss14A, 14B and 14C by ss70 and 71 Criminal Justice and Public Order Act 1994 enable a Chief Constable to apply to his local authority (in London, the Home Secretary) for an order banning 'trespassory assemblies' on the grounds that they may give rise either to serious disruption to the life of the community, or where the land or a building or monument on it is of historical, architectural, archaeological or scientific importance and significant damage to the land, building or monument may occur. An assembly is a trespassory one if it consists of at least 20 persons meeting in a place to which the public has no, or limited, right of access. The ban is for a maximum period of four days, and covers an area, so that peaceful, non-obstructive and static assemblies within that area may also be caught by the ban, even if they take place on a public highway within that area: *DPP* v *Jones* [1997] 2 All ER 119.

3 The Official Secrets Act 1989 protects specified categories of official information from disclosure if a certain degree of harm to the public interest is likely to result from such disclosure. For example, information relating to the defence of the realm must not be disclosed if it would damage the national interest, for example by impeding the efficiency of the armed forces. The offence will be committed if the discloser knew or could reasonably be expected to have known that the disclosure would be likely to cause such harm. There is no specific defence of disclosure in the

public interest, in contrast to American law which protects 'whistle blowers' who infringe law of secrecy in order to expose abuses of power or other activity harmful to the public interest. It is also no defence under the 1989 Act to show that the information had already been disclosed in the UK (unless the defence could show that no further harm was likely to result from further disclosure). Again this is in contrast to American law where information that comes into the 'public domain' can be freely discussed.

Liability arises under the 1989 Act for disclosure of protected information. It is no longer an offence merely to receive unauthorised official information.

4 An arrest must be based on reasonable suspicion (s24 PACE), and the arrested person must be told of the fact that he is under arrest and the reasons for the arrest (s28 PACE). He should be cautioned as to his right of silence, ie that he is not obliged to say anything but that it may harm his defence if he does not mention when questioned something which he later relies on in court, and that anything he does say might be given in evidence: Code of Practice, Code C, para 10.

When at a police station for interrogation the suspect should be placed in the special care of a 'custody officer' who is responsible for ensuring the proper treatment of the suspect and for deciding whether there is sufficient evidence to charge the suspect. The suspect is entitled to have someone informed of his arrest (s56 PACE) and to consult privately with a solicitor (s58 PACE). Under ss40–44 PACE the suspect can be detained without charge for questioning, though reviews of the detention must be carried out at regular intervals in the early stages to see if detention is necessary, and for detention beyond periods of 36 hours and 72 hours separate warrants authorising such detention must be obtained from a magistrate's court at which the suspect has the right to appear. Detention without charge cannot extend beyond 96 hours under PACE 1984. Special safeguards exist for the questioning of 'vulnerable' suspects such as juveniles or mentally incapacitated persons. All interrogations must be tape recorded.

5 The trial judge *must* exclude from the trial any confession obtained from the accused as a result of oppression or which is otherwise unreliable as a result of anything said or done to the accused improperly inducing him to confess: s76 PACE. The trial judge *may* exclude from the trial any evidence illegally or unfairly obtained if satisfied that its admission would have such an adverse effect on the proceedings that it would be unfair to admit it. Much will depend on the methods used to obtain the evidence. All 'undercover' operations by the police will involve some kind of trickery to trap suspects, but there is no general defence of entrapment in English law and no general rule that evidence so obtained must be automatically excluded: *R* v *Christou* [1992] 3 WLR 228; *R* v *Khan (Sultan)* [1996] 3 All ER 289. However, the trial judge ought to take a serious view of flagrant breaches of PACE or the Codes of Practice if such breaches prevent the accused from receiving due process of law, eg if the police lie to the accused's solicitor as to the evidence they have so as to influence the solicitor's legal advice to his client: *R* v *Mason* [1988] 1 WLR 139 (evidence excluded under s78 PACE).

SUGGESTED ANSWER TO QUESTION ONE

General Comment

This question deals with the restrictions upon the freedom of association and expression. Students are asked to advise the local chief constable as to his powers and duties in respect of the march to the Royal Air Force base and the resulting obstruction of the highway, and also the threats by the travellers to attack the marchers. This will mainly involve a discussion of s137(1) Highways Act 1980, breach of the peace, s5 Public Order Act 1936, the *Beatty* v *Gilbanks* principle, and mention should also be made of the Official Secrets Act 1911. Students are reminded to keep to the constitutional law implications of the question and not to get involved in discussion of the criminal law generally.

Key Points

- The basic rule of freedom to demonstrate
- Duty of the chief constable to keep the highway free for passage - powers available to achieve this object
- Duty of the chief constable to keep the peace - possible public order offences committed by the travellers - powers available to deal with threats to breach public order
- The possible application of the *Beatty* v *Gilbanks* principle and the exceptions to it which might apply in the present case
- Discussion of possible breach of s1(1)(a) Official Secrets Act 1911

Suggested Answer

The basic rule is that anyone is free to assemble for the purposes of demonstrating provided that no law is breached. The law in this area consists in essence of the restrictions that Parliament and the courts have felt necessary over the years to impose on the freedom to assemble in public, in the interests of maintaining order.

The first duty of the chief constable is to keep the highway free for lawful passage. The march to the Royal Air Force base will generally be lawful provided the marchers keep to the public highway and do not cause any obstruction. When the marchers surround the base, however, and block all the roads in the vicinity, their actions become unlawful. Under s137(1) Highways Act 1980 it is a criminal offence wilfully to obstruct the free passage along a highway. If the highway is obstructed then a constable can arrest those causing the obstruction. Obstruction in this context is a very flexible term. In *Homer* v *Codman* (1886) it was held that it is no defence to show that there was a way around the obstruction. In *Arrowsmith* v *Jenkins* (1963) Arrowsmith was arrested for obstructing the highway under s121 Highways Act 1959. She argued that the prosecution had to show that she had an intention to obstruct the highway. The court rejected this argument, holding that if a person does an act according to her free will which results in an obstruction, it will be sufficient for the offence of obstruction.

The marchers therefore are committing an obstruction of the highway and when asked to move on by the police they refuse to do so. In these circumstances the chief constable has the power to order the arrest of those persons committing the obstruction, under the Highways Act 1980, or they may be charged with wilfully obstructing a police officer in the execution of his duty, under s89 Police Act 1996.

The reaction of the travellers to the obstruction caused by the marchers raises the prospects of public order offences being committed. The travellers threaten to attack the marchers and run them down. A breach of the peace therefore seems likely. The travellers may also under these circumstances be committing an unlawful assembly and also breaching s5 Public Order Act 1936, which makes it an offence to use threatening, abusive or insulting words or behaviour in a public place or meeting with intent to provoke a breach of the peace or whereby a breach of the peace is likely to be occasioned. The chief constable, like all citizens, has a duty to prevent breaches of the peace occurring. If the police reasonably apprehend an imminent breach of the peace they may take any action which is necessary to control or prevent it, including arresting those travellers who are responsible.

The threat to the peace comes not from the marchers but from the travellers. The question arises therefore whether the chief constable can, as a preventative measure, disperse the marchers if they themselves are committing no threat to the peace. Under the principle stated in *Beatty* v *Gilbanks* (1882) a lawful act does not become unlawful merely because other persons decide to offer unlawful reaction to it. But while the principle in *Beatty* v *Gilbanks* still stands today, its operation has been modified. There may be situations of actual disorder where, if order is to be restored swiftly, the police are entitled to stop someone doing what he would otherwise be entitled to do. For example, in *O'Kelly* v *Harvey* (1883) a magistrate was held to be entitled to disperse a lawful meeting since he had reasonable grounds for supposing that those opposed to the meeting would use violence and that there was no other way in which the peace could be preserved.

Therefore, if the *Beatty* v *Gilbanks* principle applies, the threat of the travellers will not justify the disposal of the marchers. But, if a breach of the peace is threatened and no other way of preventing such a breach exists, the police may dispose of marchers, as in *O'Kelly* v *Harvey.* In any case it is doubtful that the *Beatty* v *Gilbanks* principle will apply in this case beacuse the marchers have directly provoked the travellers by their own illegality in obstructing the highway. If the police did decide to disperse the marchers because they reasonably apprehended a breach of the peace, and if the marchers refuse to co-operate with the police, then, as in *Duncan* v *Jones* (1936), they may be charged with the wilful obstruction of a police officer in the execution of his duty.

If the marchers intend to act for any purpose prejudicial to the safety or interests of the state while in the vicinity of the Royal Air Force base this also raises the possibility of a breach of s1 Official Secrets Act 1911. Under s1(1)(a) of the Act it is an offence, punishable with 14 years' imprisonment, if any person for any purpose prejudicial to the safety or interests of the state, approaches, inspects, passes over or is in the neighbourhood of, or enters any prohibited place within the meaning of the Act. For example, in *Chandler* v *DPP* (1964), anti-nuclear demonstrators sought to enter an RAF base and sit on the runway in order to prevent nuclear bombers taking off. As they approached the base they were arrested and charged with conspiracy to enter a prohibited place for a purpose prejudicial to the safety or interests of the state, contrary to s1 1911 Act. The House of Lords unanimously upheld the conviction. Thus the 1911 Act is not restricted to spying but includes acts of sabotage and other acts of physical interference. However, it is unlikely that the chief constable will be able to rely on this offence in respect of the marchers from the Peace in Britain campaign. If their intention is merely to hold a protest meeting outside the Air base it may be difficult to establish that this in itself constitutes an act which is prejudicial to the safety or interests of the state.

SUGGESTED ANSWER TO QUESTION TWO

General Comment

This is a potentially wide-ranging question and the student should direct his/her attention to the area of assemblies and not be diverted into discussing other areas of public order such as processions. The main statutes to be familiar with are the relevant sections of the Public Order Act 1986 and the Criminal Justice and Public Order Act 1994. In addition, candidates should be aware of the available common law powers to curb an assembly, as well as any other statutes which might be utilised for this purpose.

Key Points

- The issue of 'rights' in English law
- Section 14 Public Order Act (POA) 1986
- Criminal Justice and Public Order Act (CJPOA) 1994 - trespass, trespassary assemblies, 'raves'
- Common law powers to control assemblies
- Highways Act 1980
- Conclusion

Suggested Answer

According to Dicey (*Law of the Constitution* (1959, 10th ed)), rights are regarded as residual. This means that the individual is permitted to do something provided it is not forbidden. When one examines the law relating to peaceful assembly this necessarily entails an analysis of the restrictions which may be imposed on individuals or groups. The restrictions in this area take the form of statutory and common law curtailments on freedom of assembly.

Unlike the law relating to processions, the Public Order Act (POA) 1986 imposes no requirement to obtain permission from the police in order to organise an assembly. A public assembly is defined by s16 POA 1986 as being 'an assembly of 20 or more persons in a public place which is wholly or partly open to the air'.

While, however, no permission is needed to organise an assembly it has to be in the words of art 11 a 'peaceful' gathering. If a senior police officer reasonably believes that the assembly will result in serious public disorder, serious damage to property or serious disruption to the life of the community, or the purpose is the intimidation of others, he may impose conditions on the organisers relating to the duration of the assembly and the maximum number of people who may make up the meeting: s14 POA 1986. What constitutes the reasonable belief of the senior police officer (presumably the senior police officer present) as to these factors is not defined in the Act. One may suppose that the belief is a combination of subjective/objective reasonableness. That is, did the police officer have an honest and reasonable belief as to the facts and would a police officer in those circumstances have reasonably formed this view? What is certain is that a police officer cannot arbitrarily forbid an assembly.

A much more far-reaching statute in this area is the Criminal Justice and Public Order Act (CJPOA) 1994. This Act was passed in response to a number of public order issues ranging from 'New Age Travellers' to 'rave' parties on disused airfields. Associated with these groups and events is the issue of trespass and trespassory assembly. The POA 1986 attempted to deal with some of these issues by providing a senior police officer (ie the most senior present) with powers to direct trespassers to leave land: s39 POA 1986. These could only be invoked if the police officer believed that two or more persons had entered the land as trespassers with a common purpose of residing there, that they had not heeded reasonable steps, by the occupier, to leave and that they had caused damage to the property on the land or that they had used threatening, abusive or insulting words or behaviour towards the occupier or his agent. The police officer could also direct the trespassers to leave the land if they brought 12 or more vehicles on the land: s39(1)(b).

The above proved inadequate to deal with a number of increasingly popular gatherings in the 1980s and 90s. Section 61 CJPOA 1994 went further than s39 POA 1986. By s61, even in the case of individuals who entered the land by invitation, if the invitation is withdrawn they are then categorised as trespassers and can be asked to leave. Moreover, while s39 talked about damage to property, the CJPOA talks about damage to the land. Damage may presumably be caused by cars driving onto fields and the number of vehicles has been reduced from 12 or more (in s39) to six. The use of the definition of land has now been extended and, for instance, common land and bridleways are included. Gatherings at historical monuments may also be curtailed, a move designed to prevent the gathering of people at the time of the summer solstice at Stonehenge. By s70 CJPOA 1994 the relevant chief police officer may apply to the local council for an order prohibiting for a specified period the holding of all trespassory public assemblies in a specified area, provided the Secretary of State consents. One of the specified areas described in the statute is an area of historical monuments, provided that a case is made out of potential damage to the said structures. A s70 order will cover all trespassory assemblies, even those that are peaceful and do not obstruct the highway: *DPP* v *Jones* (1997).

Assemblies may also be prohibited if their aim is to disrupt or obstruct a lawful activity by trespassing on land in the open air with that aim in mind. This new offence of 'aggravated trespass' (s68(1)) is designed to include the activities of, for instance, hunt saboteurs.

Finally, the CJPOA has prohibited assemblies in the open air where amplified music is played during the night, provided there is an attendance of 100 or more people: s63. Moreover, the Act gives the police a new power to stop somebody they reasonably, believe is travelling to such an assembly or 'rave'. This power can only be utilised within five miles of the boundary of the assembly: s65.

In addition, English law has extensive common law powers which in effect curtail an assembly. The test is whether there will be a breach of the peace or a reasonable likelihood of breach of the peace at the gathering, rather than what is the intention of the organisers or those attempting to reach the assembly. In *Moss* v *McLachlan* (1985) the Divisional Court held that the police had reasonable grounds for apprehending a breach of the peace as imminent when they stopped a group of striking miners from going to attend a mass picket. The miners were arrested for obstruction of the police. It is not necessary in such a situation to argue that the meeting is unlawful, but rather whether the natural consequence of the meeting will be a breach of the peace. If, however, the natural consequence of an assembly is not to provoke violence then it would appear that it is legitimate to proceed. Such reasoning is an echo of *Beatty* v *Gillbanks* (1882) in which the court emphasised that so long as the participants at a gathering were 'quiet and reasonable' then the unlawful actions of the other participants were not deemed to be the 'natural consequences' of the event .

Further to the above, a peaceful assembly may fall foul of additional legislation which may have been passed with other situations in mind. The Highways Act 1980 is a piece of legislation which falls into this category. Designed to provide for free passage along the highway it has also been utilised to curb demonstrations and assemblies. For example, in *Hubbard* v *Pitt* (1976) consumers who protested against an estate agent outside his shop on a narrow pavement were prohibited by an injunction from doing so under the Highways Act 1959 (the forerunner to the 1980 Act), although use of the 1980 Act was not successful when directed against animal rights protesters who were protesting on a spacious pedestrian precinct in a shopping mall: *Hirst* v *Chief Constable of West Yorkshire* (1987). The Court of Appeal in this case seemed to give more weight to the 'freedom to demonstrate reasonably' argument.

In conclusion, the individual may attend a peaceful assembly but the constraints are numerous. Legislation has been passed in response to such phenomenon as New Age Travellers and rave parties; in their desire to preserve public order statute and common law have limited the opportunity to convene an assembly.

SUGGESTED ANSWER TO QUESTION THREE

General Comment

Potentially a very long answer, so it is suggested that attention should be concentrated on the Official Secrets Act 1989, the Contempt of Court Act 1981 and the Broadcasting Act 1990, which are three significant statutes concerning the balance between state security and freedom of expression.

Key Points

- Impact of Official Secrets Act 1989

- Main provisions of the 1989 Act
- Impact of Contempt of Court Act 1981
- The 'Death on the Rock' television documentary
- Effect of the Broadcasting Act 1990

Suggested Answer

It is right that certain secrets must be kept in any state, but if we view the function of the democratic state to be that of the efficient protection of information so that the country is run properly - not just refusal to disclose information - then the Official Secrets Act 1989 can be severely criticised. The test to be applied is the balance struck between access to information to citizens and protection to servants of the state so that they can in fact run the country properly.

Under the Official Secrets Act 1989 no new rights to information are provided for and ministers will continue to be able to withhold information embarrassing to their case. It is true that the vast bulk of information will no longer be protected by the criminal law but in the past civil servants were more likely to be disciplined or sacked for breaches of the Official Secrets Act 1911 rather than facing criminal prosecution (except in exceptional cases like Tisdall and Ponting). Many breaches of the old statute went unpunished.

The 1989 Act makes it an offence for a member of the security and intelligence services or retired members to disclose any information relating to that work he has obtained while so employed. There is an offence relating to other Crown servants or government contractors who make damaging disclosures of information they have obtained about the security services. Damaging disclosures in relation to defence and international relations are also offences by Crown servants. A Crown servant also commits an offence if he discloses information he has received as such which results in the commission of an offence, facilitates an escape from custody or inhibits the detection of crime or arrest of offenders.

Where information is leaked from a foreign source and where information 'likely to be useful in the commission of a crime' is leaked it is outside the ambit of the Act.

The concept of absolute offences is less strict than under the Official Secrets Act 1911. The areas covered have been reduced but there is no prior publication defence. Therefore it is of no avail to show: (i) no harm was done; or (ii) that the matter was already widely published. This is particularly disturbing - an editor can be caught for repeating words forbidden today which had been widely published yesterday but not then forbidden.

No public interest defence will be allowed - so information revealing exceptional abuse of authority will not be a defence. The Home Secretary has said that a form of public interest defence will exist because in some areas the prosecution would have to show a disclosure caused 'harm to the public interest'. The Act itself does not use the words 'public interest' so if a specific form of harm can be shown, a jury will have to convict. For more than a century a public interest defence has existed. In the *Spycatcher* case, Lord Griffiths (in a dissenting judgment) continued to defend this principle - in exceptional circumstances a civil servant could be 'relieved of his duty of confidence' so that he could 'alert his fellow citizens to the impending danger': *Attorney-General* v *Observer Ltd* (1988).

A case can be made, therefore, that the 1989 Act should seek to uphold this principle because secrecy can be damaging in these 'exceptional circumstances'.

Contempt of court is another area where freedom of expression can be curtailed. The position is now governed by the Contempt of Court Act 1981. This Act was partly in response to an appeal made by the *Sunday Times* to the European Court of Human Rights. The European Court had said that the test was too widely drawn in the United Kingdom and had the effect of unlawfully silencing a newspapers right to freedom of expression: *Sunday Times* v *UK* (1979). Under the Act there can be contempt regardless of 'intent to do so', this is the 'strict liability rule', however, there are defences under s3 eg 'innocent publication ... etc'. Contemporaneous reporting and reporting a discussion 'in good faith of public affairs' are two further defences.

The protection of journalistic sources is given a limited defence only. (See *Secretary of State for Defence* v *Guardian Newspapers Ltd* (1984).) This limited defence is provided for in s10 Contempt of Court Act 1981. Disclosure will not be required 'unless it be established' (that disclosure) 'is in the interests of justice or national security or for the prevention of disorder or crime.'

The 'Death on the Rock' programme screened by Thames Television on 28 April 1988, against the government's wishes, illustrates a crisis with regard to freedom of expression.

This programme was 'a lightning conductor for the intense feelings that the Gibraltar shootings evoked in the minds of the British public ... The conflict was essentially one of divergent personal attitudes and value rather than of party political divisions. Some people felt that the security forces were fully entitled to take such measures as were necessary to protect the people of Gibraltar and the Royal Anglian Regiment from planned assassination. Others, whilst abhorring the IRA's objectives and tactics, felt that the security force's actions (whether in Northern Ireland or elsewhere) fell outside the specific limitations of the rule of law by which they are bound. The question was whether the programme 'Death on the Rock' offended against impartiality requirements? The Windlesham Rampton Report vindicated the objectivity of the television programme.

However, the Broadcasting Act 1990 provides that where the minister is of opinion that an item to be broadcast would promote or incite crime or undermine the authority of the state, he may order a person/company not to broadcast such item. The Home Secretary can issue an order under this Act requiring all television companies to refrain from broadcasting the forbidden item. This will include an interview or discussion of a person who appears or is heard on the particular programme and the person is representing or purports to represent a terrorist organisation or where the words support such an organisation.

To try to curtail terrorism is perfectly understandable in any civilised society, but it might be more practical to leave the discretion in the hands of the directors of the various television companies.

SUGGESTED ANSWER TO QUESTION FOUR

General Comment

This question presents a very challenging task in subjecting the relevant law to a critical analysis. Familiarity with the Police and Criminal Evidence Act (PACE) 1984 and the Codes of Practice is essential, and the ability to be selective in highlighting issues and illustrating by reference to cases is also crucial. The effect of the Criminal Justice and Public Order Act (CJPOA) 1994 should be touched on, but clearly the question requires concentration on the effect of PACE 1984 and its interpretation in the courts. Despite the apparent invitation in the question to give a personal view, every effort should be made to present a dispassionate, clinical analysis giving equal weight to both sides of the argument.

Key Points

- Definition of the conflict of interests between protection of the public and safeguards for suspects
- The purpose of PACE 1984 and the Codes of Practice
- An appraisal of whether the purpose was achieved and (in outline only) the reasons for the passage of the Criminal Justice and Public Order Act 1994
- An outline of suspects' remedies for abuse of police powers
- A detailed analysis of the effect of a breach of PACE and/or the Codes of Practice on admissibility of evidence
- The rule on confessions in s76 PACE
- The exclusionary discretion under s78 PACE
- Case law conflicts of authority on the interpretation of s78
- Comparisons with USA law on entrapment and the 'Miranda' principle - a critical conclusion on whether English law ought to adopt the USA approach

Suggested Answer

Presumably the interests of the community may be defined as protection of the public from criminal activities through the effective detection, investigation and prosecution of criminal offences. The rights and liberties of suspects may be defined as protection against abuse of the powers granted for the purposes of detecting, investigating and prosecuting, including protection against oppressive or inhumane exercise of authority. The purpose behind PACE was to strengthen police powers to combat crime, but at the same time preserve and strengthen the safeguards against abuse of such powers. Whether that purpose was achieved and the proper balance struck remains a highly contentious political issue. The Conservative administration which enacted PACE evidently came to the view (urged by the police) that PACE had tilted the balance too far towards the interests of suspects, and hence increased police powers and a modification of the right of silence have occurred as the result of the Criminal Justice and Public Order Act (CJPOA) 1994. Critics from civil liberties organisations argue that PACE did not protect suspects' rights as effectively as the Government contended, and that consequently the CJPOA 1994 represents a further undermining of human rights.

One of the problems for a suspect is that his rights depend on whether the relevant provision under which he was stopped and searched, or arrested, or questioned in police custody, is contained in PACE or one of the Codes of Practice issued by the Home Office under the authority of PACE. Breach of a statutory provision would be treated as a serious matter and likely to give rise to a cause of action in tort, or even form the basis for a criminal prosecution against the police. However, breach of the Codes of Practice is expressly declared by s67(10) PACE not to give rise to any civil or criminal liability; instead the suspect is expected to complain to the Police Complaints Authority so that, for minor breaches, he would be assured of at least an apology, and for more serious breaches he might be assured that appropriate disciplinary action would be taken. Since the police investigate accusations of police malpractice on behalf of the Authority there is a suspicion that this might not prove an effective remedy.

Even more problematic is the effect of a breach of PACE and/or the Codes of Practice on the admissibility of evidence obtained as a result of such breach. The suspect is assured by s76 PACE that involuntary confessions made as the result of oppression, and unreliable confessions made as the result of an improper inducement, would be inadmissible at his trial. However, all other evidence, including dubious confessions obtained otherwise than by oppression or improper inducements, might be admissible at the trial judge's discretion depending on the character of the breach of PACE and/or the Codes of Practice and the effect of the admission of such evidence on the fairness of the trial: s78 PACE.

The interpretation of s78 has given rise to conflicts of authority. In *R* v *Samuel* (1988) it was robustly stated that a suspect's right to consult privately with a solicitor under PACE, s58, is of fundamental importance, and that evidence obtained after unreasonable denial of such access should be excluded from the trial under s78 PACE. However, this rule of exclusion was not to apply if the police had adequately informed the suspect of his rights (*R* v *Alladice* (1988)); or if the suspect was a 'hardened criminal' well aware of his rights (*R* v *Dunford* (1990)). These decisions appear to make a mockery of the safeguard Parliament intended all suspects to have when held in police custody at a police station.

Trickery by the police in order to obtain incriminating evidence may be a ground for excluding such evidence under s78 PACE, but the difficulty is that PACE, unlike USA law, does not clearly outlaw various forms of 'entrapment' by the police. The more extreme kinds of trickery involving bad faith on the part of the police have resulted in the exclusion of evidence under s78 PACE on the ground that they involve flagrant breaches of the Codes of Practice, eg *R* v *Mason* (1988), where the police had lied to the suspect and his solicitor about the evidence they had against him, thereby unfairly influencing the legal advice given to the suspect. Similarly, undercover operations in which police officers questioned suspects without cautioning them or acted as 'agents provocateur' in procuring, inciting or counselling a crime, have resulted in the exclusion of evidence: *R* v *Bryce* (1992) and *R* v *Smurthwaite*, *R* v *Gill* (1994). But if the police malpractice takes a less extreme form, and it can be said that the criminal applied himself to the trick rather than the police applying the trick to the criminal, then evidence obtained as a result of the trick may be admissible: *R* v *Christou* (1992) and *Williams* v *DPP* (1993). Evidence obtained by bugging a police cell, or even a private house, may also be admissible since PACE and the Codes of Practice appear to be silent on suspects' rights to privacy apart from when consulting with a solicitor (*R* v *Bailey* (1993) and *R* v *Khan (Sultan)* (1996)), though see now ss91–108 Police Act 1997.

It follows that those who support civil liberties' philosophy will not be satisfied unless and until English law adopts the USA 'Miranda' principle of automatically excluding from evidence any material obtained illegally or improperly by the police. Those who subscribe to the view that the paramount need is to protect the public from crime will argue that such a step would be harmful to the interests of the community, and that the discretion allowed to exclude such evidence, together with the existence of disciplinary machinery over the police, provide an appropriate balancing of the competing interests.

SUGGESTED ANSWER TO QUESTION FIVE

General Comment

The question requires a good knowledge of Part I of the Police and Criminal Evidence Act (PACE) 1984.

Key Points

- Powers of the police to stop and search - s1 PACE
- Effect of Codes of Practice on 'reasonable suspicion'
- Grounds for arrest without warrant
- Legality of the search - s32 PACE

Suggested Answer

Section 1(2) PACE 1984 gives a general power to constables to search a person, provided the constable 'has reasonable grounds for suspecting that he will find stolen or prohibited articles 'as a result of the search (s1(3)). Ultimately the existence of such 'reasonable grounds' must be a question of fact, although the Code of Practice for the Exercise by Police Officers of Statutory Powers of Stop and Search issued under s66 of the Act, and of general application in its interpretation, gives guidance. The constable need not be certain that an unlawful article is being carried, nor does he have to be satisfied of this beyond reasonable doubt. But there must be some concrete basis for the constable's suspicion, related to the individual concerned which can be considered and evaluated by an objective third person. Reasonable suspicion may arise from the nature of the property observed or being carried or suspected of being carried, coupled with other factors including the time, place and suspicious behaviour of the person concerned or those with him.

It would appear that there is nothing in Angelo's behaviour to mark him out as a suspect. Hurd's explanation for his searching him would appear to be due to the fact that he is a student, of somewhat scruffy appearance. But the Code provides that reasonable suspicion cannot be supported on the basis simply of a higher than average chance that the person has committed or is about to commit an offence, merely because he belongs to a group within which offenders of a certain kind are relatively common, eg scruffily dressed people. Thus it is likely that there was no basis for the stop and search. Nor do the requirements of ss2 and 3 appear to have been complied with.

Where a constable has reasonable grounds for suspecting that an arrestable offence has been committed, he may arrest without a warrant anyone whom he has reasonable grounds for suspecting to be guilty of an offence either: (a) for which the sentence is fixed by law; or (b) for which a person of 21 years of age or over (not previously convicted) may be sentenced to imprisonment for a term of five years. The situation is one that would have been intended by the legislature to fall within its provisions: someone is suspected of committing an act of criminal damage. Hurd rightly tells Angelo that he is under arrest, and the ground for the arrest as required by s28. He does not say that Angelo was guilty of the offence of damaging laboratories and spraying the buildings with slogans (criminal damage), merely that he was 'connected' with it. This is rather flimsy, and may lead one to suppose that Hurd had inadequate grounds for making the arrest.

Once a suspect has been arrested he must be taken to a police station as soon as practicable after his arrest: s30(1). Hurd is probably within his rights in searching Angelo's room while he is in the area. An officer is entitled to search premises in which the suspect was arrested, or in which he was present immediately before his arrest, in order to discover evidence relating to the offence for which the arrest was made, if the arresting constable has reasonable grounds for believing that such evidence exists: s32(2) and (6), but Angelo was not in his lodgings. Therefore such a search must be justified under s18. This enables premises in Angelo's control to be searched for evidence relating to the offence or other similar or connected offence. Arguably the lecture notes do not come within this category, and their service would not be justified.

Therefore it may be that the lecture notes could be excluded under s78, since in all the circumstances of the case, to admit them as evidence would have an adverse effect on the fairness of proceedings.

With respect to Hurd's attempted search of B's rooms, s17 only empowers him to arrest a person for an arrestable offence or for one of a number of specified offences. Again Hurd may have criminal damage in mind as an arrestable offence. In addition, under subs17(1)(e) powers of entry and search are only exercisable if the constable has reasonable grounds for believing that the person whom he is seeking is on the premises. But in cases where premises consist of two or more separate dwellings (eg two rooms in a house or hostel) the powers are limited to any parts of the premises which the occupiers of any dwelling comprised in the premises use in common with the occupiers of any other such dwelling. Bertie is thus fully within his rights to obstruct Hurd.

SUGGESTED ANSWER TO QUESTION SIX

General Comment

A straightforward problem-type question on police powers. Familiarity with the detailed provisions of the Police and Criminal Evidence Act (PACE) 1984 and the Codes of Practice issued under it is essential. Students should concentrate on issues directly arising from the facts and avoid a general narrative of the law of police powers.

Key Points

- Stop and search powers under ss1–4 PACE
- Seizure and retention of evidence under s22 PACE
- Arrest powers under ss23 and 24 PACE
- Duty to give reasons for the arrest under s28 PACE
- Consequences of unlawful arrest
- Terms of the caution on the right of silence under Code C, para 10
- Consequences of failure to caution properly
- Rules on detention and questioning of young persons at a police station
- Access to a solicitor under s58 PACE
- Inducements to confess and unreliable confessions under s76 PACE
- General exclusionary powers under s78 PACE
- Conclusions

Suggested Answer

The first issue is the stop and search of Terence prior to his arrest. This is governed by ss1–4 Police and Criminal Evidence Act (PACE) 1984. A stop and search is permitted if the police officer had reasonable suspicion that Terence had stolen something or was in possession of a prohibited article, such as an instrument of theft or burglary. On the facts that police could argue that there was a reasonable suspicion (a 'concrete basis') for believing that Terence's behaviour indicated that he and a colleague (Jonathan) were engaged in picking pockets on tube trains. Since the search appeared to produce evidence of stolen money and credit cards, the police had power under s22 PACE to seize such evidence and to retain it for as long as it might be needed for evidence at a trial.

Seizure of such evidence would also give the police grounds for arresting Terence without a warrant under ss23–24 PACE, since theft is an arrestable offence (being punishable by at least five years' imprisonment) and there was reasonable suspicion (not a mere hunch) that Terence had committed such an offence. The police officer was under no obligation to delay the arrest in order to question Terence or to conduct further enquiries to confirm his suspicion. He was entitled to take the view that Terence was more likely to tell the truth when in custody at the police station: *Mohammed-Holgate* v *Duke* (1984). However, no written record of the stop and search was kept as required by PACE.

There is also doubt as to whether the officer complied with his duty under s28 PACE to inform Terence of the reasons for his arrest. He probably did enough to convey the fact of arrest by indicating that Terence was no longer free - 'we have to take you in' - but he probably did not do enough to explain the reasons for arrest - 'it's obvious what you've been up to' - since s28 requires the provision of reasons even though they may appear obvious! The arrest was therefore unlawful at that point and continued to be unlawful detention (tort of false imprisonment) up to the time when reasons were eventually supplied (presumably when Terence was charged with theft, if not earlier than that): *Lewis* v *Chief Constable for South Wales* (1991).

The police officer was also in breach of Code C, para 10 of the Code of Practice issued under PACE, in failing to caution Terence in appropriate terms. Paragraph 10 states that the caution is: 'You do not have to say anything. But it may harm your defence if you do not mention when questioned something which you later rely on in court. Anything you do say may be given in evidence.' Code C provides that minor deviations do not constitute a breach of para 10 provided that the gist or sense of the caution is preserved. It is suggested that the wording of the officer's caution was more than a minor deviation because it failed to indicate the positive nature of the right of silence and was also misleading in suggesting that anything Terence might say could only be used against him at trial, when in fact it could also be used in his favour if that proved to be the case.

The failure to caution properly does not give rise in itself to remedies in civil law, but it might affect the issue of admissibility of evidence at Terence's trial, depending on all the other circumstances of Terence's treatment.

When Terence was questioned at the police station a number of breaches of PACE and the Codes of Practice appear to have occurred. First, he should have been placed under the responsibility of a custody officer (of the rank of sergeant) who has not been involved in the arrest. The custody officer is responsible for Terence's treatment in custody and for charging him when there is sufficient evidence to do so. Code C requires that young persons such as Terence (aged 15) should only be questioned in the presence of an adult (not being a police officer) who can reasonably be expected to look after their interests. The interview with Terence should have been tape-recorded. Terence should have been informed of his rights under ss56 and 58 PACE to have someone informed of his arrest and the place where he was being held, and to have access to a solicitor for confidential advice in private.

Questioning a young person non-stop for two hours might also be regarded as oppressive. There was certainly an improper inducement to Terence to confess by holding out the prospect of release from custody if he gave the police his 'partner's name'. Such an inducement renders Terence's subsequent confession to participation in theft with Jonathan unreliable and inadmissible under s76 PACE, though *other* evidence obtained as a result of the confession (the money found at Jonathan's home) may be given at Terence's trial. The fact that such evidence seems to confirm the reliability of his confession is, however, irrelevant since s76 is designed to stop police malpractice in extracting confessions, so the discovery of such evidence cannot make the inadmissible confession admissible.

It is possible, however, that *all* the evidence against Terence will be excluded from the trial if the trial judge uses his general discretion under s78 PACE to exclude evidence which has such an adverse effect on the fairness of the trial that a judge ought not to allow it to be given. There remains controversy as to the scope of s78 but it is now settled that unfair treatment of a suspect may be relevant to the exercise of the discretion, depending on the nature of the treatment. Denial of access to a solicitor by itself is regarded as fundamental unfairness and a breach of a constitutional safeguard of great importance: *R* v *Samuel* (1988). Taken together with the unlawful arrest and other breaches of the Codes of Practice (especially the failure to caution Terence properly), it is suggested that the evidence against Terence may well be excluded from the trial under s78 PACE in which event, of course, the case against Terence will collapse.

SUGGESTED ANSWER TO QUESTION SEVEN

General Comment

This is a very detailed and lengthy question which requires a thorough knowledge of the Police and Criminal Evidence Act 1984 and the connected case law. A question of this type should always be read thoroughly and a careful plan made so that a well structured answer can be given.

Key Points

- Legality of police stopping the three parties
- Legality of arrest
- The following should be discussed for each detainee where applicable
  - legality of search
  - conditions of questioning and detention
  - admissibility of evidence
- If issues have been discussed in relation to one person, it is not necessary to repeat your points - simply refer the examiner to the relevant issues and your previous discussions

Suggested Answer

The introduction of the Police and Criminal Evidence Act (PACE) 1984 and the accompanying Codes of Practice was designed to safeguard the rights of detainees by clarifying the exact extent of police powers on a statutory basis. It is the details of that legislation that must be discussed here in relation to each of the parties.

Turning first to the action of the police in stopping Jonathan, Trevor and Orville. Sections 1–3 PACE give the police a power to stop and search anyone they have reasonable grounds to believe is carrying stolen or prohibited articles. These include articles intended or made for use in connection with theft. The police must have reasonable grounds for suspecting they will find these articles. This must be something more than a hunch, something concrete. While PACE and the Codes do not say exactly what would constitute a 'concrete' reason, it is clear that the suspect's personal factors or stereotyping by the police are not sufficient. They should be looking at the behaviour and location of that person, and at the time of day. From the information given there would appear to be no grounds for suspicion at all other than the fact that they are black, which is clearly insufficient. Therefore, this initial action by the police would appear to be in breach of PACE.

Orville is then searched and, following the discovery of the lead piping and wallets, the three are apparently arrested. The legality or otherwise of the search is dealt with below. The power of arrest is established by, inter alia, s24 PACE which provides that a constable may arrest anyone he has reasonable grounds for suspecting has committed, is committing or is about to commit an arrestable offence. Arrestable offences are also defined by s24 and include theft related matters. The basis of the reasonable grounds of suspicion is presumably the articles found in Orville's pack. If the grounds are the arrestee's race, this would not be sufficient, as discussed above. When exercising the power of arrest, the police must make it clear that they are arresting that particular person and on what grounds. No technical language need be used, but, if the arrest is to be lawful, it must be clear to the arrestee: *Edwards* v *DPP* (1993). It is debatable whether the words used here are sufficient to fulfil that need for clarity, but this would be a matter for the magistrate or jury to decide at any subsequent trial.

It is now proposed to deal with the treatment of the parties individually.

Orville

The actions of stopping and arresting Orville (O) have been dealt with above. This still leaves the question of the legality of the search. Sections 1-3 PACE also provide the grounds for detaining a person in order to search them, providing the grounds already discussed are fulfilled. Furthermore, the Codes of Practice emphasise the need to gain the detainee's permission to search whenever possible, to always state a reason for the search and to make a record of the search and reasons as soon as is practicable. On the facts given, it would appear that a 'demand' was made of O rather than a request. No details are given on the issues of grounds being given or records being made, but it is clear that failure to give a valid reason for the search will lead to it being unlawful. There is, therefore, a strong case to suggest that the search of O's pack is unlawful.

However, this does not necessarily make the evidence obtained inadmissible. Under s1 PACE the police are within their powers to seize anything obtained as a result of the search. Here, s78 PACE is important in providing for the exclusion of unfairly obtained evidence. This preserves the common law discretion of the court to exclude evidence which it considers unfair, having regard to the circumstances in which it was obtained. In dealing with this area, the judges have varied in their approach. Often a breach of PACE is looked for (clearly an issue here), but in *R* v *Keenan* (1990) the court suggested that a breach did not automatically lead to exclusion, and in *R* v *Mason* (1988) the Court of Appeal pointed out that the courts were not the place to discipline the police. However, Lord Lane LCJ in *R* v *Alladice* (1988) said that where the police have acted in bad faith the courts will have little difficulty in ruling any confession inadmissible under s78 (if not s76, discussed below). If this evidence against O is to be excluded, he must hope that the court follows Lord Lane's approach to s78.

The only other matters in relation to O are his departure in the police van, which of itself does not suggest any problem, and the statement of Jonathan, which is discussed below.

Trevor

One of the first things we are told about Trevor (T) is his age. However, at 17 he is technically an adult for the purposes of PACE (a juvenile being someone under 17) and so there are no special rules regarding his treatment.

The legality of his arrest has already been discussed, and so the main issue is the lawfulness of his detention. On the facts given it is assumed that the custody officer complied with all the requirements of PACE on T's arrival at the police station, including the right to have someone informed (s56). The key fact is the refusal of access to legal advice. We are told that T clearly asked for and was refused access to a solicitor. Section 58 PACE established the right to legal advice for all detainees if they so choose (and clearly T has done so). Only in exceptional circumstances can this access be delayed. These are detailed in s58 and apply where the police are dealing with a serious arrestable offence and have reasonable grounds for believing that access to a solicitor would lead to evidence or witnesses being affected, or accomplices being alerted. Serious arrestable offences are specified in s116 and do not include the facts in question. Furthermore, the courts have shown the seriousness with which they regard this right, especially in the case of *R* v *Samuel* (1988) where it was emphasised that delay would only be justified in exceptional circumstances. It would appear, therefore, that there has been a blatant breach of s58 in relation to T.

There is no information given regarding any evidence being obtained from T so admissibility is not in issue here. We are told that he was released after two hours of questioning; this is just within the guidelines of the Codes which specify a break every two hours.

Jonathan

By far the most important issues in this case surround the treatment of Jonathan (J). At only 14 he is clearly to be regarded as a juvenile and, while this does not require any special treatment with regard to the powers of stop and search and arrest, there are very important requirements regarding detention.

Again, it is assumed that the custody officer has complied with the initial requirements, including s56. However, in addition to s56 there is an extra requirement which places the onus on the police to make sure an appropriate adult is informed of the juvenile's arrest and detention. For the purposes of the Act, an appropriate adult is a parent, guardian or a social worker, or any other appropriate person unconnected with the police. Furthermore, that adult should be present throughout any questioning and has the right to intervene on the part of the juvenile or to ask for legal advice on his behalf.

It is apparent from the facts that initially the police did not know J's age. However, the Codes of Practice suggest that whenever a detainee *appears* to be a juvenile, he should be treated as such until he is *proved* to be older. This makes the duty on the police more onerous and undermines any defence by the police that they did not realise J was a juvenile, especially since he was some years under 17. As soon as the police apparently realised J's age they attempted to find someone. This would perhaps absolve them from initial fault. Nevertheless, when they confirmed J's age, they still failed to fulfil requirements by bringing in the police typist who clearly is not an appropriate adult as defined above. They are, therefore, again in breach of PACE on this matter, even if only towards the end of J's detention.

Another issue which the facts raise is J's refusal of a solicitor. This is prima facie not a problem provided he clearly understood his right to legal advice and the nature of that right. His attitude suggests he may not have done, although there are insufficient facts to corroborate or refute this point.

We are also told that it was during the 'second day' that the police discovered J's age. This immediately raises issues regarding the length of detention. Section 41 of PACE allows an initial period of 24 hours. After that, further detention must be authorised in accordance with ss42 or 43 and is only permissible where dealing with a serious arrestable offence. It may be that J is still within the 24-hour limit depending on the time of arrest, but this is not clear from the facts, and the fact that he is being detained for a second day clearly suggests a considerable time in detention.

We are also told that J is questioned extensively. Again, although no specific facts are given, the length and conditions of questioning may be a problem. The Codes suggest a break every two hours with regular meals and proper sleep.

By the time J makes his statement he is clearly distressed. At the very least, there has been one breach of PACE with the failure to have an appropriate adult present (note that his brother has long been released by this stage). The main issue is the admissibility of that evidence. Here, ss76 and 78 of PACE may both be applicable. Section 76 specifically provides that the court must exclude confessions obtained by oppression (s76(2)(a)) or which are unreliable (s76(2)(b)). It is submitted that the most appropriate point here is the issue of unreliability. The Codes of Practice themselves suggest that juveniles by their very age may be prone to giving unreliable evidence (hence the need for an appropriate adult). However, the unreliability must be as a result of something said or done by someone rather than the state of the detainee himself. In the present case we must look at the actions of the police and the breaches of PACE that have taken place in relation to J. Furthermore, the circumstances to be considered are those prevailing at the time (ie J's youth and distress) and not what the police perceived them to be. There would seem to be a strong case for arguing for exclusion under s76(2)(b), but this would be for the decision of the court.

Section 78 is also applicable in this matter. Although it deals with all evidence, it clearly includes confessions. As discussed in relation to Orville, the case law in this area is not conclusive. However, in the case of *R* v *Delaney* (1989) the failure to provide an appropriate adult was considered a sufficient ground for exclusion. Again, the approach of Lord Lane in *Samuel* (above) offers the most assistance to the defence here. While both sections may be pleaded together, and both would probably use a voir dire (arguments in absence of the jury) to decide the issue (though this is not compulsory with regard to s78), s76 has an advantage for the defence as the burden is placed on the prosecution to prove that the statement is not unreliable rather than on the defence as is the case under s78.

In conclusion, the police actions throughout suggest breaches of PACE of varying severity and would appear to provide potentially strong arguments for the exclusion of evidence. Apart from this, Jonathan, Trevor and Orville may well wish to consider a civil action against the police or a complaint to the Police Complaints Authority based on their treatment.

10

Civil Liberties II: The European Convention on Human Rights

Introduction

This chapter is concerned with the traditional way in which civil liberties have been protected in the UK's unwritten constitution and the movement for reform that has demanded better protection through a 'Bill of Rights' enforceable in the ordinary courts. For many years the UK has been a signatory to the European Convention on Human Rights and has permitted UK citizens to petition the European Court of Human Rights for redress. It has been a source of embarrassment to successive governments that so many decisions of the European Court have found English law to be defective in the protection of human rights: see especially Lester [1984] PL 46. The Labour Government, elected in May 1997, has committed itself to incorporation of the European Convention into English law so as to give individual citizens easier access to remedies from domestic courts. However, incorporation raises several important constitutional issues:

a The effect on parliamentary sovereignty. The best guarantee for human rights is an 'entrenched' Bill of Rights on the lines of the American constitutional arrangements, but the traditional concept of parliamentary sovereignty would appear to make such entrenchment impossible.

b The value of a non-entrenched Bill of Rights. If, as seems likely, the Labour Government incorporates the European Convention into English law in a non-entrenched form (on the New Zealand model) will it provide any better protection than that already existing under statute law or as a result of common law developments? See *Derbyshire County Council* v *Times Newspapers Ltd* [1993] 1 All ER 1011.

c Will incorporation of the European Convention politicise the work of the judiciary? Traditionally judges have adopted a narrow, literalist approach to the interpretation of legislation so as to avoid accusations of 'making law' through the formulation of new principles, but a Bill of Rights on the model of the European Convention will contain declarations of general principles which will need to be refined and applied – a positive invitation to judges to create new rights and remedies, eg a general right of privacy. Will such judicial activism undermine the impartiality and independence of the judges?

Essay questions on the European Convention and the need for a British Bill of Rights are annual favourites with most examiners and they are likely to continue to appear on a regular basis in view of the topical debate concerning the legislation to incorporate the Convention into English law during 1998. It is useful to be familiar with the main contents of the European Convention and some of the case law involving the UK heard by the European Court. There is plenty of material available in the law journals and recent contributions include: Lord Lester [1996] PL 5 (the European Convention); Penner [1996] PL 104 (Canada's Charter of Rights); Kentridge (1996) 112 LQR 237 (South Africa's experience); Cockrell (1997) 60 MLR 513 (South Africa's experience); Ison (1997) 60 MLR 499 (Canadian Bill of Rights); Beatty (1997) 60 MLR 481 (Canadian Charter of Rights); Krug and Starmer [1997] PL 223 (indirect incorporation); Kentridge [1997] PL 96 (incorporating the European Convention); Wadham [1997] PL 75 (incorporating the European Convention); Andrews (1997) 56 CLJ 243 (UK cases before European Court); Bamforth (1997) 56 CLJ 480 (UK cases before European Court); Palmer (1997) 56 CLJ 469 (UK cases before European Court); Milmo [1997] NLJ 1631 (new rights to privacy); Leach [1997] NLJ 1595 (Government proposals to incorporate the European Convention); Wadham [1997] NLJ 950 (the Canadian system).

Questions

INTERROGRAMS

1 Outline the main methods by which the European Convention on Human Rights could be incorporated into English law.
2 What has been the traditional status and influence of the European Convention in English law?
3 Outline the main arguments in favour of incorporation of the European Convention.
4 Outline the main arguments against incorporation.

QUESTION ONE

'I do not relish the prospect of the judiciary being invested with the ultimate power to declare invalid the laws emanating from the will of Parliament on any subject at all and certainly not on human rights ... I would prefer it should not be given the tasks beyond its scope which are more properly left to other organs of the constitution.' (Lord Lloyd of Hampstead).

Discuss.

London University LLB Examination
(for external students) Constitutional Law June 1985 Q5

QUESTION TWO

'Incorporation of the European Convention on Human Rights into domestic law is unnecessary and undesirable in view of the right of individual petition to the Commission in Strasbourg.'

Discuss.

London University LLB Examination
(for external students) Constitutional Law June 1989 Q5

QUESTION THREE

In A V Dicey's view, individual rights are best protected under the common law. To what extent does the record of the United Kingdom under the European Convention on Human Rights uphold or deny this view?'

London University LLB Examination
(for external students) Constitutional Law June 1993 Q6

QUESTION FOUR

'For [Dicey] there was no need for any statement of fundamental principles operating as a kind of higher law because political freedom was adequately protected by the common law and by an independent Parliament acting as a watchdog against any excess of zeal by the executive.' (Wade and Bradley, 1993).

To what extent does Dicey's view require revision to meet the needs of today's society?

London University LLB Examination
(for external students) Constitutional Law June 1994 Q7

Answers

ANSWERS TO INTERROGRAMS

1 The main methods are:

a *Full entrenchment*, under which the Bill of Rights cannot be repealed or altered without observing special procedures different from the ordinary legislative process, eg two-thirds majority of the elected House or consent of the people in a national referendum. Judges would have the power not only to interpret the Bill of Rights but also be veto legislation that conflicts with it. It is doubtful whether full entrenchment is possible in the British Constitution without first having a complete constitutional re-settlement.

b *Semi-entrenchment*, under which judges have the power to veto legislation that conflicts with the Bill of Rights but where Parliament retains ultimate sovereignty to override the veto by using express language to exclude the operation of the Bill of Rights (the Canadian model).

c *A Bill of Rights as ordinary legislation*, under which judges use the Bill of Rights as a kind of Interpretation Act, ensuring that other legislation is interpreted consistently with the Bill of Rights as far as possible. Since the Bill of Rights is given the same status as ordinary legislation it will be subject to the usual doctrine of express and implied repeal, thus fully preserving traditional notions of parliamentary sovereignty (the New Zealand model).

2 Since 1952 the European Convention on Human Rights has been binding on the UK in international law, and since 1965 individual UK citizens have been able to bring petitions to the European Court complaining that English law fails to meet the

requirements of the Convention. If a petition is successful the UK government is bound in international law to bring in reforming legislation to deal with the requirements laid down by the European Court. Although traditionally the Convention has not been directly enforceable in the UK courts, British judges have often taken it into account as an external aid to interpretation of ambiguous legislation or as a device for resolving conflicts of authority at common law, but have been unable to use it where the position is unambiguous for fear of being accused of undermining parliamentary sovereignty: *R* v *Secretary of State for the Home Department, ex parte Brind* [1991] 2 WLR 588 (HL). Sometimes judges have declined to use the Convention if other persuasive precedents, eg from America or Commonwealth jurisdictions, provide a better solution: *Derbyshire County Council* v *Times Newspapers* [1993] 1 All ER 1011 (HL).

3 The main arguments in favour of incorporating the European Convention (even in the minimum non-entrenched form of the New Zealand model) are:

 a it should provide an educative force in moulding society's views by encouraging a political atmosphere which discourages the violation of human rights;
 b it should restrain abuse of power by public bodies and protect minority rights of all kinds;
 c it should provide minimum standards of protection for all citizens;
 d it should bring the UK into line with its international obligations by offering direct access to remedies for UK citizens in UK courts.

4 The main arguments against incorporation of the European Convention in any form are:

 a incorporation is unnecessary because individual rights are already adequately protected by Parliament's legislative abilities and by the evolutionary character of English common law (the traditional Diceyan view);
 b a Bill of Rights would lead to unnecessary litigation, encouraging frivolous applications and wasting public money and judicial time;
 c a Bill of Rights would 'politicise' the judiciary, which would lose its appearance of impartiality by being called upon to decide politically sensitive issues, such as the extent to which individuals should enjoy rights of privacy;
 d a Bill of Rights would lead to the loss of judicial independence since there would be pressure for future judicial appointments to be made on the basis of a candidate's political beliefs in order to obtain a balanced 'Supreme Court' or a senior judiciary acceptable to the government of the day.

SUGGESTED ANSWER TO QUESTION ONE

General Comment

A very difficult question which seems to encompass inter alia the doctrine of parliamentary supremacy, the question of a Bill of Rights for the United Kingdom, and the role of the judiciary in enforcing such a Bill of Rights as against inconsistent legislation. Like all such essay questions students may find difficulty in identifying the relevant issues and covering all the possible points raised in the time available. Therefore, unless you are absolutely sure that you know the specific area concerned and have sufficient information to write without straying from the point, such questions are best avoided.

Key Points

- Introduction (supremacy of Parliament, residual nature of civil liberties in the United Kingdom and the role of the common law in protecting individual liberty)
- Proposals for a Bill of Rights (difficulty of entrenchment) - incorporation of the European Convention of Human Rights into United Kingdom law
- Role of the judiciary in enforcing a Bill of Rights (objections and practical difficulties likely to result from judiciary declaring Acts of Parliament invalid)
- Role of the legislature in checking breaches of human rights by executive policy

Suggested Answer

Two fundamental features of the unwritten constitution of the United Kingdom are the legislative supremacy of Parliament and the role played by the common law, particularly in the field of protecting individual freedoms. In the United Kingdom individual freedoms are not guaranteed in any formal document, they are residual; the individual being free to do as he wishes provided that he does not commit any civil wrong or any criminal offence. Further, under the principle ubi jus ibi remedium, for every wrongful encroachment upon the liberty of an individual there is a legal remedy available before an independent court of justice.

Therefore in the United Kingdom, individual liberty is largely protected by the ordinary courts of law applying the common law. However, the protection afforded by the courts in this way is necessarily limited because of the operation of the doctrine of parliamentary supremacy, under which there is no legal limitation upon the legislative competence of Parliament. The Queen in Parliament may legislate upon any subject. No Parliament can bind its successors or be bound by its predecessors, and once Parliament has legislated no court or other person can pass judgment upon the validity of the legislation. In the field of individual liberty therefore, Parliament, by enacting legislation can take away, suspend or alter the fundamental freedoms hitherto enjoyed by the individual citizen and the courts will be bound to give effect to that legislation, no matter how repugnant it may seem to traditional English values.

Since the early 1970s there has been growing disenchantment with this typically British approach to safeguarding individual liberty, and much discussion has taken place regarding the possibility of enacting some form of Bill of Rights to protect the fundamental freedoms of the individual from executive encroachment. In particular, Lord Scarman, in his Hamlyn lectures in 1974 (***English Law - the New Dimension***), called for the enactment of entrenched and fundamental laws protected by a Bill of Rights, 'a constitutional law which it is the duty of the courts to protect even against the power of Parliament'. But, of course, such a measure, even if desirable, is easier said than done.

Under the present constitutional system of the United Kingdom, it is impossible to entrench legislation in the face of a supreme Parliament which cannot bind its successors or be bound by its predecessors. Whatever 'Bill of Rights' one Parliament enacts, another Parliament can amend or repeal. However, ignoring the largely sterile academic argument as to whether or not entrenchment is possible in the United Kingdom, various practical propositions have been put forward for enacting a new Bill of Rights in the United Kingdom. The Canadian Bill of Rights 1960, illustrates that it is possible to have a Bill of Rights enacted as an ordinary statute. Under the Canadian Bill Federal legislation was to be so construed and applied as to conform to the Bill except in an emergency or unless an Act expressly stated that it was to take effect notwithstanding the Bill of Rights. Further, the United Kingdom is a party to the European Convention on Human Rights and Fundamental Freedoms. It has been widely canvassed that the convention should be assimilated into English law, for example under a similar arrangement to that by which EC law was assimilated by the European Communities Act 1972. The Labour Government, elected on 1 May 1997, proposes to incorporate the European Convention in a non-entrenched form and without giving judges the power to invalidate legislation: Human Rights Bill 1998 (expected to become law during 1998). Even with this method of incorporation judges will enjoy increased power to develop new rights and remedies.

A Bill of Rights could, especially if difficult to amend, lead to government by judges. Governments, frustrated by judicial intransigence, could start to make political appointments to the bench thus causing public confidence in the impartial administration of justice to dwindle. The very independence of the judiciary would thus be threatened and conflict created between the organs of government. Delay and uncertainty in the law would also follow, because the politicians will not be sure what they are entitled to do until the judges have told them. There would be an increase in litigation. Many critics also adopt Dicey's view (*Introduction to the Study of the Law of the Constitution* (1959, 10th ed), p198) and see a Bill of Rights as something alien to the British Constitution. Such Bills may be all right for foreigners, but in the United Kingdom, with our long history of responsible governments, the rule of law, an independent judiciary, the safeguards of the common law and the residual nature of our freedoms, they are unnecessary and irreconcilable with our ancient traditions.

Therefore, while some of the more adventurous judges would not perhaps share Lord Lloyd's reticence, his objection to the courts being given the task of challenging executive policy as expressed through legislation, does have a degree of merit, especially as the controversy surrounding human rights is almost certainly going to give rise to confrontation and possible conflict between the judiciary and the executive. His Lordship supports the traditional role of the judiciary vis-à-vis statute, ie if the statute is duly enacted by the Queen in Parliament it cannot be questioned by the courts. The only power the courts have in respect of validly enacted Acts of Parliament is one of statutory interpretation in cases where the wording of the Act is ambiguous or uncertain. Lord Lloyd also makes the valid point that any check on executive encroachment or breach in the field of human rights is the task of the other organs of the constitution, ie the legislature. If the House of Commons were reformed so as to reassert its independence and remove the government's dominance and control, or if the House of Lords were reformed and perhaps given more powers to block legislation, then there would be no need for a Bill of Rights or the involvement of the judiciary in declaring statutes to be invalid. The check on Executive policy implementations would take place in the proper constitutional forum, ie Parliament itself.

SUGGESTED ANSWER TO QUESTION TWO

General Comment

The question has become a topical one in view of the current debate over the Labour Government's proposals to incorporate the European Convention on Human Rights into English law during 1998.

Key Points

- Features of the UK's unwritten constitution
- Pressure for incorporation of the European Convention on Human Rights
- Opposition to incorporation
- Likely reforms

Suggested Answer

Two basic features of the (unwritten) constitution of the United Kingdom are: (i) the legal supremacy of Parliament; and (ii) the common law which protects individual freedoms. In the United Kingdom, therefore, individual freedoms are not guaranteed in any formal document, they are residual. Provided the individual does no civil or criminal wrong, he may do as he wishes. A person also knows that for every wrongful encroachment upon his liberty there is a legal remedy available in an independent court of justice.

In the United Kingdom, therefore, individual liberty is protected by the ordinary courts of law using common law. This protection of the courts is limited by the doctrine of Parliamentary sovereignty. The Queen in Parliament may legislate upon any subject so that whatever liberties are given today may be taken away tomorrow.

The traditional unwritten constitution founded as it is partly on Acts of Parliament and judicial decisions, partly upon political practice, and partly upon detailed procedures established by the various organs of government for carrying out their own tasks, provides a complex and comprehensive system of government which some would argue has served the United Kingdom well. In particular, as all law in the United Kingdom, including laws relating to the constitution, may be enacted, repealed or amended by the Queen in Parliament using the same legislative procedure, our constitution is highly flexible and can adapt to meet changes in social, moral and political circumstances. Indeed this facility for gradual evolution has been one of the major contributions to the political and social stability of the United Kingdom.

Nevertheless in recent years there have been increasing calls for reform of the United Kingdom constitution by adoption of a written Bill of Rights and the model most often suggested is the European Convention on Human Rights, to which the UK has been a signatory since 1951 and which has been in force since 1953. In the UK, unlike other European countries such as West Germany, the Convention did not, merely by signature, become part of our domestic law. An Act of Parliament would be required to effect this, and the Labour Government proposes to pass such an Act during 1998. Until the passage of the Human Rights Act 1998 the issue of breach of the Convention cannot be raised before a British Court. If a individual or group feel that they have discovered a breach of the convention then, since 1966, it has been possible for this to be raised with the European Commission on Human Rights. States too may refer another signatory to the Convention to the Commission if a breach of the Convention has occurred. However in a number of respects it may be argued that these rights to refer an alleged breach are insufficient protection for our human rights. First if an individual wishes to complain he must first exhaust all his rights under the national law before complaining within one year of the final decision in a British court. Since legal aid applies only in such a small number of cases it will in many cases be prohibitively expensive to take a case as far as the Lords before a reference to the Commission (in itself an expensive undertaking). It is also an extremely lengthy procedure, which again deters potential complainants. Once the European Court makes its judgement then,although an individual case may be settled, if English law does not coincide with the Convention there may be further delay before the necessary reforming enactment is introduced.

In *Attorney-General* v *Times Newspapers Ltd* (1974) the House of Lords made a pronouncement that the European Court subsequently decided conflicted with article 10 of the European Convention on Freedom of Expression, but not until 1981 was the substantive law reformed by the Contempt of Court Act 1981.

The level of complaints to the European Court of Human Rights against the British Government and English law has been consistently high and that together with anxieties over the situation in Northern Ireland and the defects of the system mentioned above has caused many to believe that incorporation of some Bill of Rights is now necessary and desirable.

The opponents to incorporation of the European Convention put forward a number of arguments. First that since the UK is already bound to its provisions in international law there is no need to go further, second that to have such a Bill of Rights would put too much power into the hands of the judiciary and third that to incorporate the Bill would be futile since the doctrine of Parliamentary sovereignty means that any later Parliament could simply choose to depart from its provisions.

The second objection is based on the view that even if judges are not given the power to invalidate legislation which conflicts with the new Human Rights Act, they will still have great potential to use the new Act as a basis for developing new rights and remedies. This leads to the debate over whether judges, being unelected, unaccountable and unrepresentative can be trusted to perform this task adequately in a democratic society.

Proponents of the European Convention argue that for it to be fully effective as a safeguard of human rights it should be entrenched in some way against later repeal. However this would, of course, be difficult from the constitutional point of view because of the doctrine of Parliamentary Sovereignty which includes as one concept the idea that no Parliament is bound by its predecessors. To achieve entrenchment it would probably be necessary to adopt a written constitution adjusting the relationship of Parliament and the Courts. Even so some more limited form of legislation could be attempted and it appears that the Labour Government's proposed Human Rights Act will be in a non-entrenched form but nevertheless serving as a strong declaration of civil liberties and a highly persuasive tool for the judges when interpreting other laws. Academics such as Professor Michael Zander contend that even a non-entrenched Bill of Rights will be of value in 'changing the political atmosphere' in favour of fundamental rights and freedoms: *A Bill of Rights* (1997, 4th ed).

SUGGESTED ANSWER TO QUESTION THREE

General Comment

It is important to note the emphasis of the question which is rather more narrow than might appear at first glance. It is tempting to run through all the well-rehearsed arguments for and against incorporation of the Convention on Human Rights, but the examiner wishes the student to concentrate on a particular issue: would a UK citizen's individual rights be better protected under incorporation than at existing common law? Note the reference to Dicey and try to commence the discussion with reference to Dicey's Rule of Law and the emphasis he gave to judge-made law as the basis for constitutional rights. It is expected that legislation to incorporate the Convention into English law will come into force during 1998.

Key Points

- Dicey's concept of judge-made constitutional rights
- UK's position under the European Convention on Human Rights (ECHR)
- Violations of the ECHR by UK law (useful reference can be made to academic research on this point)
- Effect on sovereignty of Parliament of incorporation of ECHR
- Alternative views on UK's record under ECHR
- Common law use of ECHR to resolve ambiguous domestic law
- Position where domestic law is unambiguous and the need for an elected body to have the last say on contentious issues of policy
- Conclusions

Suggested Answer

In Dicey's exposition of the theory of the rule of law emphasis was placed on the role of the judge as defender of civil liberties; indeed Dicey went as far as to assert that the British Constitution, in its aspects relating to basic rights and freedoms, was a judge-made one. Historically Parliament built on the foundations laid by the common law. Since 1952 successive British governments have ratified the European Convention on Human Rights (ECHR) and since 1965 individual United Kingdom citizens have been permitted to petition the European Court of Human Rights at Strasbourg to obtain remedies for breaches of the Convention by UK governments. The experience has been cited by many authorities as evidence that English common law, as adapted by statute law on a piecemeal basis, no longer provides adequate protection of individual rights, and that therefore incorporation of the Convention into domestic law so as to give United Kingdom judges greater powers to protect fundamental freedoms is urgent and necessary. The Labour Government, elected at the General Election on 1 May 1997, has accepted this argument and legislation to incorporate the Convention into English law is expected to come into force during 1998.

In a devastating critique, Anthony Lester argued that the United Kingdom has the worst record of violations of the European Convention:

> '... no other country which belongs to the Convention has been faced with so many cases of such importance': [1984] PL 46.

His catalogue includes cases involving inhumane treatment of prisoners generally and of terrorist suspects in particular; inadequate safeguards against invasion of privacy; unfair sex and race discrimination, especially in the fields of employment and immigration law; inhumane punishments for school children (cane in English schools, tawse or strap in Scottish schools); nationalisation without fair compensation; oppressive interference with free speech through the laws of contempt of court and confidentiality; and so the list goes on. In all these examples the government of the day was usually obliged to enact new laws to comply with the ECHR rulings, but Lester argued cogently that such slow reform could be avoided if the Convention were directly enforceable by UK judges, who would be able (and indeed obliged) to adapt common law and statute law to comply with the jurisprudence of the ECHR and the precedents set by ECHR, which would become the supreme court for the United Kingdom on human rights.

Naturally incorporation would involve setting limitations to the powers of Parliament, but Lester argued that a mature Parliament should be able to accept constraints on its sovereignty so far as those constraints are necessary to protect human rights: 'The Convention sets those limits in relation to fundamental rights and freedoms, protecting minorities against the tyranny of elected majorities, and ordinary men and women against the misuse of administrative and judicial discretion.'

Even if one accepts the latter view for the sake of argument, there is still a large bone of contention at the heart of Lester's analysis and reasoning. It concerns the issue of whether individual rights would be better protected under an incorporated Convention. At first sight Lester's catalogue of British inadequacies would appear conclusive, but in fact his case is rather misleading. Although it is true that the United Kingdom has the worst record of violations, this should be set in the context that the United Kingdom allowed the right of individual petition as long ago as 1965, whereas others of the 1952 signatories allowed their citizens such access much later, eg France in the early 1980s, so that the inadequacies of the French system are only now coming to light (bearing in mind the typical wait of four to five years before a case reaches judgment at ECHR).

Another factor which could be used to counter Lester's argument is that United Kingdom judges already take account of the ECHR when interpreting ambiguous common law and statute law; indeed it has been said that it is mandatory for judges to do so when deciding how to resolve conflicts at common law: see per Butler-Sloss LJ in *Derbyshire County Council* v *Times Newspapers* (1992). Indeed, the Law Lords went further afield than the Court of Appeal by taking account of the American Constitution and Commonwealth authorities! This signifies how alert and willing the senior judges are when it comes to protection of human rights in the face of out-of-date common law or statute laws. In the *Derbyshire* case both the Court of Appeal and the House of Lords held that local authorities could not sue for libel in respect of their reputation for administration because otherwise such a right of action would stifle legitimate public criticism of their activities and impose an unnecessary restriction on freedom of expression in a democratic society. Lord Keith, in the leading judgment, managed to reach his conclusion without finding the need to rely upon the European Convention: 'I find it satisfactory to be able to conclude that the common law of England is consistent with the obligations assumed by the Crown under the treaty in this particular field.' Who needs the ECHR to give a ruling of this kind when common law is capable of giving it? As Lord Denning often said in his career on the bench, common law is capable of evolving from precedent to precedent so as to move with the times and to meet the needs of society.

Of course such reconciliation of English law with the obligations under ECHR is not possible if English law is unambiguously in conflict on the point in issue, particularly if it is statute law which is unambiguous: see *R* v *Secretary of State for the Home Department, ex parte Brind* (1991). But, as Lord Ackner pointed out in that case, that is the price for preserving a degree of national self-government and independence, and to ensure that the people are ruled by their elected legislature and not by the unelected (and very unrepresentative) judiciary. Further, it would be rare for a government to legislate so as to flout international opinion and domestic wishes; the practical and political constraints on a sovereign legislature are usually sufficient to deter such behaviour. The United Kingdom has survived for centuries without an American-style Supreme Court and a European-stvie Bill of Rights and, when violations of human rights are compared on a fairer and more scientific basis than in Lester's critique, the United Kingdom probably emerges with a reasonably good record, a place to which many still wish to emigrate.

SUGGESTED SOLUTION TO QUESTION FOUR

General Comment

A general question which, again, illustrates the dangers in question-spotting, since a good answer requires the adoption of an overall perspective. The question is sufficiently wide as to admit of an almost infinite number of approaches. Here, the intention is to concentrate on the protection of civil liberties (or human rights) in a system based on parliamentary sovereignty. Hence, the bill of rights debate is important to the answer, and it should be noted that legislation to incorporate the European Convention on Human Rights into English law is expected to come into force during 1998.

Key Points

- Common law and civil liberties (general position; case law - *Dr Bonham's Case*; *Pickin* v *BRB*; *Malone* v *MPC*; *Malone* v *UK*; *Spycatcher*)
- Parliamentary sovereignty and civil liberties - scrutiny of executive
- A bill of rights? - the ECHR as a model

Suggested Answer

It is submitted that Dicey's view does indeed require revision to meet the needs of today's society. It is questionable whether or not his statement was accurate when first made and mention will be made of this point below. Dicey based his assertion that there was 'no need for any statement of fundamental principles operating as a kind of higher law' on two propositions: the first, that common law provided adequate protection; the second, that Parliament was an effective check on the executive. It is proposed to discuss these propositions in their turn, pointing out the inadequacy of both in the light of contemporary society. It will be suggested in the conclusion that the most effective form of revision would be the incorporation of the European Convention on Human Rights as part of English law, as a prospective 'higher law', and this indeed is the policy of the Labour Government, elected at the General Election on 1 May 1997.

Whether or not common law has ever provided adequate protection for political freedom is a matter for debate. It may once have done so, in those days when, if an Act of Parliament was 'against common right and reason, or repugnant', the common law could 'control it and adjudge such Act to be void' (*Dr Bonham's Case* (1610)). But even when Dicey wrote, the doctrine of the sovereignty of Parliament was well-recognised. And, of course, in today's society, the idea that an Act of Parliament could be disregarded in so far as it was contrary to such fundamental principles as the 'the law of God or the law of nature or natural justice ... has become obsolete': *Pickin* v *British Railways Board* (1974).

The common law does, it is true, recognise fundamental principles, particularly in the area of civil liberties: 'England', it has been said, 'is not a country where everything is forbidden except what is expressly permitted: it is a country where everything is permitted except what is expressly forbidden': *Malone* v *Metropolitan Police Commissioner* (1979) per Sir Robert Megarry. And, thus, freedoms of speech, of assembly and of religion, for example, are inherent in the common law. But Sir Robert Megarry VC's dictum fails to inform us as to what restraints, if any, the common law can impose on prohibitions. Is there anything, any 'kind of higher law', to prevent everything being 'expressly forbidden'? It is suitably ironic that in Malone itself this principle of liberty was used to deny restraints on the powers of government to violate an individual's privacy: Mr Malone's only recourse lay outside the United Kingdom, before the European Court of Human Rights in Strasbourg: *Malone* v *UK* (1982).

But these liberties are not necessarily protected from erosion, even by the common law itself. In *Attorney-General* v *Guardian Newspapers (No 1)* (1987) *(Spycatcher)*, for example, the House of Lords upheld an interlocutory injunction restraining freedom of expression because, on balance, the common law regarded the protection of confidential government secrets as a more worthy goal. Lord Bridge's famous dissent that the decision marked a 'significant step down that very dangerous road' to a totalitarian regime hardly suggests that the common law always guarantees adequate protection of political freedom.

Nor, more problematically, can the judiciary stand against the will of Parliament. Parliament can, and does, enact restrictions on civil liberties and, although the judiciary can apply presumptions such as those against alteration of the common law or in favour of individual liberty, ultimately, the concept of some 'kind of higher law' higher than an Act of Parliament has been alien to English constitutional thought since at least 1688. As Lord Scarman has argued, the common law is ultimately helpless 'in the face of the legislative sovereignty of Parliament which makes it difficult for the legal system to accommodate the concept of fundamental and inviolable human rights': *English Law: the New Dimension* (1974). This was also the theoretical position when Dicey wrote.

There was, however, more force in Dicey's second proposition, at least when he wrote. Parliament in the mid-nineteenth century enjoyed something of a golden age, when it truly did exercise a degree of control over any 'excess of zeal by the executive'. It was far from uncommon for governments to be forced to resign through loss of a vote of confidence. Since then, as Wade and Bradley pointed out, 'the inexorable growth of the party system and its attendant discipline has seen the executive increasingly gain control of the House of Commons' (*Constitutional and Administrative Law* (1993, 11th ed), p411); the House of Lords was effectively neutered by the Parliament Act 1911. While it would be an over-simplification to assume that Parliament could not restrain executive zeal in extremis, the practical likelihood of it doing so in the case of a gradual erosion of civil liberties is not great - one need only refer to the controversy over the enactment of the Criminal Justice and Public Order Act 1994.

Even if we accept that Dicey's view does require revision, and there is now a need for some 'statement of fundamental principles operating as a kind of higher law', the question remains how this need might be met. Proponents of this revisionist view rely strongly on the argument that Britain needs a new 'Bill of Rights' and usually look for it in the European Convention on Human Rights. Even if the European Convention on Human Rights were to be incorporated, while political considerations might influence a government seeking to legislate in an area impinging on rights contained in the enacted Convention and although a degree of entrenchment might be achieved on the model of s2(4) European Communities Act 1972, ultimately Parliament - for which read the executive - could not be prevented from repealing this purported 'higher law'.

There is, in conclusion, little doubt that Dicey's view is no longer adequate to explain away the absence of any fundamental higher law in the United Kingdom. At the very least, the ability of the common law to protect political freedom and of Parliament to control the executive has been significantly eroded. Although incorporation of the European Convention on Human Rights would, as explained above, be no panacea, it might nevertheless go some way to satisfy the need for a statement of fundamental principles operating as a kind of higher law. That need is as great today as it was when Dicey wrote; and it is submitted that he himself would have revised his views had he been writing on the needs of today's society.

